PHILADELPHIA.

SCALE OF FEET

D1209628

Monographs
of the Rutgers Center of Alcohol Studies
No. 13

Monographs of the
Rutgers Center of Alcohol Studies

This monograph series was begun as Monographs of the Yale Center of Alcohol Studies and Numbers 1, 2 and 3 in the series were published at Yale. Beginning with Number 4 the series has been continued as Monographs of the Rutgers Center of Alcohol Studies. The change conforms with the transfer of the Center from Yale to Rutgers University. The works published in this series report the results of original research in any of the scientific disciplines, whether performed at Rutgers or elsewhere.

Liquor and Poverty

This washing up was a thoroughly odious job—
not hard, but boring and silly beyond words. It is
dreadful to think that some people spend their
whole decades at such occupations. The woman
whom I replaced was quite sixty years old, and she
stood at the sink thirteen hours a day, six days a
week, the year round; she was, in addition, horri-
bly bullied by the waiters. She gave out that she
had once been an actress—actually, I imagine, a
prostitute; most prostitutes end as charwomen. It
was strange to see that in spite of her age and her
life she still wore a bright blond wig, and darkened
her eyes and painted her face like a girl of twenty.
So apparently even a seventy-eight-hour week can
leave one with some vitality.

GEORGE ORWELL
*Down and Out in Paris and London**

* New York; Harbrace Paperbound Library; 1972, *p.* 69.
Copyright 1933 by George Orwell, 1961 by Sonia Pittman.
Quoted by permission.

Liquor and Poverty
Skid Row as a Human Condition

by
Leonard U. Blumberg
Thomas E. Shipley, Jr.
and
Stephen F. Barsky

PUBLICATIONS DIVISION
RUTGERS CENTER OF ALCOHOL STUDIES
NEW BRUNSWICK   NEW JERSEY

Library of Congress catalog card number: 76-620080

ISBN: 911290-46X   ISSN: 0080-4983

Contents

Tables

Figures

Chart

Acknowledgments

Temple University granted faculty research leaves to L. U. Blumberg and T. E. Shipley, Jr.

A grant from the Center for Metropolitan Studies, U.S. National Institute of Mental Health (Grant No. MH 15081) from 1967 to 1972 provided some typing services, research assistants, and some travel funds.

The following agencies, their executives, and their staffs were unfailingly helpful once we got beyond the necessary bureaucratic formalities. Their courtesies and interest were heartwarming; this is particularly the case where records were stored in safes and attics:

National Archives, Washington, DC
Historical Society of Pennsylvania
Family Service of Philadelphia
Society to Protect Children, Philadelphia
White-Williams Foundation, Philadelphia
Grace Baptist Church–Baptist Temple, Philadelphia
Bureau of the Census, Pittsburg, Kansas
Archives of the City of Philadelphia
Library Company of Philadelphia
Friends Historical Collection
Swarthmore College Library
Presbyterian Historical Society, Philadelphia
Church House, Episcopal Diocese of Pennsylvania,
    Philadelphia
Methodist Historical Center, St. George's Methodist
    Church, Philadelphia
The American Foundation, Philadelphia
Methodist Community Service Center, Philadelphia
Friends Neighborhood Guild, Philadelphia
Free Library of Philadelphia
American Philosophical Society
Octavia Hill Association, Philadelphia
Library of Congress, Map and Geography Division

Social Welfare History Archive Center, University of
Minnesota Libraries
Philadelphia Historical Commission
Detroit News
Burton Historical Collection, Detroit Public Library
Archives of Labor, History and Urban Affairs, Wayne State
University

The contents of this volume are solely the responsibility of
the authors. They are not the responsibility of the Department
of Health, Education, and Welfare, of Temple University, or of
the various agencies whose libraries and archives were con-
sulted.

The following persons were of assistance:
Executives and staff of the Diagnostic and Rehabilitation
Center/Philadelphia: Irving W. Shandler, James Rooney,
Leonard Moore, Shelly Silverstein, Joseph O. Moor, Jr., James
Cassidy, Barbara Christmas, Marilyn Whitt and Stephen Roche.
Temple University: Dr. Michael Lalli, Howard Spivak, Ar-
lene Sing, Sallie Boyer, Irene Best, Grace Dessureau, and Mary
Bortnyk.
And others: Marjorie Blumberg, Dennis Clark, John Strock,
Dr. Harold E. Cox, Prof. Henry Miller, Jim Baumohl, Linda
Scherr.

In association with each chapter, we have appended the
names of those who assisted us in some more specific manner. For a research project which has extended for at least 14
years, it is easy to make unintentional omissions; we offer our
apologies in advance for any slight or oversight in our acknowl-
edgments.

We have used, with permission, the *Genealogy of Philadelphia County Subdivisions*, compiled by John Daly, Archival
Examiner, and Allen Weinberg, Archivist of the City of
Philadelphia. We also acknowledge use of maps from the Library of Congress Map and Geography Division.

Finally, parts of this book rely on articles previously published in the QUARTERLY JOURNAL OF STUDIES ON ALCOHOL.

Introduction

The past decade has witnessed a spate of new books on Skid Row, including *Skid Row and its Alternatives* (1973), which was coauthored by two of the authors of *Liquor and Poverty*. One might conclude that the dozen or so new volumes on Skid Row and its inhabitants would suffice for the present, or at least render redundant this latecomer.

But *Liquor and Poverty* is not merely more of the same. It is a creative, useful contribution in at least four ways. First, it is comparative; the reader encounters not only the Philadelphia Skid Rows, both major and minor, stereotypical and incipient, but also those of Detroit and San Francisco. Second, its historical documentation is far better than that of any recent Skid Row study; it is comparative in time as well as in geographic scope. The detailed history of Philadelphia's slums, its Tenderloin (the urban district where illicit activities such as prostitution, gambling and drug use are concentrated) and the Skid Row is a substantial work that will be cited frequently. Third, *Liquor and Poverty* is action-oriented, treating questions such as "Where will the next Skid Row occur?", "How can Skid Row-like people be identified and helped before they leave their home neighborhoods?" and "Which populations are most likely to produce the next generation of Skid Row residents?" Finally, and most ambitiously, it proposes a significant conceptual change in the definition of Skid Row.

In *Skid Row and its Alternatives*, the authors described the homeless men of Philadelphia, evaluated programs designed to assist and rehabilitate them, and recommended principles and practices that would help Skid Row people to live more normal, productive lives. In that book, Skid Row was seen as "a special kind of slum" occupied by the unfit, the unfamilied, the poor, the personally inadequate, the aged and the chronically ill, especially those afflicted with alcoholism or tuberculosis.

In *Liquor and Poverty* Blumberg, Shipley and Barsky continue to view Skid Row as a special kind of slum. It is the extension of that perspective which permits them to make their conceptual leap, from viewing Skid Row as a neighborhood to defining "skidrowitis" as a malady affecting everyone in some degree. If Skid Row represents a sore on the body urban, these authors would have us search elsewhere for the source of the infection, and not pay too much attention to its ugliest and most visible manifestation.

In fact, the book is a direct assault on the traditional definitions of Skid Row and its people. The "natural area" perspective is explicitly rejected; Skid Row, they argue, is not merely or even primarily a specific neighborhood. Rather, "Skid Row-like" people are found wherever there is poverty, in the slum neighborhoods, the low-income ethnic enclaves, even in the suburbs.

The appeal to abandon the traditional definition of Skid Row is not an idle, abstract notion derived from armchair theorizing. It stems directly from the authors' attempts to predict where the next Skid Row in Philadelphia would be. Their rationale for rejecting the traditional definition is not merely the pedant's preference for one term over another; it is that the old definition does not "work" for them, that it impedes, confuses and misrepresents reality. The traditional definition, they say, has so limned the population of disaffiliated, poor and alcoholic peoples that most of those who need help have not been within the purview of the established helping institutions.

Even the problem of prevention has been miscast. Only if it is defined as city-wide in scope, and not a neighborhood clean-up problem, will it be possible to prevent the deterioration of incipient Skid Row neighborhoods into true Skid Rows and of incipient homeless alcoholics into Skid Row denizens. Preventive efforts must be located in the slums and suburbs, with programs directed to identifying Skid Row-like people before they have used up their social margin, before the "neighborhood drunk" has been transformed into the "Skid Row bum."

In support of their reconceptualization, Blumberg and his associates treat the reader to an impressive diversity of evidence, and the journey through that evidence is enriching even if one remains convinced that there is justification for retaining the label "Skid Row" for certain urban neighborhoods. Their arguments are securely footed in historical detail: in addition to the chapters on the slums and Skid Rows of Philadelphia and Detroit, there are illuminating appendices on the history of social welfare agencies in Philadelphia and on the relationship between Chinatown, the Red Light district and Skid Row. Among the numerous fascinating historical tidbits which, by themselves, almost justify this book's existence, are the following:

In Philadelphia in the 1870s paupers and vagrants in "the lowest sections of the city" were arrested on Saturday nights, "carted by the car load" to Moyamensing prison where they were "kept from the gaze of the Sunday public," and then on Monday mornings they were released once more to the community.

As early as 1864 the Philadelphia Department of Police contained a "Vagrant Department" and hired special "Beggar Detectives" or "Vagrant Detectives" to find and arrest vagrants and to help the deserving homeless persons they encountered. Among their assignments as recorded in 1886 were "hunting up young girls who have absconded from home and taken refuge in houses of ill repute," and "conveying vicious and incorrigible children to the House of Refuge."

The Magdalen Society of Philadelphia, originally established (1799) for the rehabilitation of prostitutes, gradually changed its objectives and programs in the direction of respectability, first limiting its mission to only the "younger and more deserving" girls, and finally abandoning the idea of reforming prostitutes and instead working to prevent girls under 16 from dropping out of school.

To protect themselves from the "vicious poor" the Union Benevolent Association (founded in the early 1830s) investigated the worthiness of applicants for charity, and by 1855 there had been compiled a "black book of imposters who mulcted the charitable."

In 1821 the Michigan Territorial Legislature mandated that "idle, vagrant, lewd, drunken or disorderly persons" could be delivered up to a constable to be hired out for wages for a period of up to three months, with the wages being used for the support of the poor of the County.

Firemen who answered a call in Philadelphia's Chinatown in 1905 discovered a cubicle hotel for members of the Tong in the floors above a local grocery store.

The historical analysis tests and largely confirms accepted notions about the emergence of Skid Rows in American Cities (that following the Civil War various economic and social forces operated to concentrate in a single neighborhood services and disaffiliated people who formerly had been more widely dispersed). But the authors go beyond the question of when the Skid Row first appeared and ask more difficult questions, notably, "Why did the slum develop separately from the Skid Row?" In the end, the answer to that depends upon how Skid Row is defined. And the authors assert that to limit the definition to the traditional geographic one—the "homeless workingman's area"—is far too shortsighted both historically and with reference to present-day needs of disaffiliated people. They urge that any area where Skid Row-like people live should qualify for attention, thus including the Tenderloin as well as Philadelphia's major slum areas as prime targets for major rehabilitation programs.

As long as the geographic definition prevails, Skid Row can be "renewed" with little attention to the disaffiliates who live there, and none to the more numerous "Skid Row-like" people elsewhere in the city. Historically, cleaning up Skid Row has usually meant ejecting the homeless inhabitants. But for Blumberg, Shipley and Barsky, "cleaning up Skid Row" means helping Skid Row-like people wherever they live, and working to prevent others from falling into "Skid Row status."

Liquor and Poverty is especially persuasive because the authors are not content to make informed suggestions; they have actually applied some of the techniques they recommend. They attempted to detect "pre-Skid Row" conditions by identifying the location of bottle-gang activity and monitoring those locations over several years, and by analyzing police records on the incidence of Skid Row offenses. They searched the records of social welfare agencies and hospitals, talked to real estate agents and evaluated long-term changes in neighborhood housing and real estate quality, assessed trends in real estate valuation via inspection of City tax records for the period 1915 to 1971, traced the histories of slum neighborhoods and surveyed clients of the Philadelphia Travelers' Aid Society. Yet the combined result of these and other efforts was not sufficient to permit identification of the neighborhood most likely to become the city's next Skid Row. However, they do conclude that all areas of the city which are deteriorating both commercially and residentially, or which seem likely to do so, are incipient Skid Rows. Consequently they urge increased attention to the long-run trends of urban blight and slum formation.

The keys to prevention are identifying incipient Skid Rows early and then acting to prevent the neighborhood from being

defined by the public as a Skid Row. Because public definitions about an area are so important, the authors are scrupu-
lously careful to avoid contributing to any self-fulfilling prophecy by labeling specific neighborhoods as incipient Skid Rows,
and therefore use pseudonyms to refer to the places they
studied.

The authors also show how "Skid Row-like" people may be
found and helped. One of their means of locating Skid Row-like
people on their home turf was a three-month experiment in
aggressive outreach casework which demonstrated both the
feasibility of reaching potential clients this way and an unex-
pectedly wide range of problems. The caseworker provided referral services, help with money management, counseling and
information. Many of his services, once people came to trust
him, were not related to alcohol problems but instead were
elemental problems of survival in the city, such as knowing how
to use transportation lines, how to clean house, shop for
groceries, pay a bill or apply for needed social services. The
description of the active casework underscores the finding that
the differences between Skid Row-like people and other poor
people are often minimal. Perhaps this conclusion is only a
repetition of the cliché so often applied to the Skid Row person,
"There, but for the grace of God . . . ," but coming as a perspective from the experiment in aggressive preventive social work it
seems to strike home with extra force.

The call to stop looking at neighborhoods as homogeneous
units and instead to look for people in trouble so expands the
"Skid Row problem" that it may be resisted on these very
grounds. I am reminded of a welfare administrator's reaction to
the finding, based on a statistical analysis of records of potter's
field burials, that there were perhaps 10 times as many homeless men in New York City as had been enumerated on the
Bowery. He insisted that those who lived elsewhere were not
true Skid Row men; the problem could not be that large. The
finding had to be an artifact of faulty definition by the researchers. The idea that the Skid Row-like population was
many times larger than that within the boundaries of the stereotypical Skid Row was unsettling and, he seemed to think, its political implications for him and his program were negative. He
had responsibility for the Skid Row people; these multitudi-

nous others, an unknown and unserved group, might place his program in an unfavorable light, or make it appear less effective than he thought it was. So he dismissed the finding as additional evidence that researchers tend to be isolated from the real world, and their conclusions inappropriate to his rehabilitation programs.

The memory of that encounter seemed especially relevant as I read *Liquor and Poverty*. For in expanding the definition to include the human condition of "Skid Row-like," these authors may have so enlarged the target population as to invite administrators of existing programs and agencies to reject their new definition. It is one thing for the researcher to say that there are many more Skid Row-like people than live on Skid Row. It is quite another for a welfare administrator charged with combating the "Skid Row problem" to be asked to make a 10-fold increase in the number of his potential clients, especially when the budget may be too small to serve the present clients adequately. True, the more inclusive definition may serve as justification for increased funding and personnel. But possible future improvements are problematic, and may not be seen as commensurate with the increased responsibilities which will accompany the proposed redefinition.

Also, if Skid Row is defined in more abstract, nongeographic terms, there is likely to be less interest in doing something about it, rather than more. For more of the pressure to clean up Skid Row neighborhoods comes from the merchants and residents of the area. It is a direct consequence of the geographic definition and of real estate owners' and residents' concern with improving a specific neighborhood.

Of course Blumberg and his associates have already considered these arguments, and perhaps that explains their frequent repetition of the theme that Skid Row must be defined as a human condition, and that caseworkers must begin to care for the "pre-Skid Row" people they have overlooked while bound by the residential definition of Skid Row.

Their recommendations for action reflect their assumption that the Skid Row problem stretches throughout the slums and suburban areas of the modern city. The "disabling conditions" which foster disaffiliation reduce, in the main, to two: poverty and addiction. Their two "preventive checks," aimed at these conditions, are an end to poverty through the enactment of a guaranteed income and an end to addiction through some unspecified means. Because they are unwilling to prescribe prohibition or high tax penalties for alcohol use, in the end they can only wish for an end to addiction. The kinds of measures which would limit public access to alcoholic beverages, or discourage the development of a taste for them, they see as undesirable. Nor are they very sanguine about the possibilities that a guaranteed income program will be enacted soon. A more realistic line of action is their list of "positive checks" aimed at making "Skid Rowness" more pleasant and manageable.

They argue for the decriminalization of the typical Skid Row offenses and the establishment of a civilian public service corps to replace the police in dealing with vagrancy, public drunkenness and other petty violations. Their most original proposal is the creation of a "comprehensive social, political, economic and residential services agency for those Skid Row-like people who would use such a place." The aim of this institution is to meet the people's needs and at the same time to avoid profiteering from human misery. Its multiple services would be citywide, and the nonprofit, well-supervised facility would even include a liquor store. It is viewed as being as essential to the welfare of the metropolitan community as the schools, libraries and organized charities. Its services would be widely advertised and it would serve as a resource center from which outreach casework would be directed. Presumably its comprehensive facilities would provide services without stigmatizing clients as "Skid Row people," and the facility might even provide some political leverage for disaffiliated people if its career manager were given cabinet-level rank in city government.

To be sure, some of these proposals seem visionary by present standards. To urge attention for all the Skid Row-like people in a metropolis may be multiplying the task of social service agencies beyond capacity. Or, more probably, it may be asking for more charity and concern for human needs than our agencies, accustomed to dealing with only the most pressing, obvious and politically relevant problems, are capable of delivering. The political clout of the Skid Row-like, even defined in the inclusive terms of these authors, may not be sufficient to merit a high priority in city budgets.

There are also some problems with the reconceptualization itself. Not only is "Skid Row-like" verbally awkward, but if "Skid Row" as a neighborhood and as a label is stigmatizing, then surely "Skid Row-like" is also stigmatizing, and a more neutral term should be substituted. In my view, the term "disaffiliate" meets necessary neutrality criterion and also serves to generalize the problem beyond the boundaries of the traditional Skid Row.

Books are memorable because they contain material previously unavailable, or because they cast existing knowledge in a different light, or because they provoke controversy and the reexamination of accepted ideas. *Liquor and Poverty* rates high marks on each of these criteria. Its historical accounts and research procedures will be widely appreciated and used, its conceptual proposals and recommendations for civic policy will be a focus for spirited debate.

In *Liquor and Poverty* we have that uncommon situation where a sequel is a more important contribution than the original release. I believe that eventually the disaffiliates of American cities will be better off for having been labeled "Skid Row-like" by Blumberg, Shipley and Barsky, and that is far more than can be said for most of the modern literature on Skid Row.

HOWARD M. BAHR

Brigham Young University
Provo, Utah

Preface

As research began in anticipation of the redevelopment of the Philadelphia Skid Row area, several problems were posed: What kind of people lived in the Skid Row section of the city? Where will Skid Row move next? What kinds of programs should be recommended for the rehousing and general care of the homeless men of Skid Row that would be helpful to them and at the same time prevent the formation of another Skid Row somewhere else? *Skid Row and Its Alternatives* (23) described the homeless men of Philadelphia's Skid Row area, presented an analysis of a program designed to persuade the homeless men to come to a social service agency for a variety of services, evaluated the effectiveness of rehabilitation services that were a part of the activities of the Diagnostic and Rehabilitation Center/Philadelphia, and made a series of recommendations directed to "What can be done about Skid Row men?"

While many Skid Row residents are not "drunken bums," there is enough public drunkenness among Skid Row area residents to support the stereotype. Alcohol facilitates the dissolution of past economic, familial and social relationships, while it is also the tie that binds together many of those who adopt a Skid Row-like lifestyle. The bottle wrapped in a brown bag and passed around the circle is the hallmark of bottle gangs that are found not only in Skid Row neighborhoods but other low-income sections of the big cities. The big glass of cheap port wine poured from the gallon jug often is breakfast, lunch and supper for the Skid Row-like resident of the urban slum or the neighborhood that is "going downhill."

The present volume elaborates on the view that Skid Row is the intersection of alcohol and poverty. That is, Skid Row is a lifestyle. Alcohol and poverty are central to that lifestyle whether it is found in the Skid Row area or elsewhere.

We reached this conclusion as we changed our orientation from the description of Skid Row men and their "rehabilitation" to the prediction and prevention of Skid Row. The predictive–preventive orientation is manifested differently in different parts of the book. Chapters 1, 2 and 3 examine the development of the Skid Row areas in Philadelphia and Detroit. The conjunction of drunken and vagrant men, women and children in the development of both cities raises a question about the meaning of the term Skid Row itself. The Skid Rows of both Philadelphia and Detroit developed in the last decades of the 19th century as Skid Row sections became differentiated from earlier slum–prostitution–high-drunkenness areas. The historical data suggest that future Skid Rows in our major cities are already well on their way before redevelopment projects are undertaken in the old Skid Row areas.

One cannot casually overturn earlier conclusions on the basis of two case histories, but we believe that an examination of the basis of these earlier generalizations will suggest that they are poorly supported by data. Furthermore, we recognize that each city has its unique history; ultimately the job of the social scientist is to separate the specific from the general. What we argue is that Philadelphia has developmental characteristics which are typical of the East Coast cities and that Detroit has characteristics which are typical of midwestern industrial cities. At the very least, our studies of Philadelphia and Detroit challenge earlier conclusions about when big-city Skid Rows developed and the process associated with the development of Skid Rows. If the scientific endeavor is cumulative, and we believe that it is, we trust that there will be others who will put the present alternative conclusions to further examination by comparative studies of still other Skid Rows.

Chapters 4 and 5 examine the problem of prediction in our own time. They report on efforts to find indicators of the actual recurrence of the Philadelphia Skid Row as physical clearance took place. The location of bottle gangs, police arrest data for drunkenness and vagrancy, neighborhood descriptions, and real estate tax data are examined as possible predictors. The efforts of public officials in Detroit to prevent the recurrence of the Skid Row area and the movement of San Francisco's Skid Row to the area just outside the boundaries of redevelopment are examined. Again, the conclusion is that the prevention of Skid Row areas is a long-term process of intervention through urban planning and urban renewal. One might say that the seeds of the future Skid Rows already exist in our major cities.

Chapters 6 through 8 discuss Skid Row-like people and where we might look for them. They suggest that we take another look at women who are living a Skid Row-like lifestyle though not usually found in significant numbers in the stereotyped Skid Row neighborhoods. They also suggest that social scientists, social welfare workers, social welfare policy makers and public officials have neglected homeless Black people who are also living a Skid Row-like lifestyle within the racially segregated districts of our cities.

In addition to women and Black people, there are homeless youth who are living a Skid Row-like lifestyle but who tend to be viewed as "hippies," "drop outs," or "street people." The consequence of this examination of populations which have been omitted from the stereotype of Skid Row is a call for a reorientation of what we mean by the term Skid Row. The differences between the stereotyped homeless Skid Row person and a variety of different kinds of urban poor people are slight, and once the stereotyped Skid Row area is cleared from the land it is difficult to make sharp distinctions. Rather than limiting the concept of Skid Row to the homeless male residents of a certain area which has Skid Row institutions, the argument is advanced that the issue of Skid Row prevention be viewed in terms of the Skid Row-like condition wherever it is found in the city.

Chapter 9 picks up this theme. It presents the results of a pilot project to locate and assist people living a Skid Row-like lifestyle in a neighborhood that is not locally perceived as a Skid Row neighborhood. The modest success of the project urges that it be repeated on a larger scale and more systematically. The search for people living a Skid Row-like lifestyle, in which heavy alcohol usage is a central feature, is extended into a suburban county. In the suburban county, Skid Row institutions tend to be dispersed if for no other reason than that the density of Skid Row-like people is relatively low. But alcoholism clinic case records give evidence that there are, indeed, people living a Skid Row-like lifestyle in suburban communities that are similar to the deteriorating sections of the central city. What is more, there are substantial numbers of people who appear to be drifting into a Skid Row-like lifestyle. For most, though not all of these people, the heavy use of alcohol is a significant factor in the process.

In the formation of public policies to "deal with the Skid Row problem," this monograph suggests that the relevant question is not so much, "Where will Skid Row move next?" as it is, "What kind of social policies and programs are necessary and desirable to inhibit the development of a Skid Row lifestyle?"

Part I

The Origins of Skid Row

Chapter 1

Slums, Prostitution and Vagrancy: The Post-Civil War Hypothesis[1]

THE HOBOHEMIAS and Skid Rows of the American cities were considered a post-Civil War phenomenon by most social scientists. A variety of explanations for the development of the distinctive homeless-workingmen's areas have been offered by Lovald (107), Wallace (217), Vander Kooi (213) and Rooney (170): (1) the economic growth and change of the United States after the Civil War, including the rapid expansion of the country, the demand for a large mobile labor force in such industries as railroading, farming, logging and seafaring, banking–commercial panics and depressions of the economic system, and seasonal unemployment; (2) the development and rapid expansion of new modes of transportation, including urban street railways and inter-city steam railways; and (3) the demographic changes in the country that were correlated with these factors, such as the rural–urban migration of the population, and the large-scale immigration that took place in the period between the Civil War and World War I. Another explanation is that, as a latent consequence of the Civil War, many men never again "settled down" into "normal community life" and an unknown number of people, especially young men, were caught up in wanderlust.

This chapter and the two that follow have dual objectives. They examine the past of Skid Rows in Philadelphia and Detroit in the hope that they can provide a basis for policy recommendations with respect to the prevention of Skid Rows in the future and they seek to provide a test of previous generalizations made about the development of Skid Rows in American cities.

[1] Appreciation is expressed to Leonard Moore whose enterprising interest in "junk" found us the critically important *Philadelphia Press* article of 18 March 1872.

1

Facts to verify the development of Philadelphia's Skid Row were not readily available, so a correlative approach was used. If completely satisfactory references on the homeless workingmen's area could not be found, then perhaps data on the Tenderloin could be used as an indicator of the development of that area. We were especially interested in (1) where homeless people lived before the Civil War and the relationship of the area to the Tenderloin and the Skid Row, (2) where and when the Tenderloin developed, and (3) whether the homeless workingmen's area developed before or after the Civil War.

William Penn's town plan was based on a gridiron scheme found in Richard Newcourt's plan for London and in smaller cities in the British Colonies (161, *pp. 204–223*). For its day the plan was innovative and undoubtedly was meant to convey an attitude of orderliness in this as well as in all things. Front Street ran parallel to the Delaware River's edge. Numbered streets were parallel to Front and ran north and south; the principal east and west streets were named for trees and ran river to river. The plan had additional symmetries: The main east–west street extending from Front was Market Street.[2] It was intersected roughly halfway between the Delaware and Schuylkill Rivers by a major north–south street, Broad Street. At the intersection of Market and Broad was a public square, but this was preempted late in the 19th Century for the present City Hall buildings. In the center of each quadrant created by the intersection of Market and Broad streets a public square was planned, subsequently called Washington, Rittenhouse, Franklin and Logan.

Logically there should have been an equal number of streets on all sides of the Squares, but actually the city boundaries went north only as far as Vine Street at the northern edge of Franklin Square, while the southern boundary extended to South Street, 3½ blocks south of Washington Square. This was consistent with the early growth of Philadelphia, which first tended to be along the Delaware River extending several blocks inland. As the early town grew it tended to be to the south and west, largely because Dock Creek was south of Mar-

---

[2] Whenever feasible, the present names of streets are used; see Appendix B for previous names.

ket Street and that initial settlement clustered near Dock Creek.

Penn's initial landing was at Dock Creek, a stream that ended in a tidal pond near the present Fourth and Market streets. To the south of Dock Creek, there was a small Swedish village that was probably an attraction to settlement in that direction. The next creek up the Delaware was Pegg's Run. Because farmers brought their produce along the river to Dock Creek and Pegg's Run, produce and meat markets were early established in the immediate vicinity. When the tanyards completely polluted both creeks, they were covered and became Dock Street and Willow Street, respectively, but the market areas remained. By 1816 Washington Square had become the residential locus of Philadelphia's rich and powerful, and their complaints led to the relocation of the cattle market from the Seventh Street side of Washington Square to the Hay Market at Sixth and Callowhill streets, which was at that time outside the northern city limits (128, *Vol. 2, p. 86*). In 1842 the fish market moved from Front and Market to Front and Noble streets, not far from the Callowhill Street market area (12, *p. 257*). The dominance of the Dock Street produce market was established early and it continued to be the city's chief wholesale market until the late 1950s, when a new Food Distribution Center was built far to the south. The Callowhill Street area was an important produce and meat packing center down into the 1950s and continued to be a locale for meat specialties down to the early 1970s.

During the colonial and early national period wealthy merchants often lived over their places of business on Water Street and Front Street, parallel to the Delaware. Even men of standing, such as Supreme Court Justices, continued to live on Water Street at the River's edge. But the yellow fever epidemic began on Water Street in July 1793, and when it was over the wealthy had moved to Market Street, going as far west as Seventh Street (218, *Vol. I, p. 225*). By the time of the War of 1812, however, Market Street had become commercialized and Chestnut and Walnut streets became the residential areas of Philadelphia's upper class, with Washington Square as the focal point (11, 26, 87, 94, 97). As the town expanded, upper-class Philadelphians retreated to Rittenhouse Square where they remained until they began major moves to the western suburbs along the main line of the Pennsylvania Railroad in the 1880s or to the inner-city suburban Chestnut Hill section in the late 1890s. To live "north of Market Street" was to be outside the area of élite society, although the Quakers on Arch Street were a partial exception because in many ways they approximated a distinctive ethnic group. South of the upper-class streets were the middle class on Spruce and Pine streets, while the area between Pine and Lombard was marginal middle- and working-class. By the time of the Civil War, the eastern part had become a region of sailors' boardinghouses as well as an impoverished workingmen's area. The entire section from Lombard Street south for about four streets and extending from the Delaware to about Ninth Street became notorious for its bad housing and vice, and as the principal location of the city's vagrants. In this present discussion, it is referred to as the Lombard–Southwark–Moyamensing section.

Perhaps the most graphic description of the bad housing conditions in the Lombard–Southwark–Moyamensing area was published in 1859 by Benjamin T. Sewell, missionary at the Bedford Street Mission:

"As we passed down the street, she turned up a dirty alley into a still dirtier yard, built up on each side with what I supposed to be cow stables. . . . But not cows were lodged in these sheds, which were *ten feet* and six in height. A little round hole cut in front of each, was the only admittance for air and light, except the doors, which although fastened by a padlock, swung two or three inches away from the posts. They were really not good enough for animals, and yet they were used as *boarding* houses for those poor human beings, who had no homes of their own in this populous district. . . . These incomparable lodgings are rented out at ten cents a night, invariably in advance" (182, *p. 91;* also, 174).

Sewell's statement on tenement conditions in 1859 is also worth repeating:

"Though you may not believe it yet it is nevertheless true, that there is a family in every room of almost every house in this vicinity. The exceptions are but few. In some houses there are from ten to sixteen families stowed away, whilst many others have eight and ten; and in some places I know of two and three men and their wives living, cooking, eating and sleeping in one room. . . . All these tenants pay by the week, or night, counting six nights to the week, and paying invariably in advance: the rent ranging from six to twelve cents per night. If a cellar has no floor in it, it can be had for six or eight cents; if there is a floor, then twelve cents per night can be obtained very readily for its use. If the rooms above ground are plastered, and a good many are not . . . the rent is twelve cents per night" (182, *pp. 323–324*).

Nor had these conditions developed just before the Civil War, for the western part of the section, south of Pine Street and west of Sixth, was a shanty-town as early as 1807 (218, *Vol. I, pp. 482–483*).

As early as 1816, the area also had a reputation for crime and vice. In that year there was an unsuccessful plot to kidnap the Governor (36, 46). The scheme involved the rescue of a man condemned to hang for killing the husband of his sweetheart; the husband was a drunken sea captain. The widow recruited members of one of the gangs in Southwark and planned the expedition. She was later acquitted because no kidnapping had taken place. Ann Carson thereafter drifted into a career of cheating, theft and passing counterfeit money and ultimately died in prison. Throughout most of the time she lived in various houses in the Lombard–Southwark–Moyamensing vicinity. In 1817 the reputation of the area for "degraded indolence and vice below the level of brute creation" was justification for the establishment of a Presbyterian Church in Southwark by the Rev. Francis Ballentine, Missionary for the Female Domestic Missionary Society of Philadelphia for the Support of the Gospel in the Alms House (64, *1817, 1818;* 66, *p. 53*).

Prostitution was characteristic of the Lombard–Southwark–Moyamensing section throughout the entire pre-Civil War period. Thus George Foster, writing in 1848, speculates that "the keepers of five notorious brothels, all in a row, in Elizabeth Street [Bartram] would probably not be tried because it would not be possible to find witnesses to testify." Foster placed the center of this activity at Dandy Hall, located on Monroe Street, between Third and Fourth streets. According to Foster, Dandy Hall was a dance hall, a "regular house of resort" for Black women and their "fancy men" [pimps], as well as for Irishmen. It was also a groggery and a hotel–house of prostitution that was used by sailors who were very likely to be robbed in the place (67, *pp. 23–72*). That this was indeed an area of ill repute is corroborated by an anonymous commentator of the same period who says that in Rodman Street below Fourth there were numerous houses of prostitution "of the lowest order, the names of the inmates we have in our possession, but, as they would only occupy space for no good purpose, we shall not mention them" (240). This does not deny the presence of better-class houses of prostitution elsewhere in the Philadelphia area. While the listing is incomplete, it suggests that the most desirable houses of prostitution were located in sections of what later became Wards 7, 8 and 14. Further, the 1852 annual report of the managers of the Rosine Association, an organization of women who attempted to assist "girls in trouble," doubted that the police would do much to suppress active prostitution in Philadelphia (Appendix D). They pointed out that the keepers of 25 houses of prostitution in the vicinity of Fourth and Monroe had been indicted 4 months before, but the operators had simply moved out and opened elsewhere and thereby voided the case (172, *1852, p. 10*).

Southwark was also a principal area of poverty and vagrancy. Matthew Carey and the matron of the Provident Society of Philadelphia both commented on the poverty in Southwark (34, 35). And we have a report of the Library Committee of the Pennsylvania Society for the Promotion of Public Economy which, from the results of a questionnaire that it had circulated to knowledgeable persons, concluded in 1817 that pawnbrokers, commonly found in poor working-class sections, were numerous in Southwark (136, *p. 19*). Indicative of the poverty of the area is the fact that in 1820 the managers of the Alms House established in Southwark a special asylum for the children of the poor. Its main building was between Spruce and Pine and Tenth and Eleventh streets and thus just north of the slum zone.

That the section had a reputation as the principal location of the city's vagrants is witnessed by the solemn warning of Benjamin Sewell (182) in 1859 to young men and women about town who drank in fashionable places on Chestnut Street. He warned them that while they might be drinking mint juleps through a straw today it would not be long before they would be gathering mint in the swamps and going from groggery to groggery selling it for three cents a bunch and then limping back to Kater Street or Pemberton Street, "to spend their pennies with ragged loafers and after they have broken their father's heart by their dissipation and degradation, the sheriff in all probability, will break their necks . . . or, if they not get that high in the world, they will live in some cellar with a gang of dirty men and dirtier women, and with a hooked stick go from street to street, and from lot to lot, in search of rags and bones, or with a bucket in hand pick cinders from ash barrels along the curbstones, or else go from door-to-door begging cold victuals to satisfy their hunger, or for old clothes to cover their nakedness" (pp. 124–125). To young women, he directed the warning that they "should take care . . . you are in the road to Baker [Pemberton] Street . . . in these haunts of vice, after an apprenticeship in Pine Alley [Rodman Street]." This echoes Rev. Francis Ballentine who observed in 1817 that "almost every house in these streets and lanes is converted into a grog-shop or oyster-house. When the passions become inflamed by the intoxicating draught, those poor unhappy wretches are prepared for every species of crime" (64, 1817).

The Lombard–Southwark–Moyamensing slum continued to have a reputation as a vice area through much of the post-Civil War period. In 1897 the Rev. M. H. Williams, pastor of the First Presbyterian Church on Washington Square, observed:

"Into this region criminals of all kinds gravitated. . . . Many frame structures were erected before the Revolutionary War and antedating the fire laws. Not a penny was spent for repairs. Cellars were filled with water and refuse and boarded over. Stairs were worn through. Bricks were tumbling from the dilapidated chimneys; and when all respectable tenants had forsaken the neighborhood, it became the haunt of criminals, classes given over to every imaginable form of lowest vice. Extra doors were put in to make convenient 'badger houses.' Holes were cut in the fences through which anyone fleeing from police officers could make his escape into winding alleys. Murders were frequent, robberies too numerous to chronicle, and sometimes a hundred and fifty arrests would be made in a single night. . . . Still lower down in the city was the old Shippen [Bainbridge] district where abandoned women would persuade sailors on shore to marry them and make over their advance pay, but when the sailor returned from his voyage, the wife was not to be found. She had married several other sailors in the interim" (226, pp. 54–55).

The minister of the First Presbyterian Church was very much aware of these conditions for, as president of the Christian League, he led the "clean up" campaign against them (Appendix C).

To take an example from the case records of the Society to Protect Children, in 1879 a drunken mother on Kenilworth Street was neglecting her children, but the agent complained that the neighbors would not testify against her because the neighborhood was one of "infamy and degradation."[3] In September 1883 a resident of Norristown, Pennsylvania, went "scudding around the downtown slums . . . was enticed into 614 St. Mary [Rodman] Street [and] was robbed." Two years later, a girl was "enticed" into this same house, which is described as a "notorious rookery." Disorderly lodging houses (noisy, carousing at all hours, often sexual promiscuity) and low lodging houses (cheap, dirty, sexual promiscuity) were common in the area. A pool hall at 313 Bainbridge Street was "right in the midst of a number of houses of prostitution. . . . The place is filthy dirty."[4] In August 1892 a 15-year-old girl was found in a "low lodging house" on South Street east of Second Street. She told of having been seized and raped by four men in an alley off a street below S. Hancock running from Bainbridge to South, east of Second. The lodging house was known as "Louse Harbor."[5] In 1890, Reese Street was reported to be the home of a woman involved in prostitution and the badger game.[6] Finally, the *Evening Bulletin* of 5 January 1905 reported that a Kensington man had visited the "red light district" downtown several evenings before and had been robbed of $265. The police arrested two Black women where the man said that he had visited them.[7]

After the Civil War the area was still characterized by poverty, drunkenness and vagrancy. The first Wayfarer's Lodge and Woodlot of the Society for Organizing Charity was at 1719 Lombard within convenient walking distance of the heart of the slum section. Its location was analogous to the location of the Diagnostic and Rehabilitation Center in Philadelphia in the

[3] 509 Kenilworth, SPC case no. 968, 11 June 1879.
[4] 104 Delancey St., 20 South St., 723 S. 4th St., 317 S. 2nd St., 215 Pine St., northeast corner Front and Bainbridge St., 602 Penn St., 608 Penn St., Philadelphia *Public Ledger*, 22 July 1885; SPC case no. 7109, 18 August 1885; no. 9490, 13 July 1889; no. 10344, 12 August 1890; no. 10380, 26 August 1890; no. 10483, 5 October 1890; no. 11532, 16 December 1891; no. 12319, 23 October 1892; no. 14302, 4 February 1895.
[5] SPC case no. 12157, 19 August 1892.
[6] SPC case no. 10177, 13 June 1890.
[7] 247 S. Schell St.

early 1960s—just a few blocks away from the Skid Row; convenient to reach but not subject to the direct influences of Skid Row itself.

The heart of the Lombard–Southwark–Moyamensing section in the post-Civil War period was Rodman and Kater streets. Rodman Street was located in the western part of the Fifth Ward and the eastern part of the Seventh Ward, while Kater Street was located just below South Street in the Fourth Ward. These two streets were the center of those function shops and low lodging houses which occasioned the greatest moral outrage in the 1880s. (A function shop was a place where food was sold that had been collected by beggars.) The *Record* of 18 January 1879 reported the case of a poor mother and child who were brought to the magistrate. "We bum for grub," said the child. Under the child's direction a reporter went "into the classic region of Seventh and South streets" and found the function shop of Mrs. Haughey where the mother sold the food she begged. "Besides serving lunch, 'the establishment' also affords 'lodging to such as pay ten cents' for a night's lodging on a filthy covered floor."

There was another function shop on Rodman Street above Seventh. On 18 January 1882 the *Monthly Register* of the Society for Organizing Charity quotes a reporter of the Philadelphia *Times* who "recently found these lodging houses filled with men and women, in the very lowest stage of degradation, sleeping eight and ten in one room, color and sex mixed promiscuously. . . . Old clothes, given to entire strangers, do the same vicious office, being almost invariably sold for means to buy liquor, before the day closes. Let those who doubt this statement pay a careful visit to the South Street old clothes' shops, or to Mrs. Huet's or Pat O'Brian's 'Hash Shops' on St. Mary Street" (186, *Vol. 3, no. 3, p. 20*).

The Lombard–Southwark–Moyamensing slum section was not perceived as Philadelphia's Tenderloin area; this developed primarily in the eastern half of the old Spring Garden District and the adjacent streets of the pre-Consolidation City (before 1854 the city boundary was at Vine Street). This too was a marginal area and there are indications that it was subjected to some of the same influences as the opposite boundary area of the city. At the time of the Revolution there was a tavern on the north side of Vine Street (and hence outside the city limits) between Seventh and Eighth streets which "was for years the great rendezvous for the enlistments for the Army in the Revolution, and for the Indian Wars afterwards" (218, *Vol. I, p. 470*). Still later it was heavily used by cattle drovers. As we have noted, the cattle market was not far away at Sixth and Callowhill for some years before it was moved further north. The vicinity of Ninth and Vine streets was especially under such influences, for in 1846 an ordinance was passed which declared Ninth Street from South to Chestnut and from Market to Vine a "Station for horses and vehicles in which people from the country may expose for sale the produce of their farms and gardens, free of rent" (12, *p. 257*). (The remnants of this practice may still be found in the Ninth and Christian–Washington Street area of Philadelphia.)

In the 1830s there were also slum conditions in the easterly part of the section north of Market Street (35, *p. i;* 135, *p. 466*).[8] A citizens' committee found 64 tenements with 92 families and 437 inhabitants. Of these, 30 (with 55 families and 250 other people) had no privy; pots were used and the contents thrown daily into the river or into the streets. The privies in the remaining buildings were either in cellar vaults or under the streets.

There were sailors' boardinghouses on Front Street just north of Market and extending up to Arch which were notorious as "sailor town" as early as the colonial period (218, *Vol. I, p. 470*). Also some one-story houses on the west side of Third Street extending south from Race Street, locally known as "Helltown," were presented for prosecution by the Grand Jury in 1744 as "disorderly houses."

While it may be concluded that an incipient Tenderloin existed north of the Market Street area, we are fairly certain that an organized and officially sanctioned Tenderloin area was not recognized before the Civil War. The 1867 report of the Board of Managers of the Magdalen Society (114, *p. 9*), an organization to assist "fallen women," argued against proposals for "what is termed in England, the 'Continental System' or the system of license, as a means of lessening the evil we are combatting" (Appendix D). The report argues that not only were the licens-

---

[8] Also, the *Public Ledger*, 15, 18 April 1836.

ing features of the Continental System a failure, but the sanitary features as well. The issue was intensively debated during the period (154, *pp. 59–62*). This does not mean that police collusion was absent with respect to prostitution. In 1852 the annual report of the Managers of the Rosine Association (172) commented on the failure to obtain convictions with the observation that "The houses were indicted, the Police absorbed all the money that could be drained from the unfortunate women, and they were then released to open houses of the same character in other parts of the city" (*p. 10*).

The Tenderloin defined as a high-density vice district seems to have been a post-Civil War phenomenon. It may have been a consequence of the Sanitary Fair that was held in Logan Square in 1864 to help raise money for the care of the sick and wounded, but the data are not clear. For a less respectable good time, those who came to the Fair could find it readily along Arch, Race or Vine streets. For example, Miller's Variety Theatre at 720-27 Vine Street at the corner of Franklin was one of the more notorious forerunners of the "night club," then called a "Variety Theatre," and featured entertainment, alcohol and women. The *North American* of 24 June 1862 reported that it was raided after the complaint of a nearby hotel keeper on a charge of "keeping a turbulent place." Apparently Miller had so much trouble with police officials that he sold out or used someone else as a front, for an advertisement in the *Public Ledger* of 6 April 1868 lists "Valer's (late Miller's) Wintergarden." Ten years later the place was again known as Miller's Winter Garden. When Mayor Stokely refused to renew its license to sell liquor, he argued "that the place had extensive drinking, a low form of entertainment known as 'varieties,' a good deal of rowdyism in the place and outside, and that numerous prostitutes are attracted to the neighborhood during the said evening performance, to the annoyance of those obliged to pass said place of amusement."[9]

It seems probable that it was Miller's that was being alluded to by the author of the article that appeared in the Philadelphia *Press*, 18 March 1872, under the title "Our Boweries: Eighth

[9] SPC case no. 282, 20 November 1878; no. 1301, 19 November 1879; *Public Ledger*, 6 April 1868; *Evening Bulletin*, 11 January 1878.

Street; the Stroll of the Nymph du Pave." The article, incidentally, also documents the Civil War period change of the area.

"Within the past ten years this thoroughfare has undergone a gradual and complete metamorphosis, and now presents a moral aspect of an entirely different nature. Here, on each succeeding Saturday night, is the true school to study human nature in all its varied phases. . . . [We went to see] the sights from Walnut Street to Vine Street [where] the dazzling glare of light from brilliantly illuminated show windows reflected almost the glare of day. . . . The drinking saloons with which the street is dotted at certain intervals appeared to be driving a good business. Their illuminated and attractive lights of handsomely ornamented stained glass seemed to be enticing bait which drew the 'roystering blade,' the mechanic, and the man about town within their portals. . . . We turned our steps toward Vine Street knowing by previous experience that this was the locality. . . . Hurrying on his way to a concert-saloon around the corner on Vine Street could be seen the sturdy man of toil. . . . Standing where we do, we hear sounds of music proceeding from the free concert saloon above referred to. Clear up until midnight there is a steady throng of males and females passing in and out. As the hand of time presents on the 'wee small hours' hilarious individuals emerge from this temple of Momus and render night hideous by baccanalian songs, which are only checked by an admonition from a blue-coated guardian of the place, coupled with a threat that in case of disregard to obey such admonition certain iron doors may be closed upon the rollekers. As midnight approaches there is a noticeable diminution in the crowd of pedestrians, many having taken their departure for home, while others (especially of the male sex) are drawn into beer or drinking saloons for the purpose of a 'night cap,' which is generally equivalent to stupefying themselves with the cup that cheers but *does* inebriate. The most prominent feature at this time is the constant throng of unfortunates who, arrayed in gaudy habiliments, flaunt their shame in the face of all passers by. Standing on the corners of small streets and alleyways they can be seen until far into the morning generally in groups, but often alone, with sad dejected appearance."

Another such place was the Arcade Garden Theatre-Saloon at 255 N. 8th Street. The agent of the Society to Protect Children had it raided about 11 March 1879 as a "vile immoral place" where children 12 and 14 years of age were dancing. That there was indeed some indication of danger to the morals of children (the Society apparently limited its concern to persons under 16 years of age) is indicated in his report of a previous case on 25 November 1878. On that day, he went with a police captain to the ladies' balcony where he "was accosted by three of the many women present and with any encouragement could have made the acquaintance of any of them for they were all walking about plying their vocation."[10]

Across from Miller's, Franklin Square was also a site of these activities and had been from before the Civil War. A Rosine Association report tells of girls being picked up in the Square for purposes of prostitution in 1855. On Thursday, 13 November 1879, the matron of the Magdalen Society reported about some girls who had run away from home. The father of one of them came and discussed the matter with the matron and left the house. An hour later he brought the girls back. It seems that "as he was going down Vine Street, he felt impelled to go through 'Franklin Square.' He hadn't gotten very far in the square when he saw [his daughter] sitting talking to a man. He immediately went to them and ordered them to go with him. . . . She seemed very ashamed to think he had found them. But was fully determined to go back to her evil ways." The matron's diary of Tuesday 16 June 1891 reports on a girl from Shamokin who was arrested in the Square—"she seemed like a nice modest girl and very unlike the others" who were with her. Again, the *Sunday Transcript* on 6 September 1914 reported that two girls from Chester had gone to Eighth and Vine streets, were picked up by two young men and went to talk in Franklin Square. The girls then lived with the men for three weeks before coming to the attention of the police.

We examined the case record books of the Society to Protect Children for the period 1877 to 1895 and recorded and organized the location of houses of prostitution by wards. Ward Thirteen heads the list with about 19% of the 462 houses of prostitution; the other wards of importance were the Tenth (14%), Fourteenth (11%), Eighth (9%) and the Fifth (8%) (Figure 1). The remainder had small or negligible numbers. The Eighth and the Fifth Wards have already been discussed in the context of the Lombard–Southwark–Moyamensing section; to these should also be added the Fourth Ward. The balance that stand out are those which include parts of the Tenderloin. It was in these wards, especially the Thirteenth, that by the time of Mayor Samuel H. Ashbridge (1899–1903), politics reputedly

[10] SPC case no. 69, 25 November 1878; no. 830, 11 March 1879.

became integrated with prostitution and vice throughout the
Republican Party Organization, which also sold police protection. (The term "White Slave Syndicate" was popularly used,
but its activities also involved gambling and vote fraud. There is
no reason to assume that young Black women were excluded
from forcible prostitution, either.) Police protection reputedly
cost from $25 a month to $50 a week (77; 195, *p. 215*).[11] The
Republican Organization in the Twelfth and Thirteenth Wards
protected houses that were reported in the *Public Ledger*. The
Syndicate was said to have started out with 15 Russian-Jewish
young women bought in other cities at $100 apiece. But by 1905

FIGURE 1.—*Inner City Wards of Philadelphia.* [Source: Daley, J.
and Weinberg. A. Genealogy of Philadelphia; county subdivisions,
1963. Reproduced by permission.]

[11] Also, the *Public Ledger*, 25 December 1904.

it was said that young Italian women were also being procured; none of them could speak English, a preferred condition.[12]

The involuntary nature of the recruitment, the forcible retention of the young women, and the scale of the activities rather than the prostitution itself may have made the difference in public attitudes. Similar activities were not uncommon in the years before the Ashbridge administration: in 1879 a 13-year-old girl was abducted and placed in a house of prostitution; in 1880, a man who lived in the fashionable Continental Hotel at Ninth and Chestnut streets imported a pregnant girl of 15 from England and placed her in a house on Fairmount Avenue and, after the delivery, she was moved to a rooming house on Twelfth Street; an operator of a house on American Street regularly imported girls from Germany in the early 1890s.[13] To take another example, in 1886 a girl "from the country" who had answered an advertisement for housework found herself working in a house of assignation; within a short time she was "ruined" and escaped only by creating a disorder that led the proprietress to have her arrested and sent to the County Prison; from there she managed to get to the Magdalen Society.[14] In 1893 a 14-year-old girl went into the Lyceum Theatre at 724 Vine Street and someone persuaded her to come live at 1028 Wood Street and work as a servant; within a week, she was forced into prostitution at that address.[15] It was common to recruit a young woman to cook and then force her into prostitution:

"This girl . . . said she was accosted on the street by a Defdt [defendant] who persuaded her to go to his house as a cook. She went. After working in the kitchen for a week, Defdt advised her to take her place as a boarder for the entertainment of men, which she did. She also stated that she paid Defdt $6.50 per week board and half of what she made, so that if she made $20 per week, $16.50 went to Defdt and the balance, $3.50, went to the girl for clothes; which clothing is kept under lock and key by Defdt and worn by girls only when Defdt per-

---

[12] *Public Ledger*, 25 January 1905; *Evening Bulletin*, 25 January 1905.

[13] 240 S. 12th St., 1012 Fairmount Ave., 20 N. 12th St., 444 N. American St.; SPC case no. 1275, 8 November 1879; no. 2054, 18 October 1880; no. 11715, 1 March 1892.

[14] Magdalen Society, Matron's Diary, 1885–1889, Thursday, 22 April 1886, p. 47.

[15] SPC case no. 12912, 13 July 1893.

mits, and do not become their property until paid for which is seldom done and the girls leave without them" (117, *p. 315*).[16]

Young Black women were also forced into prostitution: the Society to Protect Children found a 16-year-old Black woman who two years before had been forced to cohabit with a White man, and, since that time, the adult defendant (a Black woman) had attempted to force the girl to do it again.[17]

We may assume that the city officials and law enforcement agencies were thoroughly corrupt before Ashbridge took office. There was, for example, the case of Agnes King (probably a pseudonym) who had been operating a house of prostitution at 1731 Filbert Street at least since 1893. After 18 months of vigorous citizen protest, warrants were issued in early November 1897 for her arrest and for the arrest of a city real estate assessor who had leased the house to her.[18] Agnes King was sentenced to a fine and a jail term of 60 days, but the city real estate assessor went free because the magistrate did not think that the testimony was strong enough. During the course of the testimony, however, the names of public officials who visited the place were mentioned, so that it is hard to believe that the city assessor did not know what the premises were being used for, and one may infer that the magistrate was, in fact, a part of a corrupt political system. Furthermore, during the testimony it was suggested that Agnes King was the common-law wife of a public official—a health officer of the city. Public protest led to his resignation by the end of the year, but he continued to be a political power in the Twelfth Ward, on the basis of "the many lodging houses now in that ward, which are packed about elec-

---

[16] 345 N. 6th St., SPC case no. 7489, 7 February 1887; other cases: 624 N. 3d St., *Public Ledger*, 25 December 1904; SPC case no. 7699, 29 April 1887. The control of prostitutes through control of their clothing was also practiced in other cities: in New York City, a young woman who ran away from a house was taken to a magistrate for stealing clothes and sentenced to 60 days in the workhouse.

[17] 633 Delancey St.; SPC case no. 7906, 8 July 1887.

[18] He was subject to prosecution under P.L. 382, Section 43, Act of 31 March 1860: "If any person shall keep or maintain a common bawdy-house, or place for the practice of fornication, or shall knowingly let or demise a house, or part thereof to be so kept, he shall be guilty of a misdemeanor, and on conviction, be sentenced to pay a fine not exceeding One Thousand Dollars and to undergo an imprisonment not exceeding Two Years."

tion time with foreigners, some of whom know enough to buy naturalization papers; others simply vote on a tax receipt, promise of work on a city job, or general promise of being taken care of, being a sufficient inducement for them to support the machine."[19]

There were perennial protests and attempts to suppress the Tenderloin, all with little lasting effect. In 1875, for example, the Board of Managers of the Magdalen Society complained to Mayor Stokely (1872–1881) that prostitution could be eliminated if it were not for the fact that some well-known citizens put up bail before the magistrates (114, 1876, p. 12). Mayor Stokely responded to the appeals by ordering raids which apparently drove some prostitutes into hiding (194, pp. 187, 274, 428). The diary of the matron of the Magdalen Society for 22 June 1880, for example, mentions a girl who had come several weeks before and was a "bad influence." "She is the girl that came to us on May 24, at three o'clock in the morning, to escape the raid the Mayor had ordered upon three houses of ill-repute." The Public Ledger of 7 July 1885 criticized these raids: "The disreputable houses where 'lewd women congregate' can be overhauled by the police and their occupants put under bond for their better behavior, as we find on the odd occasions when raids are made. But why should raids be necessary on them or upon any others? Whenever such necessity is supposedly to exist it argues an antecedent neglect or loose administration of the law. There should be steady enforcement of all laws, then those inclined to break them would get into the habit of observing them, and these spasmodic 'raids' would be unnecessary." The implication that such activities continued with the tacit or active consent of the police and public officials is clear.

The Jewish and Christian middle and upper classes were up in arms (98, 1881 ff.).[20] The Jewish community organized its charitable activities to assist girls who were rescued from the houses. The Christian community's principal vehicle for action

[19] City and State 4: 98, 18 November 1897; 98, 134, 140, 2 December 1897; 201, 30 December 1897; 5: 282, 27 January 1898; Minutes of the Philadelphia Board of Health, 31 December 1897.

[20] Also, the Public Ledger, 18, 19, 20, 21, 25 March; 15 April; 9, 10 June 1890.

was the Law and Order Society, organized in 1881 to focus on Sunday liquor law violations. Under the leadership of D. Clarence Gibboney, it put considerable pressure on Mayor Weaver (1903–1907) as evidenced in the report of David J. Smyth, director of the Department of Public Safety, that, in 1904, 163 proprietors and 480 bawdy-house inmates were arrested and many sent to the House of Correction. Police also closed 227 disorderly houses, arrested 1173 gamblers and 101 proprietors of gambling houses. The effort to suppress streetwalking led to 785 arrests.

Much of this activity was due to the Law and Order Society which hired its own detectives, made it own citizen arrests and took its cases directly to the magistrates, thereby circumventing the police. This near vigilantism was facilitated by P.L. 382, Section 43, Act of 31 March 1860. However the Society was not able to resist counterpressure. Mayor Weaver (143)[21] publicly questioned the methods of the Society and, after a large raid late in March 1905, the Law and Order Society, and its near vigilantism, ceased operations for all practical purposes.

The Philadelphia Tenderloin was officially abolished in 1914. The Vice Commission of Philadelphia, a self-appointed body, began its work about 1 August 1912 and issued a report (216) early in 1913.[22] The Commission concluded that there was no special section of the city set apart for prostitution. It pointed out that in the 15 blocks of "more notorious streets of the city there were 1,542 children between the ages of six and sixteen years, and a total of 2,500 minors in these blocks." That is, prostitution was common in poor residential sections and there was no particular section of the city given up exclusively to vice. But the fact remains that the concentration of such activities was apparently higher in the Tenderloin than in other parts of the city and on 6 May 1914, on the orders of reform Mayor Rudolph Blankenburg (1911–1916), a "quarantine" on the "so-called segregated district of the Tenderloin" in Philadelphia was declared. Evidently Blankenburg and Public Safety Director Porter believed in the existence of a Tenderloin from the

---

[21] Also, the *Evening Bulletin*, 9, 21, 25, 26, 30 January; 31 March 1905.
[22] The Commission was probably instigated by the Pennsylvania Society for the Prevention of Social Disease. See Appendix D.

north side of Vine Street to the south side of Poplar and from the west side of Sixth Street to the east side of Broad, i.e., the Thirteenth and Fourteenth Wards. This was the Eighth Police District. In this area the Vice Commission had reported about 200 houses of ill repute with an average of 5 inmates, or from 900 to 1000 women. It estimated that each house took in about $300 a week or about $60,000 a week for the entire area.[23] The *Evening Bulletin* noted that the quarantine had an immediate effect: "The elaborate places on Callowhill Street near 12 were closed as tightly last night as the more notorious ones in Percy and Noble street." It was reported that any woman under police surveillance, who was seen "flirting" on the street, was also subject to arrest during this crackdown, and a "notorious" restaurant hangout for thieves, pickpockets, gamblers and cadets at 319 North Eighth Street was raided.[24] The police were deeply implicated in the vice activities, and it was not surprising that an inspection committee found that houses on the main streets were closed while those on the side streets were still operating. Despite only partial success in this one area, the Mayor and the Director of Public Safety put the entire city under quarantine on 12 May. Gambling, speakeasies and prostitution were banned, and a desultory campaign against vice was conducted.

Possibly the beginning of the "cleanup" was August 1912, when a raid was made on the Mutual Republican Club on Spring Garden Street near Seventeenth Street and its slot machine confiscated. Blankenburg's reform administration raided the Mutual Republican Club at the behest of the wives of the workingmen of that locality who complained bitterly that their men were losing their week's wages in the Club and were coming home empty-handed. But the Club was more than a gambling house. In 1904, when it was located at 706 North Franklin Street, it was reported to be the interface between the Republican Organization and the Syndicate, being the Thirteenth Ward Republican Headquarters and also the headquarters of the "White Slave Syndicate" (77).[25]

[23] *Evening Bulletin*, 7 May 1913.
[24] *Evening Bulletin*, 8, 17 May 1913.
[25] Also, *Evening Bulletin*, 3 August 1912; *Public Ledger*, 25 December 1904.

The reformers lost the next election and prostitution, gambling, liquor and drugs continued in a Tenderloin which now had no official standing. Our most detailed information about these activities at the time comes from the *Sunday Transcript*,[26] whose editor, apparently a heavy drinker, lived in a vaudeville boardinghouse near Franklin Square. The *Transcript* published the names and addresses of 82 cases involving prostitution, gambling or illegal liquor sales from 1911 through 1917, almost all of which were from the Tenth, Twelfth, Thirteenth or Fourteenth Wards.[27] The police also arrested a group of homosexuals who used Washington Square as a meeting place (they referred to it as "Fairyland").[28] Police raided a "complete opium layout" at 244 North Tenth Street which also had supplies of cocaine.[29]

If prostitution is used as an index, the Tenderloin to which the Vice Commission gave special attention and which was of initial interest to Mayor Blankenburg was in Wards Thirteen and Fourteen. Why Ward Ten was not given the same initial attention is hard to say. The continued importance of Ward Thirteen as the most central Tenderloin Ward is suggested by the listing in the *Sunday Transcript* of 1 April 1923 and later during the same year as part of an apparent attempt to put pressure on Mayor Moore during his version of the "quarantine." (The campaign was not taken up by Mayor Smith, Blankenburg's successor.) The 1923 listing gives names and addresses of 60 wide-open places, almost all of which dealt in girls, with some dealing in "hooch," gambling and opium. Of these places, all but 2 were in the Thirteenth Ward.

In addition to the information published by Mark Mason in the *Sunday Transcript*, there is a more comprehensive but less detailed source in the Philadelphia Hospital and Health Survey of 1926 (59, *Ch. 4*). While the data are not readily comparable with the Society to Protect Children case records listing discussed above, they do give an indication of the location of the more readily available places over a number of years. The Thir-

---

[26] *Sunday Transcript*, 1 September 1914; 26 June, 3 July 1921; 16 April 1922.

[27] *Sunday Transcript*, 12 May 1918, city edition. (The early edition takes the data back to 1907 but is less complete.)

[28] *Sunday Transcript*, 19 July 1914.

[29] *Sunday Transcript*, 10 July 1915.

teenth Ward had about 23% of the 107 houses of prostitution known to the Survey in 1926; other wards of importance were the Seventh (19%), the Fourteenth (12%) and the Eighth (11%). Thus, the Thirteenth Ward continued to be important, and when it is considered along with the Fourteenth Ward it is evident that the old Tenderloin lingered on. The Seventh Ward was relatively more important than the data of the Society to Protect Children suggested. The Seventh Ward was the heart of the Lombard–Southwark–Moyamensing slum and, while the policy of repression may have been a qualified success in the sense that the scope of overt prostitution had been greatly reduced, the persistence of the Lombard–Southwark–Moyamensing strip as a vice area is worthy of note. The conclusion is clear that a distinctive Tenderloin became recognized north of Market Street that continued well into the 20th Century.

It is also evident that a concentration of vagrants and homeless workingmen and related institutions developed in the Race–Vine Street area adjacent to the Tenderloin. We have discussed the characteristics of the Skid Row population of Philadelphia in the 1960–1970 period in some detail elsewhere (23). Our immediate question is when such a Skid Row developed in Philadelphia. Available evidence leads to the conclusion that the distinctive homeless workingmen's area became differentiated quite late in the 19th Century. Thus, the Philadelphia *News* of 25 December 1887 commented that Philadelphia was the "winter haven" for the tramps of the East Coast and continues:

"The Western Pennsylvania breed are principally Germans, and as they strike town make for the five cent eating houses and ten cent lodging houses along New Market Street [in the vicinity of the Callowhill food market area]. The blooded tramps eat and lodge on Market Street, while the very low down break for the St. Mary slums and Pat O'Brien's function shop. No matter where he sleeps, however, whether it be an unburied water main or a fifteen cent lodging house, the tramp by 'instinct' finds the city's best hunting grounds within an hour after arrival. It is the theatre district, the public buildings district and the promenade district here existing all in one and included between Chestnut Street and Arch and Eighth and Seventeenth."

Presumably those with a little more money could stay in hotels that might charge 25 cents. Such hotels could also be found at 310 and 624 Race Street.[30] Furthermore, a cheap lodging house charging 10 cents a night and operated in conjunction with a drinking bar could also be found at 643 Callowhill Street.[31] Thus we conclude that in the 1880s the tramps and vagrants lived in several places in the Tenderloin section, on its edge, and south of the Market Street slum. A distinctive homeless-man area apparently had not yet emerged.

By 1890 there were cheap lodgings for homeless men on Race and Vine streets. In that year there was a rooming house at Second and Vine streets in which an elderly man lived: "It was learned upon investigation that Defdt lives on the 3rd floor at the above address, and he gets drunk on Saturday, and keeps in that condition until Wednesday following, then works for 2 or 3 days and earns $4 per week."[32] This is a typical Skid Row lifestyle. Again, a few months later, an agent of the Society to Protect Children reported on a place at Sixth and Race streets: "Defdt keeps a house which she calls a 'home' or 'shelter' under the garb of Charity. In agts opinion from what he saw it is nothing more or less than a 'Bum' lodging house or 'Function Shop.' There are people of all ages from 4 to 60. They are a hard looking crowd and it is not a fit place for children."[33] And, in 1895, there was a raid on a cheap lodging house located at 808 Race Street which found 60 men and 16 or 18 boys "who lodged there nightly paying 10 or 15 cents each for the privilege of sleeping on the floor."[34]

That the area had been transformed is evidenced in the commentary on a hoped-for merger between the Arch Street Presbyterian Church (located at Fifth and Arch streets) and the West Arch Street Presbyterian Church (at Eighteenth and Arch) that finally took place in 1897. An undated newsclip not long before the merger comments that "The families which used to gather . . . their dwellings hereabouts had long given place to business houses, hives of industry, and boarding houses, and a floating population now occupied the alleys, nooks, and upper rooms."[35]

[30] *Public Ledger*, 2 July 1885; 23 November 1889.
[31] *Evening Call*, 20 September 1883.
[32] 226 Vine St., SPC case no. 9991, 1 April 1890.
[33] 630 Race St., SPC case no. 10361, 18 August 1890.
[34] SPC case no. 14233, 4 January 1895.
[35] "A Dream? Union With West Arch Street Church." [Presbyterian Historical Society.]

Near the end of the decade, speaking of the Tenth Ward, the *Monthly Register* in 1898 commented: "a great change has come over this district in consequence of the growth of the industries of the city and the transformation of the old-time residential districts into business houses, boarding and lodging houses. . . . Where once were streets of houseowners and householders enjoying congenial society, active in good works, useful members of flourishing churches, interested in large business concerns, now the lodging house flourishes and the cheap boardinghouse shows its untidy front . . . in short, the situation is such that it requires faith and courage to [carry on] in the doubly necessary work of our organization. For the ward is poorer, its destitute more numerous, its demands on charity more urgent, while its resources diminish day by day" (186, *Vol. 20, p. 11*).

The civic leaders of the day, then, understood that the process of urban growth, both in residential and commercial-industrial terms, had led to the impoverishment of the ward. The 22d annual report of the Tenth Ward Association notes this and the emergence of the homeless-man area: "The district of the ward where there is the most poverty and distress now covers a much larger area than it did five years ago, having rapidly encroached upon the more prosperous neighborhood that surrounds it. This can be seen at a glance, in a walk through the northeast section of the ward, while, in fact, the whole ward has felt the blighting effect of the influx of 'the undesirable' " (191, *1900*). It is hard to believe that the change was as sudden as this suggests, but the 14th annual report (191) in 1892 does not mention the deterioration of the ward and has a satisfied tone of effectiveness and shared responsibility, describing most people in the ward as "workers" with few wealthy residents, but having a concern for neighborly care (185). Of course, this could be the blindness of the perennially optimistic.

One final datum suggests a conservative answer to the question at hand. The city persuaded the Legislature to pass the Lodging House Act in 1885 which covered those places "not licensed as a hotel, inn or tavern, in which ten or more persons are lodged at a price, for a single night, of twenty-five cents or less for each person." The license cost $2. In the first year of operation, 1896, 250 properties were inspected with a bed capacity of 5619; however, only 83 licenses were granted, involving 1045 rooms with a maximum capacity of 3037 (138, *pp. 16–17*). A large percentage of the lodging houses were rejected because beds and bedding, filthy and unclean, were crowded into rooms that were equally filthy. Useful data from City Controller reports are available from 1896 through 1907 (when the fee structure apparently changed). There are also parallel data from the Board of Health reports of 1896 through 1900. While there are unexplained discrepancies between the 2 sets of data, and the Board of Health statistics are lower in all years than those of the City Controller, at least 119 licenses were issued under the Lodging House Act in 1899.

In the annual report for 1899, the Chief Inspector of Nuisances of the Board of Health wrote: "The extreme poverty of many of the applicants in the Fifth and Eleventh Wards has prompted some consideration to the licenses where poor unfortunates, almost without the pittances for a night's lodging, are admitted; otherwise the station house must care for them or they are forced to roam the streets at night." This is an indication of the continued existence of low lodging houses occupied by homeless people in the Fifth and Eleventh Wards at the turn of the century. We must conclude, therefore, that while the decade of the 1890s seems to be when a distinctive homeless-man area became discernible north of Market Street, it was not a sudden developing but a gradual decline of cheap boarding and lodging places outside the immediate vicinity of the Race–Vine Skid Row area. Furthermore, the Tenderloin section seems to have developed well before the Skid Row area on its edge.

In sum, our examination of the data makes clear that the Tenderloin and the homeless-man area were different but closely related aspects of urban life. Historically, the Philadelphia Skid Row developed on the fringe of the Tenderloin. But this was not always the case, for the Lombard–Southwark–Moyamensing section was a slum, Tenderloin and homeless-persons area as well. It was identifiable as such at least as early as 1815, possibly earlier in that part which is located from the river to Fourth Street. While the Tenderloin and Skid Row north of Market Street were predominantly White, the Lombard–Southwark–Moyamensing area was racially mixed and apparently had been so for the entire period in question. The data support the conclusion that were was no Tenderloin in the area north of Market Street before the Civil War. This does not mean that there was no prostitution, gambling or crime, for there surely was. However, we have found no basis for the conclusion that these activities were concentrated in the area, and the evidence suggests that it was well into the fourth quarter of the century before they became highly organized. Nor do we mean to say that there were no slum conditions in the area north of Market Street, for there were.

The Civil War seems to have been a turning point for the area north of Market Street. The official sanctioning of the Tenderloin came much later and was a political act which simply recognized a civic condition, although it probably intensified the trend toward the concentration of such activities once the scheme was put into operation. By the mid-1880s, the Tenderloin had developed in the area north of Market Street and continued at least into the early 1920s.

Finally, the data support the conclusion that there was no distinctive homeless-workingmen's area north of Market Street before the Civil War. It developed on the fringe between the Tenderloin and the central business district no earlier than the mid-1880s and possibly the early 1890s. It gradually became consolidated as a distinct section of the city and has continued to exist, slowly dying, until the present time, when the remnant was cleared by a combination of urban renewal and highway construction projects.

Chapter 2

The Great Antislum Campaign in 19th Century Philadelphia[1]

THE SLUM, the Tenderloin and the Skid Row in Philadelphia developed as part of the changes—the "urban process"—that took place in the city. Because of the paucity of adequate information we do not know why they developed where they did. Nonetheless, enough data are available to reach tentative conclusions which may be considered as hypotheses for future research.

This chapter examines the following questions: How can we account for the development of the Lombard–Southwark–Moyamensing slum section? Why did the White vagrants and alcoholics move away from it? Why did the Tenderloin and the Skid Row develop in the section north of Market Street on the other side of the central business district?

THE ORIGINS OF THE SLUM

The beginnings of the Lombard–Southwark–Moyamensing slum are attributable at least in part to the "moralistic" English and German settlers of Philadelphia and the surrounding area. The colonial theaters escaped control by locating in Southwark, on the south side of South Street. When the theater became more socially acceptable, as evidenced by the location of the "new Theatre" at Sixth and Chestnut streets in 1794, South Street lost its standing as a "first run" location. A pattern had been established, however, in which socially and politically disapproved activities tended to locate in Southwark, just out of reach of city control.

This reputation was reinforced by the location of a Federal Navy Yard in Southwark in 1880–1801 which gave an impetus for the growth of the area, albeit in the direction of maritime occupations. The Yard was the anchor point for maritime activ-

---

[1] We express appreciation to Dennis Clark and Eric Blumberg for their encouragement and suggestions.

ity that extended upriver for several miles; in the immediate vicinity new streets were rapidly opened as far as
Fourth and Fifth streets and extended southward below Washington Avenue. Not very far from the Yard, with Bainbridge
Street as its axis, an area of grog shops, rooming houses and
houses of prostitution developed.

The slum was influenced by the maritime trades for many
years. Eastburn's Mariner's Church, the first of a number of
such establishments, was built on the east side of Water Street
(between Walnut and Chestnut) in 1828. Enumeration sheets of
the 1850 Census show that people engaged in maritime trades,
e.g., sailors, mariners, watermen, stevedores, carpenters, rig-
gers and coopers, lived close to the Delaware River although
they also lived as far west as the eastern wards of Moyamensing
Township (Eleventh Street). Within the city the riverfront
wards had a number of cheap boardinghouses and hotels that
were used by seamen and by persons in other semiskilled occupations. It would seem probable that the Bainbridge Street
houses of prostitution and saloons developed in response to the
demands of sailors and other workingmen in the area. The
lower end of Bainbridge Street continued to be an area of prostitution and heavy drinking for many years after the Civil War.

In the early 1800s growth extended south on Second Street
to Moyamensing Road, where it turned in a southwesterly direction into the "Neck"—a low-lying area of swamps and farms
between the Delaware and the Schuylkill Rivers. Meat and
produce moved into the area to supply both the wholesale and
retail markets that developed in the Dock Street section: the
Second Street Market from Pine to South Street, the Wharton
Market (on Moyamensing Road from Christian to Ellsworth
after 1812) and the Washington Market on Bainbridge from
Third to Fifth streets (after 1834). These activities would also
have encouraged the growth of cheap transient housing and
prostitution because of the presence of so many men.

Further west, centered on the border between Southwark and
Moyamensing (Passyunk Road), a racially mixed area developed
at least as early as 1815. Such a location was typical of Black
residential settlement in the Philadelphia area (19). Blacks had
built homes in marginal locations, such as on the edges of
swamps, railroad rights-of-way, and at the boundaries of politi-

cal subdivisions in areas that Whites did not want to occupy at the time. Blacks were removed from the Whites but not too far away, for the races were interdependent. The border area of Philadelphia with Southwark and Moyamensing was such an area from 1790 to 1830 and Blacks were permitted to move there largely beyond effective political control. Others moved into the same area who were equally poverty-stricken and rejected, notably the Irish. Later residential development flowed around the area, so that by the 1840s the gangs moved up Passyunk Road to riot in the poor Black–White residential area (55).

A major explanation for the initial development of the Lombard–Southwark–Moyamensing slum, then, was its marginality. Marginal location (i.e., location in the least desirable area) is a function of relatively low levels of social power. Once such an area is established, it will continue to be occupied by low-status people until they are ejected by more powerful elements of the society which find a "higher and better" use for the land, or their relative power changes and they are in a position to acquire or demand a more desirable location. Once the Lombard–Southwark–Moyamensing slum developed, the area continued as a slum, a "vice" district and a center for vagrants until it was finally disrupted by the cumulative effects of a scattershot reform campaign that began before the Civil War and continued after the close of the 19th Century.

Disruption of the Slum

Several modes of attack were used during the last half of the 19th Century to eliminate the slum. Taken together, they may be viewed as a trial-and-error approach to the solution of what was perceived by persons of power and influence as a major civic and social welfare problem. The final procedure was the ejection of the homeless slum residents and the introduction of an immigrant population to replace them; in present-day jargon we would call it urban redevelopment of the land for a "higher and better use." Even this ejection was only a qualified success. While the social welfare workers did shift the locus of White vagrancy, they did not eliminate the slum, nor did they eliminate the prostitutes, Black or White.

Attacks on the Lombard–Southwark–Moyamensing slum consisted of four separate but related campaigns: those aimed at vagrants, at alcohol users, at "wayward" women, and at slum families and their housing. While the movements were not officially coordinated, their cumulative effect was to make the area less hospitable than other parts of the city for White vagrants.

There were considerable efforts to suppress the population of vagrants. The House of Correction Act of 1871 was aimed at vagrants throughout the city. The floor manager of the bill, however, made it clear that he had the Lombard–Southwark– Moyamensing vagrants particularly in mind when he responded to criticism of the proposed bill with the observation that on Saturday night large numbers of paupers congregated in the "lowest sections of the city." These paupers were arrested by the police and "carted by the car load inside the walls of Moyamensing Prison, there to be kept from the gaze of the Sunday public. On Monday morning the floodgates of the prison were opened and these vagrants were let out upon the community."[2]

Part of the argument for a House of Correction was presented by the Philadelphia Chief of Police:

"The number of persons furnished with lodgings at the various station houses is enormous, amounting to 76,457. No stronger argument in favor of the establishment of a House of Correction can be furnished than these figures; the greater portion of these persons are of that class who, having no fixed home anywhere, and being able-bodied, walk the streets during the day with nothing to do, and in many cases no inclination for industrious occupation, gathering food by begging or as they can, and when night approaches, seek shelter from the inclemency of the weather in our station houses" (144, p. 505).

The "revolving door" character of the House of Correction was apparently early established: "There were 84,352 persons who sought lodging at the several station houses for a single night, being an increase over 1882 of 5,725. . . . Many of these appear night after night, and, although frequently sent to the House of Correction as vagrants, having no homes or visible means of support, they remain there but a very short time, and soon reappear in their accustomed haunts, and at night seek the station house as a shelter" (145, p. 1008). The use of police

[2] Legislative Journal of the Commonwealth of Pennsylvania, Session of 1871, 12 April 1871, p. 678.

stations for lodgings of penniless people will be dealt with in greater detail later in this chapter.

Another source of the attack on vagrants came from the Society for Organizing Charitable Relief and Repressing Mendicancy, organized in 1878. The name was shortened to "Society for Organizing Charity" the following year (Appendix D). Consistent with its original purpose, the Society formed a special committee on mendicancy. Its emphasis was on work rather than giving direct relief—whenever this seemed reasonable from the point of view of the Society's "home visitors"—and it viewed compulsory work as a cure for the tramp–vagrant problem. In this, it followed the ethos of the times.

The House of Correction Act of 1871 specified that every person in custody who was not sick or handicapped was to be employed by the superintendent of the House of Correction in quarrying stone, farming or manufacturing items that were needed by the prison, almshouses or other public institutions of the state or city. The law also specified that those who refused to work were kept in their cells and fed bread and water.[3]

In addition to trying to make the House of Correction more effective as an involuntary way of "salvaging" the poor and of driving "professional beggars" out of town, the Society for Organizing Charity began planning early for the establishment of several semi-involuntary institutions known as Wayfarer's Lodges, which had been first developed in Boston in 1878 (100; 186, *Vol. 4, pp. 34–35*; 188, *1885, p. 5*; 190, *p. 13*). The Society secured legislation to the effect that, having been notified in advance, any able-bodied person who was fed and sheltered for the night and then refused to work up to 4 hours in return was to be sentenced for a term of not less than 30 days nor more than 90 days in the House of Correction. The Wayfarer's Lodge provided "a good, if homely supper," and a night's lodging after a required bath; the next morning the men (for most of those who used these facilities were men) were required to saw and split about an eighth of a cord of wood, on pain of imprisonment. The first Lodge and Woodlot was opened in March 1884 on the edge of the Lombard–Southwark–Moyamensing section. The second was opened where it would catch vagrants of the

[3] P.L. 1301, 2 June 1871.

Race–Vine, New Market–Northern Liberties, and Kensington sections. "At first the Lombard Street Lodge was overcrowded by 'tramps,'" reported the Society's Board of Directors, "but as the system became better organized this class was sifted out" (186, *Vol. 5, p. 57*; 188, *7th*). The policy of suppression was apparently not successful but probably did make the vagrants more transient.

A second approach to the amelioration of social problems in Philadelphia came through attempts to regulate the use of alcohol. Temperance workers tried to eliminate what they considered to be alcohol misuse through a two-part campaign of therapy and exhortation. The Temperance Movement was also unsuccessful.

In 1872 the Franklin Reformatory Home (Appendix D) opened at Ninth and Locust streets as a project of the Temperance Movement. This location was south of the élite section and north of the slum. The buildings that were acquired had formerly been the Newsboys Home; evidently Philadelphians no longer perceived homeless youth—"street arabs"—as a problem of general social welfare concern and the Home was discontinued.

The original plan of the Franklin Reformatory Home was much like a present-day detoxication and halfway house and its program was similar to that developed by the Washingtonians in the 1840s and Alcoholics Anonymous nearly a century later. While it claimed a "success rate" of 40%, it seems doubtful that many of its residents were the "hard core" vagrant alcoholics from the slum. The annual reports of 1883 and 1884 express concern for this type of person:

"This class is composed of the drunkards who have wasted their substance, alienated their family and friends, lost their own self-respect and that of their fellow-men, and by steady progression from bad to worse, first walk the streets for want of shelter, then hide from the police in barrels, or behind lumber piles on the docks, begging nickels and dimes for food (which are almost invariably spent for *whiskey* in some free *lunch* den), till finally they land in the House of Correction, where for want of liquor they stop drinking for a time. Their discharge from this institution at the expiration of their sentence, in nearly every case, finds them without reformation, and returning to their old habits and associates, they repeat the process till again interfered with by the law" (68, *11th, p. 15*).

The annual report of 1884 provides an account of 8 men who had been selected and persuaded to move into the Home, but it cautions that neither the Home nor the Godwin Association (the "outpatient" program) had had much experience with them. Neither later reports nor the available records make mention of this program and it seems reasonable to infer that it met with no success. The reports do not state where the vagrants came from, but in 1881 Samuel P. Godwin, president of the Franklin Reformatory Home, reported that of "60 persons, Black and White, dirty, vicious and lazy, whom he once found occupying a single room in the 4th Ward, every one was a pauper through intemperance"; it is highly probable that the vagrants who were recruited came from the same vicinity (186, *Vol. 2, p. 5*).

The Woman's Christian Temperance Union (WCTU) was also active in Philadelphia. In 1866 the WCTU held 150 gospel temperance meetings in and near the Lombard–Southwark–Moyamensing slum.[4] The WCTU also provided some support for other social welfare organizations; in 1879 a girl was admitted to the Magdalen Society (an organization dedicated to the "reform" of prostitutes) after referral from a WCTU member.[5] We infer that mutual referral was a customary procedure.

A third element in the social reform movements was the attempt to rescue wayward girls and fallen women. Both the Magdalen Society and the Rosine Association had been in existence since before the Civil War and were not specific to the Lombard–Southwark–Moyamensing district (Appendix D). After the end of the War, several other organizations opened facilities in the district and began to take up this aspect of reform.

The Midnight Mission was organized in 1867 and located its home in the 900 block of Locust Street and in 1881 established a branch at 609 Rodman Street. The original purpose was to hold mission meetings in the vice district at midnight "for the recovery of fallen women." (By 1890 it had changed its purpose to the assistance of women and girls with illegitimate babies and had moved its headquarters to Germantown.) Shortly thereafter, another mission to the prostitutes had arrived, the Flor-

---

[4] 609 Rodman St.; 729 Lombard St. (232, *12th, p. 12*).
[5] 609 Rodman St.; Magdalen Society, Matron's Diary, Monday, 26 May 1879.

ence Crittenton Rescue Mission in 1892 (Appendix D). In 1893 street meetings were held on Sunday mornings at Sixth and Rodman streets and in the fall, after having made "many converts among the depraved women and girls in the surrounding houses of shame," the Mission rented a place on Lombard Street which had been a "notorious pool and gambling room" and immediately began services. The meetings were jammed and their collections were sufficient to pay all their bills. The Florence Crittenton Rescue Band was aggressive; it even "invaded" the saloons and resorts during the midnight and early morning hours. The original plan for a combined mission and home lasted only about 7 years, then the mission aspect was abandoned and the Lombard Street building was reorganized as a home for pregnant and wayward girls. Rescuing prostitutes was not very successful in 100 years of effort, but the concentrated attempts by many social welfare agencies probably did reduce the scale of such activities.

Racial prejudice may have been one of the considerations by social welfare workers in their attention to the prostitutes of the Lombard–Southwark–Moyamensing slum. The poverty-stricken Whites lived cheek-by-jowl and intimately with the possibly more poverty-stricken Blacks. The social welfare reformers were shocked by this. Of course, there were men who would visit Black prostitutes (indeed, there were some Black prostitutes in the houses north of Market Street), but there were social pressures against it. There were also White prostitutes in the Lombard–Southwark–Moyamensing slum, but their close relationships with Blacks would have led to their rejection by many White men. Perhaps these social pressures can be illustrated from the commentary of an anonymous author of a guidebook (240) to houses of prostitution in Philadelphia in about 1849. Writing about a place for which he refused to give the address, the author reported: "Sal Boyer, alias Dutch Sal, this is the lowest house in the city—a perfect loafer hole—no gentleman visits this Sodom; it is worse than hell itself. Avoid this den, as it is a panel house of the worst description. This woman, it is said, has had connection with the lowest negro, for the small remuneration of potatoes and flour to support her boarders! Is this not enough to deter men from visiting this awful pest house!" And he wrote of a place on South Street, above Eighth: "There is a brothel occupied by a swarm of yellow girls who promenade up and down Chestnut Street every evening with their faces well powdered, and strange to say, they meet with more custom than their fairer skinned rivals in the trade of prostitution. There is no accounting for taste, however, and we have no objection to a white man hugging a negro wench, providing his stomach is strong enough to relish the infliction." Admittedly, the author writes with an apparent upper-class bias. There is little doubt that the houses of prostitution he lists (he refuses to list the "low-grade" ones) were staffed by White women, and that he reflects the preferences of the White upper class.

Another example is the report recorded in the diary of the matron of the Magdalen Society. On 3 September 1878 she observed that "a gentleman called in the morning as regards a girl now in the Almshouse. She was taken from a house kept by colored people on St. Mary's Street much diseased." Other examples are from the casebooks of the Society to Protect Children. In 1886 we find the following report: "Complt called and stated that Defdt is in a low lodging house in [613] St. Mary's St. with colored people. And she drinks a great deal and neglects her child very much. . . . Defdt has been drinking and begging on the street with this child. They were found in a room with eight colored people."[6] And, finally, there is the following in 1890: "the officer testified that near midnight last night he found Defdt in a yard on one of the numerous dens in Gillis Alley [Reese Street] and that the Defdt had been laying for sometime in an outhouse where 10 or 12 colored men had intercourse with her. The child was found in a room in the house with a colored man and two colored women. About 2 months ago Defdt was arrested in the same neighborhood in the act of having intercourse with a dirty low colored man known by the name of 'Ashes.' "[7] In these cases, the racial referent is gratuitous and is a manifestation of attitudes more than it is information for the identification of persons.

[6] SPC case no. 6888, 21 May 1886; cf. SPC case no. 5922, 17 April 1885; no. 1848, 4 December 1887; no. 2121, 27 June 1885; no. 7649, 11 April 1887; no. 13433, 31 January 1894; Magdalen Matron's Diary, Tuesday, 3 September 1878.

[7] SPC case 10177, 13 June 1890.

But such attitudes were characteristic of more than the upper classes, for racial hostility was probably a segregative factor among the working class also. Perhaps a related example will make the point. One would suppose that, in the midst of their poverty and degradation, the White residents of the Skid Row area would give up their prejudice and readily associate with Blacks living under similar circumstances. Josiah Flynt (65, *pp. 108–109*), reporting on his experiences before the turn of the century, recorded that White "hoboes" and Black "shinies" had little to do with each other. However, writing in the early 1920s, Anderson (1, *p. 8*) suggests that this was not true on the road, for in the hobo jungle, which was "the melting pot of trampdom," there was "absolute democracy," and Minehan (124, *p. 176*) in the 1930s seems to confirm this. On the other hand, there was segregation in the Chicago hobohemia during the same period and Philadelphia's Skid Row continued to be racially segregated into the 1960s. This segregation seemed to be a consequence of the attitudes of the men; to the cubicle hotel owners and managers of gospel missions, it would make little difference whether segregation prevailed or not, as long as the beds were paid for.

The fourth element of social welfare attack was the neighborhood settlement houses that developed on Kater Street (Bedford, Alaska) and Rodman Street (St. Mary). The Bedford Street Mission was founded in 1853 at Sixth and Kater streets in the heart of the slum (Appendix D). Its explicit objective was to work in "that district embracing Baker [Pemberton], Bedford, Spafford [S. Marshall], and St. Mary streets, with their vicinities; concluding that no greater amount of degradation and misery could be found in our city or district" (182, *p. 366*). Shortly after the Mission began it rented "one of the lowest groggeries that infest the neighborhood" for Sunday School space, a familiar practice in the effort to drive disapproved activities from the neighborhood (182, *p. 371*). After 1886 a nonsectarian Bedford Street Center program included a kindergarten school, baths, sewing classes, job placement and so forth, without respect to race or color. The activities on Rodman Street were similar, although the development was somewhat more complex (Appendix D). Settlement work began with a Sunday School in 1857 in a room of the St. Mary Street Presbyterian Church (204, *pp. 104–105*). In 1880 a day nursery was begun and, in 1881, a kindergarten to counter the bad influence in the neighborhood. These groups had the support of the people in power, for, in 1882, we find the following: "In consequence of reported interference with the attendance of children in the Kindergarten School, in St. Mary Street, and the demoralizing influence of a general kind that they exerted in the neighborhood, a raid on these houses was ordered by His Honor the Mayor, on application of the SPCC in connection with our Committee, and 19 of the inmates were committed to the House of Correction" (189, *p. 28*). The Committee referred to was the Fifth Ward Association of the Philadelphia Society for Organizing Charity, which obviously had a working relationship with the various groups in Rodman Street.

Only when the neighborhood settlement houses were combined with urban renewal procedures were they effective in the disruption of the heart of the Lombard–Southwark–Moyamensing slum. These urban renewal activities, with one minor exception, were undertaken by private groups with their own and not public funds. As early as 1867 there was a demand by the *Evening Star* that the city tear down the slums in the area from Fifth to Seventh streets between Lombard and Fitzwater (44, *p. 56*). Four years later, the managers of the Bedford Street Mission founded the Beneficent Building Association to rehabilitate and rent housing at reasonable prices to respectable people. While the professed objective of the Society was *not* to drive people out, but to reform them, according to the *Public Ledger* of 10 July 1879, the fact of the matter is that from the beginning, when three or four dilapidated buildings were bought and rebuilt from the ground up, the rehabilitation work did drive residents out. Thus, the same article in the *Ledger* notes with satisfaction that several gangs of thieves were driven out. The superintendent of the Fourth Ward Society for Organizing Charity reported in 1889 that "the poverty and population continued to improve" in the Alaska Street district.[8] This probably is best attributed to the massive Russian–Polish–Jewish immigration which was well underway into the

---

[8] Minutes of the Board of Superintendents of the Philadelphia Society for Organizing Charity, 16 September 1889.

Lombard–Southwark–Moyamensing section. In addition there was a continuing and increasing Italian immigration just to the south (93).

Theodore Starr initiated similar activities on Rodman Street beginning in 1880. Starr also acquired properties nearby on Naudain and Lombard streets. At first he planned to develop some model tenements, but he abandoned the idea for single-family residences. His express purpose was to drive out the slum dwellers and to replace them with more respectable people. At the eastern end of Rodman Street, Hannah Fox acquired 615–617 Rodman Street in 1886 and, with some difficulty, evicted one Mom Hewitt who operated two six-room houses as a single cheap lodging house and function shop. "Even then, she did not leave the street, but moved into a much smaller house, two doors below. At last, however, she was forced by legal measures, to leave this also, her followers were scattered and she ceased to be a notorious character" (149, p. 36).[9] In 1893 Hannah Fox's property on Rodman Street was taken over by the College Settlement which amalgamated the nursery school, the kindergarten, a branch of the Free Library of Philadelphia, and a branch of Theodore Starr's Savings Bank, and added a cooperative coal club, various clubs for women and adolescents, as well as a citizenship program (177). Thus a comprehensive settlement house program had evolved. With the support of the city council, the entire block between Sixth and Seventh streets and from Lombard to Rodman was later cleared and the Starr Garden Centre and Playground was built.

By 1893 several urban renewal approaches had developed in response to the slum. During the latter part of 1895 and 1896, the housing approach was organized more systematically and placed on a stable business basis with the organization of the Octavia Hill Association (Appendix D). The Association was a limited-dividend corporation that aimed to "improve the living conditions in the poorer residence districts of Philadelphia." To do this, it proposed both to buy properties and to act as a rental

[9] There are a number of variant spellings used in different sources, but it is almost certain that they all refer to the same woman. When she ran the function shop and "bum lodging house," Mom Hewitt was an elderly woman; can it be that she was the same Liz Hewitt who ran the "tolerable, second-rate" house of prostitution in the late 1840s on Pine Street near 12th (240)?

agent for socially concerned property owners. Wherever possible, the Association "refitted" the buildings while residents continued to live in them, so that the tenants immediately got what benefits there were to be had from the Association's ownership. The Association also urged its shareholders to take an interest in its tenants and to make unpaid "friendly visits to them." Not only would they get a better understanding of the tenant families and their problems, but they could also collect the rent, give close attention to maintenance problems, and presumably help motivate the residents to reject the influence of the slum. However successful the Association might be in the fulfillment of this ideology, it seems evident that under such close inspection "bad tenants" would be driven out one way or another and "good tenants" installed to replace them; i.e., the houses of the Association would not likely be centers for vice or for vagrants and the "undeserving poor" were driven out (129, *1897, 1899, 1907*; 130).

Part of the attention of the social workers was also a protest against the blatant exploitation of the "wanderers and bummers." Housing vagrants was profitable. The *Monthly Register* (186, *Vol. 4, pp. 42 ff.*) of the Society for Organizing Charity reported in 1883 that a house on Kater Street east of Sixth, which was "not worth $500" and was occupied by "beggars and thieves," paid its owner $80 a month rental. In the same neighborhood, the report continues, 30 men and women lived in a cellar (without a floor) measuring 16 × 30 feet. Nightly lodging charges were 10 cents and the owner was said to have an annual income of at least $1000 from that cellar.

Finally, social welfare workers gave the Lombard–Southwark–Moyamensing area so much attention during the late 1870s and thereafter because it was not conceived as a homeless-man population, but rather as a homeless population of men, women and children—sometimes as family units and sometimes not. Thus, in May 1880 the Society to Protect Children had a man arrested for child neglect "when it was clearly shown that he was in the habit of sleeping in alleys, carts and wagons in the neighborhood of 7th and Alaska, that he was a habitual drunkard, and an idle and disorderly person who paid no attention to the wants and cares of the child."[10] And in July 1882 the Society was instrumental in giving a woman living at 638 Rodman Street a sentence of 24 months in the House of Correction for drunkenness and child neglect; the "Agt recognized her as a professional 'bum' and vagrant never working, spending what money she could obtain for rum, and having been arrested a number of times before."

While vagrants were one of the chief concerns of the Society for Organizing Charity, the other was assistance to the "deserving poor."[11] Its larger philosophy was the more efficient management of charitable monies within the context of individual responsibility. Attention was given to women and children either directly or through the male breadwinner. The social theory of the period, which still prevails to a large extent today, supports such a familial orientation. It was assumed, then, as now, that "men can take care of themselves" better than women and children, that children are the future of the society, and that women need and deserve whatever protection can be afforded them. Men, on the other hand, were, and are, socially defined as self-reliant—if they are out of work or in poverty, it is assumed that it is their own fault for "there is always work that a man can do if he really wants to!" The Society for Organizing Charity took care of the eventuality that there might indeed be no work through its work-test program.

The Development of Skid Row

We can identify three sorts of factors in the development of the Tenderloin and, considerably later, the homeless-man area north of Market Street. First, those having to deal with the physical and ecological characteristics of the area, second, those having to do with the population which moved into the area north of Market, and finally, the apparent political decision to allow the area to develop as it did.

Physical and Ecological Factors. As Burgess (30), Harris and Ullman (81) and others have pointed out, economically and

[10] Spc case no. 1631, 22 May 1880.
[11] Spc case no. 3623, 28 July 1882.

socially marginal areas tend to develop in older sections of large cities near the central business districts (CBD) where land is valuable for its potential but the buildings have passed their peak of economic and social utility. In Philadelphia, there were two such areas eligible for the development of such low-quality land uses in the second half of the 19th Century: Southwark and the area north of Market. We have seen that there was a good deal of prostitution, homelessness and slum development in the southern reaches of the old city and the northern part of Southwark and Moyamensing. When concentrated efforts to eradicate these elements from Southwark were made, why did not the homeless-man area develop further south in Southwark rather than moving north of Market?

It appears that Southwark was too far from the new CBD to survive as a homeless-man area under the changed ecology of the city. As the new City Hall was being built in Center Square after 1871, the financial and commercial center of the city was moving westward using Chestnut Street as its axis. Until the 1870s, when the CBD was at Fifth and Chestnut, the vice and homeless-man area could survive in the Kater Street area. But it could not survive as the CBD moved west—it would not have had access to those central functions which it needed, such as restaurants (for scavenging food), "main stems" (for panhandling) and employment opportunities. The only other eligible and ecologically possible location was the area north of Market Street, which was closer to the developing CBD.

The movement of the homeless and vice area north of Market was supported by other ecological factors. The introduction of the streetcar in the last half of the 19th Century changed the morphology of the city. The horse-drawn and then the electric streetcar allowed workers to live as much as 4 and then 12 miles from their places of employment (84, *pp. 91–93*). Nonindustrial work became more centralized in the downtown area and, as the CBD itself migrated westward toward the new City Hall, middle-class workers found that they could have an easier journey to work if they moved out of the district north of Market to areas on the streetcar lines serving the new CBD. These residential areas were closer to city limits, and thus the migration of the workers opened areas close to the city center for new immigrants and impoverished people. Similarly, the movement from

Franklin Square to suburban and quasi-suburban city areas left large single-family houses north of Market which were converted into small apartments and rooming houses, attracting vaudevillians and other clientele who were not seen as "respectable." There was a net decline in the population of these inner areas: Wards Five and Six (north of Market) lost 37% of their 1860 population by 1900, while the city as a whole increased by 129% (49, *pp. 98–100*).

To some extent, the inflexibility of the streetcar lines was a function of multiple ownership: each ride required the payment of a new fare (no transfers). By 1895 the problem of multiple ownership had been solved through a series of mergers, but by then it was too late to save Franklin Square and other areas north of Market from becoming the new Tenderloin and Skid Row.

Buildings remaining when manufacturing establishments moved from obsolescent facilities and companies went out of business were easily turned into cheap hotels and lodging houses for the incoming lower-class population. The new establishments and the already existing market and drummers' hotels provided slightly better housing conditions than did the previous domiciles in the Lombard–Southwark–Moyamensing slum.

Wards Twelve and Thirteen had become an extensive rooming-house area by 1880. There were so many of these establishments that the *North American* of 3 June 1876 observed that "an intelligent foreigner, passing through the streets of the city the other day, took out his notebook at the end of a long walk and made a little memorandum to the effect that 89% of the population of Philadelphia are members of the powerful family of 'Rooms to Let.'" We believe that the Census was deficient in this respect, for questions were raised about whether the enumerators in 1880 had failed to list many boarders simply because they had failed to ask the householder whether there were any.[12] A rough tabulation made from the 1870 Census enumeration sheets (excluding households with fewer than 4 unrelated persons from the definition of rooming house or boardinghouse) revealed that there were

[12] *North American*, 8 June 1880.

89 rooming houses, boardinghouses or hotels in the Sixth Ward, 50 in the Eleventh, 39 in the Twelfth, 48 in the Thirteenth and 28 in the Fourteenth. Table 1 shows a more systematic count for 1880, 1900 and 1910, derived from enumeration sheets. The data suggest that relatively high population densities prevailed in the wards north of Market Street from 1880 to World War I. The Sixth and Eleventh Wards were relatively less important as boarding and lodging areas in comparison with the other wards under the impact of commercial–industrial expansion. While the Tenth Ward continued to be outstanding for the number of larger boarding and lodging places through 1910, a slow shift to the Thirteenth and Fourteenth Wards is suggested. These data are consistent with Clarence Young's report in 1912 that the lodging-house and rented-room district went from Vine to Poplar and from Sixth to Broad Street (i.e., the Twelfth, Thirteenth and Fourteenth Wards):

"The northern section of this district still contains many single houses occupied by workingmen and their families, but the district becomes gradually more congested as one goes southward. Here the familiar sign, 'Furnished Rooms,' may be found upon nearly every house. These furnished-room houses were all built for, and occupied by, single families originally, but it is not uncommon now to find a family in each room. . . . The rent of a furnished room varies from $1.50 to $3.50 a week according to size and respectability, the tenant being given the privilege of 'light housekeeping'" (235, *pp. 28–30, 129*; also, *70*).

TABLE 1.—*Number of Dwellings with 4–9 or 10+ Boarders or Lodgers in Selected Wards of Philadelphia, 1880, 1900, 1910*[a]

| Ward | 1880 | | 1900 | | 1910 | |
	4–9	10+	4–9	10+	4–9	10+
6	42	41	75	34	54	24
10	68	49	251	88	209	74
11	41	17	29	8	48	10
12	74	24	158	34	91	22
13	109	24	165	28	178	57
14	94	26	287	45	291	60

[a]Derived from the enumeration sheets of the U.S. Census of Population, 1880, 1900, 1910.

The number of men in these inner-city wards rose between 1860 and 1920.[13] In 1860 only the Sixth Ward had a male : female ratio greater than 1, while some of the other wards had a disproportionate number of women. There was a massive immigration of foreign-born people after 1880, and also a massive in-migration from small towns and rural areas of the native-born. By 1890 a relatively large number of the wards had a disproportionate number of males[14] and these trends continued after the turn of the century. Thus there were large numbers of workingmen, both native- and foreign-born, living under crowded conditions in rooming houses throughout the inner city; they provided the supportive population base for the prostitutes of the Tenderloin.

In the Arch–Race–Vine Street section located on trolley routes and convenient to Market Street and the CBD were the variety theaters, vaudeville houses and, later on, burlesque theaters. There were saloons and theaters in the élite section to the south of Market Street and there were upper-class gambling establishments as well as houses of prostitution on Samson Street, but they would not have been very receptive to the "coarser" sort of entertainment. The variety theaters would have had to locate further south in the Lombard–Southwark–Moyamensing section or in the area north of Market. The slum was inconveniently south for a population now centered on Market Street and it became even more inconvenient as time went on, for the city expanded to the north and the west more rapidly than it did to the south (49, *pp. 98–100*).

The movements of the former occupants—population and business—of the area north of Market took place because of (at that time) the almost irreversible change of the area contemporaneously with the movement of the CBD. Immigrants, especially Eastern European Jews, were creating a pressure on the area's occupants (German Jews), which those occupants found impossible to resist. The area's buildings were wearing out. The industrialization of the waterfront and Willow Street and the

---

[13] Table A-1, Sex Ratio of Philadelphia and Selected Wards, by Nativity, 1860, 1890, 1900, 1920, has been deposited with the National Auxiliary Publications Service (NAPS). To order, see Appendix A.

[14] Wards 4, 5, 6, 9, 11, 12, 13 and 14.

influx of a new population did not conform to the earlier population's idea of a land use compatible with a comfortable life and many of the wealthy residents escaped (224, *pp. 246–250*). At the same time, the industrial waterfront and Willow Street, and the Market–Second–Third Street commercial section, provided work, restaurants, liquor stores, "main stems" and other facilities for the incoming lower-class and vagrant population. Coal yards abounded, and the area was the city's center for the production of morocco leather, which uses large amounts of unskilled labor in its manufacture. Finally, the presence of rail and freight yards allowed both the employment of unskilled labor and a convenient informal transportation route into and out of town.

Population Factors. There is much evidence that there was an eligible population ready to move into the area north of Market in the latter part of the 19th Century. At least as early as 1864 there was a Vagrant Department of the Department of Police. The Vagrant Detective (at first called Beggar Detective) arrested vagrants and beggars and took wandering children and runaways back home or to private or public agencies.[15] The following statements by the Chief of Police in the mid-1880s indicate the Vagrant Detective's duties:

"Officer Allmendinger, assigned to duty as vagrant detective, in addition to arresting beggars and vagrants, is called upon almost daily to find means of forwarding sick and indigent persons to other cities, where they have relatives and friends. . . . There is no appropriation made for this purpose by the city. [He must] appeal to charities of the railway companies or solicit contributions from those about the office. Since last May, when he went on duty, he has secured transportation for 58 persons, and obtained temporary shelter with the various charitable institutions for 103" (139, *1884, pp. 19–20*).

"Officer Allmendinger . . . has his time fully occupied not only in removing beggars from the streets and securing relief for those who are deserving, but also has to find means of sending to their homes the numerous persons who, without any means, make application to this office for transportation. As the city makes no appropriation for any such purpose, he has to rely on the charity of the several railroad companies, and what money is contributed by the members of the

---

[15] The data on arrests, provision for temporary shelter, transportation or other aid given are listed in Table A-2, Activities of Vagrant (Beggar) Detective, 1865–1900, deposited with NAPS. To order, see Appendix A.

department, who are frequently called upon, and though not possessed of ample means, seldom fail to respond to deserving cases" (139, *1885, pp. 15–16*).

"Officer Allmendinger is . . . fully occupied in looking after vagrants and beggars, hunting up young girls who have absconded from home and taken refuge in houses of ill repute, conveying vicious and incorrigible children to the House of Refuge, and procuring temporary shelter and securing transportation for those unfortunates, who, finding themselves homeless and without means, flock to the Mayor's office, to be sent to some distant point where they have relatives and friends" (139, *1886, p. 17*).

Data on arrests by the Vagrant Detective should be treated with caution. All early encounters between the Vagrant Detective and his "clientele" were labeled as "arrests," but the procedure was changed around 1883 and arrests were counted only if the "client" committed a crime other than vagrancy or being a runaway. After 1884 more than half the Vagrant Detective's work was arranging for temporary shelter (in Wayfarer's Lodges), or transportation for the "deserving." Clearly, then, the Vagrant Detective worked with a Skid Row-eligible population.

An alternative to Wayfarer's Lodges was the practice of lodging the homeless in police stations. These included vagrants and the unemployed—the Skid Row-eligible. The annual reports of the Chief of Police indicate that, in the latter part of the 19th Century, the numbers of lodgers in police stations ranged from 12,000 to more than 148,000 annually; after the Wayfarer's Lodges opened the annual number dropped sharply. As Figure 2 illustrates, there was an interaction between economic conditions in the nation and city and the number of lodgers (note especially the crises of 1873 and 1883 and thereafter). The shaded sections of Figure 2 indicate the periods of economic crisis in the United States.

We have already seen the statements of Chiefs of Police on the connection between lodginghouses and the House of Correction. The following illustrate other attitudes of police officials on the problems of the lodgers:

"3036 persons were lodged in the Fifteenth District Station House during the year. . . . There are but three (3) small cells in the station house, which are entirely inadequate for the proper care of prisoners

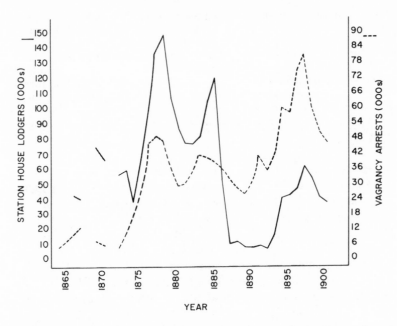

FIGURE 2.—*Police Station House Lodgers and Vagrancy Arrests during Business Cycle Contractions, 1864–1900.* Shaded areas represent depression years. Data from the annual reports of the mayors of Philadelphia, and Thorp (205, *pp. 113–138*).

and lodgers. . . . He [the lieutenant reporting] is frequently compelled to place the lodgers in the cellar of the building, which is imperfectly warmed, and devoid of sleeping accommodations; and that in consequence of this condition of affairs it is almost impossible to keep the station house clean and free from vermin" (139, *1887, pp. 32–33*).

"This [number of lodgers] is in excess of 12,082 over 1877, and of 48,874 over 1876, and can only be accounted for by the large number of persons out of employment, and the overcrowded condition of the Almshouse, many of those who seek lodgings in the Station Houses not being able-bodied, and, therefore, not admissible to the House of Correction" (139, *1878, p. 9*).

"The number of persons accommodated with lodgings for a single night, in the several station houses, was 79,620, being a decrease of 10,582. This can only be accounted for by the fact that those desiring employment have been enabled to procure it, while vagrants and those who habitually seek shelter in the station houses have been provided with accommodations in the County Prison, or House of Correction" (140, *p. 320*).

"Another question concerning the public safety is that of lodging houses. That they must exist is evident, and that a cheap lodging house properly conducted is of service to that class of the community who are better off thus housed than in a station house, is apparent" (141, *p. 18*).

It should be noted that the data are for lodgings provided and not for persons provided lodging; that is, it is improbable that the police weeded out duplications from their statistics, for every night of lodging provided was a service rendered, whether to two different persons or to the same person. Furthermore, weeding out duplications would have been difficult, because vagrants undoubtedly went from station house to station house in an effort not to wear out their welcome; for when that happened the police had them transported up the Delaware River to the House of Correction. A "census of vagrants,"[16] taken early in 1883 for the Society for Organizing Charity and with the cooperation of the police, gives us an idea of the total very poor population as perceived by those in authority who assumed some responsibility for them. The total, 10,092, should be discounted because many of the 1524 living in "cheap boardinghouses" were immigrant Italians and because it seems probable that the entire population of both the House of Correction and the County prison has been included. Lodging in the police station houses was provided for 360 persons (27 women) and 2189 (394 women) were in "cheap lodging houses." There seems little doubt that many of the vagrants drifted among the cheap lodging houses, the police station houses and possibly the House of Correction. The numbers using the police station houses were not small even though the police lodging statistics seem to give an inflated picture of the situation.

Finally, there were substantial numbers of persons who were arrested for vagrancy. After 1875 the number of vagrancy and habitual drunkenness arrests totaled at least 3000 (no doubt at least as many were not arrested as were) and, as Figure 2 illustrates, the number of vagrancy arrests seems to have some relationship to the number of lodgings provided by police station houses.[17] Both are related to the general business conditions in

---

[16] These data are presented in supplementary Table A-3, Census of Vagrants, Philadelphia, 1883, deposited with NAPS. To order, see Appendix A.

[17] Table A-4, Arrests for Skid Row Offense (breach of peace, intoxicated and

the nation and city, and, taken together, the number of lodgings, arrests for high-probability Skid Row offenses, and the activities of the Vagrant Detective (especially in finding temporary shelter) indicate a large number of Skid Row-eligible persons in the city during the latter half of the 19th Century, the number rising during business cycle contractions.[18]

Political Factors. It seems likely that there was a decision made within the city's power structure to allow the area north of Market to develop as a mixed-use residential–Tenderloin–theater–Skid Row area. In the face of Philadelphia's professed Victorian morality, the presence of the theaters (some of which were there well before the Civil War), rooming houses, houses of prostitution, cheap hotels, and a declining population consisting increasingly of Eastern European immigrants, is indicative of a political decision which, if it did not condone such an area, at least allowed such a conglomeration to exist.

Further evidence of the changes occurring north of Market can be found in the movements of the Second Presbyterian Church. In 1839, the congregation moved from Third and Arch to Seventh Street below Arch. By 1867, it had moved to Twenty-first and Walnut streets, a prestige location west of Broad Street and south of Market Street, and the church building was converted into a theater, the second-class "Philadelphia Opera House." After the building was sold by the congregation in 1871, the name was changed to "Enoch's Varieties" and it was raided by the police as a notorious place in the early 1870s and early 1880s.

The Central Presbyterian Church also relocated. In 1876, the congregation moved from Eighth and Cherry to Broad and Fairmount, probably for the reasons given by R. J. H. Munro just before the move was made:

---

disorderly intoxicated, vagrancy, habitual drunkard), 1863–1900, is available from NAPS. To order, see Appendix A.

[18] There are no satisfactory data on unemployment in Philadelphia during the various panics and depressions of the 19th Century. The following scholarly accounts about the period present some assessments in general terms: Thorp (205, *pp. 113–145*); Fels (63, *pp. 85–191*); Clark (45); Lebergott (101, *pp. 170, 178–183, 187*); Wright (234, *pp. 61–67*); Rezneck (162); Bernstein (17); Hoffman (85); Clossen (47); and Willoughby (229).

"When the site at Eighth and Cherry was selected by the Founders of the Church, the city was small; its grand future was not apparent and it was believed the Church would stand there for all time. But the rapid increase and spread of the city in all directions, the removal of the population to distant localities, and the invasion of the neighborhood by business, had gradually injured the prosperity and darkened the outlook of the Church. The marriage of the young people was a signal for their going away to live, and a baptism was almost as rare as flowers in December. There were not sufficient numbers of young people growing up in the Church itself to grasp the banner when it should fall from the hands of the older members" (39, *p. 12*).[19]

We suggest, then, a push–pull approach to the development of the homeless-man area. The homeless were squeezed out of the Lombard–Southwark–Moyamensing area. They were attracted to the section north of Market Street because cheap housing was already available: the inexpensive commercial hotels were there long before the Civil War when the center of wholesale business was on Third Street. It is probable that these hotels changed their clientele as the CBD moved west and as newer, larger, more prestigious hotels were built along Chestnut Street during the post-Civil War period. The Race–Vine strip was centrally located for the men who wanted employment as day laborers, for there were farmers' markets and commission houses and many wholesale and retail shops within easy walking distance. Further, when the wholesale houses followed the retail houses westward, the Race–Vine strip was occupied by light industrial users that required relatively large amounts of warehouse space and probably day laborers as well. There were a number of larger houses on Arch, Race and Vine streets in the pre-Civil War days, especially fronting on Franklin Square. The Arch Street residences were either converted to commercial uses or were torn down and new buildings erected. As this happened, converted and transient housing developed.

---

[19] By 1900, the supporting population of the Central Presbyterian Church had moved again. Meanwhile, Matthias W. Baldwin (of the Baldwin Locomotive Works) was the major sponsor of the North Broad Street Presbyterian Church, at Broad and Green streets, and it, too, had lost much of its membership by 1900. The congregations combined, keeping the North Broad Street Church's property, under the name of the Central North Broad Street Presbyterian Church.

There were substantial numbers of vagrant men who, for reasons of alcoholism, health, the economic depression or personal inadequacies, were attracted to the cheap lodging houses. They could get free food at the oldest of the Philadelphia gospel missions, the Sunday Breakfast Association. The "Sunday B," as it was called locally, was organized in November 1878 by 20 "reformed men," i.e., men who had given up drinking and changed their way of life thereafter. Their reformation had begun at the Franklin Reformatory Home, but they were seeking a wider population than the Franklin was reaching by means of a feeding program and evangelism.[20] The original plan of the Sunday Breakfast Association was to give a free breakfast to poor and unfortunate men who had been unable to keep out of jail on Saturday night but who were released on Sunday morning. The men got a chance to wash, were given new collars, and a hot meal at noon, after attending a 2-hour prayer meeting (52, *p. 52*; 200).[21] Its first location was in an old Methodist Episcopal Church building on the northeast corner of Eleventh and Wood streets, not far from several police stations.[22] In addition to its Sunday morning breakfasts, the volunteer leaders held Christian Temperance meetings almost every night which they reported to be highly successful. Thus, an early report stated that over 600 men had "taken the pledge" (of total abstinence).[23]

In 1882 the Sunday Breakfast Association was reorganized; it consolidated its approach to a gospel temperance position oriented more clearly to vagrants by giving free "breakfast" (i.e., a feeding program had evolved) along with holding religious services. It was estimated that at least two-thirds of those who came to the Association were directly or indirectly there because of the effects of alcohol and many "who come for a free breakfast or supper, or to have words of cheer . . . are, by reason of drink, out of work, out of situation, out of money, out of

[20] FRANKLIN REFORMATORY HOME FOR INEBRIATES. Minutes of Executive Committee, 2 December 1878 and 20 January 1879. [Historical Society of Pennsylvania.]

[21] Also, the Philadelphia *Weekly Times*, 6 March 1886.

[22] *Public Ledger*, 7 January 1879.

[23] Undated clipping in a scrapbook at the Family Service of Philadelphia, probably 25 or 26 January 1879.

friends, out of home, away from God, driven from pillar to post, ordered by the police to 'move on,' and never a kind word of encouragement from anyone; every day finds their personal appearance worse, their very condition debars them from getting even a job to white-wash a cellar; dirty, ragged and forlorn, disheartened and in despair they are pitiable objects indeed, and yet some of them, in spite of their poverty, keep themselves clean, neat and tolerably respectable in appearance" (200, *pp.* 6–7).

The increasing orientation toward homeless persons was evidenced in the 12th annual report (when the Association was located on Twelfth Street north of Race) which said that the galleries were filled, that there were hundreds of testimonials, and "never have there been so many evidences of men— women, too—reduced from lives of debauchery and wretchedness." It recorded that to date 41,749 men and 320 women had been fed; breakfast consisted of 4 corned-beef sandwiches and 3 cups of coffee with milk and sugar, costing a little less than 4¾ cents a person. And in 1889 it was reported that 19,023 had taken the pledge that year, of whom 24% said that they had no home, while of the 1101 who said that they lived in Philadelphia, "we estimate that at least 500 of these are either wanderers or live in cheap and uncomfortable houses; so that probably 1000 or more than half of those who signed the pledge are practically homeless." It seems reasonable to conclude that the Sunday Breakfast Association, in supplying the needs of this vagrant population, was also a major factor in attracting and holding the men in the area and in the development of the homeless-workingmen's area or the Skid Row north of Market Street.

We have suggested a number of factors to account for the development of the Tenderloin (and the Skid Row area that was so closely associated with it) on the other side of the CBD from the old Lombard–Southwark–Moyamensing slum that existed all during the time that the Tenderloin and the homeless-workingmen's area (or Skid Row) developed north of Market. Furthermore, it existed well before the Civil War, as a slum, as an area of crime and vice, and as a place where vagrants congregated. As in so many cases, much depends on the definitions that are imposed on the data. If one insists that a "Skid Row" or a "homeless-workingmen's area" is limited to make workingmen and vagrants, then clearly the Lombard–Southwark–Moyamensing slum was not a Skid Row, for there were homeless women and children as well. But, if the term is used to mean an area of the city with a substantial number of homeless people, an area that is well recognized for its vagrant population, then the Lombard–Southwark–Moyamensing slum should be considered a homeless-workingpeople's area or Skid Row section.

If this last interpretation is accepted, then the origins of the Philadelphia Skid Row reach well before the Civil War and the issue of the detection and prevention of Skid Rows is intimately related to the existing and longstanding slums of the city. That is, the prevention of Skid Rows needs to be seen in a wider perspective, for there are many Skid Row-like people who do not now live, nor have they ever lived, in a Skid Row locality (defined in the more limited, traditional sense). The existence of these people suggests that questions about the future of and the prevention of Skid Row may have been misdirected. Site clearance may make land available for redevelopment, but it ignores the existence of Skid Row-like people. The emergent issue is how to prevent people from falling into Skid Row status. Under conditions of urban redevelopment, Skid Row is not so much a place as a human condition which is far from desirable and can be alleviated.

Chapter 3

The Red Light District and
the Skid Rows of Detroit
A Replication

THE ORIGINS of the Tenderloin and the Skid Row in
Philadelphia were examined as a test of the proposition
that Skid Rows in American cities were post-Civil War
phenomena. In the limited sense in which the manner had
been considered in the literature, Philadelphia's Skid Row did
indeed develop after the Civil War, toward the end of the century. However, well before the Civil War, there was also a section of Philadelphia which had the attributes of a Red Light
district, a homeless-persons area, and a deteriorated housing
area. If we include homeless women as well as homeless men
in our considerations, it would seem that Philadelphia's
homeless-persons area developed before the Civil War.

To what extent are the Philadelphia findings applicable to
other cities? In this chapter, we are interested in the beginning
of Detroit's segregated prostitution district, its subsequent
growth, and its relation to the homeless-workingmen's area, or
Skid Row.

There were, and are, notable differences between the cities.
Detroit was a midwestern frontier village at the beginning of
the 19th Century when Philadelphia had already been the colonial cultural center and the political capital of the United States.
Detroit's pattern of growth was similar to that of Chicago, although the location of the latter at the foot of Lake Michigan
was a major reason why it grew more rapidly and became a
larger city. Since they were at the end of transportation lines,
Chicago's Skid Rows and Tenderloins were also larger. Nonetheless, one may argue that the general relationship between
the Red Light district and the Skid Row of Detroit was probably
similar to that in Chicago. Neither Reckless (159) nor Anderson
(1), the major authorities on the Chicago Skid Row, discusses

53

the matter in a way that facilitates a merger of their material for a unified look at Chicago. While Philadelphia may be considered representative of the eastern seaboard, Detroit may be said to be typical of the middle-western Great Lakes cities. To the extent that the Detroit Skid Row and Red Light district developed in a fashion similar to Philadelphia's, we have moved a step in the direction of generalization of the conclusions. This is not to say that two cases clinch the argument, but they may suggest hypotheses for studies of other cities.

The Ville d'Etroit was founded by Cadillac in 1701 and remained a French frontier military–trading–farming outpost until it was seized by the British in 1760. It came under U.S. control in 1796 and continued as a military outpost until some time after the Mexican War (134, *p. 665*).

After 1815–1816, the village developed rapidly on the east side of Woodward Avenue, along Woodbridge, Atwater and Jefferson (parallel to the river) and along Brush, Randolph and Bates up to Larned Street, parallel to Woodward and perpendicular to the river (31, *Vol. II, p. 1531*). By the 1830s, the Woodbridge–Atwater section was the central business district (CBD) of the town: the town pump was in the vicinity, farmers' markets were on Woodward below Jefferson (1817–1835) and at Atwater and Randolph (1830–1848). The Steamboat Hotel, headquarters for steamer and stage passengers until it burned down in 1848, was at the corner of Woodbridge and Randolph streets. The first successful newspaper in Detroit, the *Gazette*, was located (1817–1829) on Atwater Street (37, *pp. 155, 218; 62, p. 793*). The Detroit and Milwaukee Railroad depot was at Larned and Jefferson until 1852; after considerable agitation, it purchased a dock and built a terminal at the foot of Brush Street, where it continued for many years (37, *p. 162;* 56, *pp. 76–77*). (The influence of the location of this railroad on the subsequent development of the East Side Red Light district is hard to assess.)

The Woodbridge–Atwater section was the commercial section for several decades. But it seems probable that by 1850 it had slipped badly and was part of the "backwater" that is typically left as a CBD "moves up the street." One indication of this is the shift of hotels out of the area over a period of time (109, 227,

238).[1] A second is the listing along Atwater and Woodbridge of a number of wholesale grocers and commission merchants in the 1850 Directory; these activities usually occupy buildings and stores that are vacated by retail merchants who deal directly with the public as the latter move up the street.

According to the Directory of 1837, there was a concentration of sailors' residences to the east of the commercial section on Atwater Street. This lends support to the statement of Friend Palmer that Louis Moran lived at the foot of Hastings Street at the corner of Woodbridge and that "there was a line of low buildings between Moran's house and the line of the Beaubien farm, occupied principally as drinking saloons, billiards, etc." (134, p. 666). The actual date for this is not clear, but apparently it was before 1850. Some weight is lent to this conclusion by the fact that the City Directory of 1845 lists a number of unattached women on Woodbridge Street with no other notation, contrary to the normal practice of the Directory. There is a high probability that these were prostitutes or the operators of houses of prostitution.

In 1850 Detroit had a population of more than 21,000. The Detroit *Free Press* of 22 July 1850 estimated the city to have more than 100 houses of ill fame. While the Woodbridge–Atwater section was a nascent Red Light district, undoubtedly there were houses of prostitution elsewhere in the town. Of particular note is the fact that such activities had begun to infiltrate the better residential district to the north in the vicinity of Randolph and Cadillac Square. This incensed the City Fathers

---

[1] In the first City Directory (1837), of the 10 hotels that were listed, 7 were east of Woodward Avenue; in the second City Directory (1845), of the 14 hotels that were listed, 8 were in the east of Woodward area; of the 18 hotels listed in the City Directory of 1850, only 4 were on the East Side and 12 were on the West Side, most of them between Woodward Avenue and Selby in the old Second Ward. Not only was there evidence of a shift to the westward, but there was also a move to the north. Thus, in 1837, only the Railroad Hotel and the National Hotel were listed north of Jefferson Avenue; by 1845, there was also the Railroad House clustered with the other two at Campus Martius; and there were also the American Hotel, the Franklin House, and Murray's Hotel on or near Jefferson Avenue (considered "uptown" in those days). There was also the Northern Hotel located far out of town at Woodward and Grand Circus.

so much that they ordered the Town Marshall to tear down the house of ill fame at the location (31, *Vol. I, pp. 406, 415*).

In contrast to the tentative nature of our conclusions about the pre-Civil War period, there are no doubts about the post-Civil War period. The entire area from Atwater Street to beyond Campus Martius was notorious. Writing about the 1880s, Catlin (37, *p. 579*) refers to the Woodbridge–Atwater section as a "sub-cellar" for the underworld of Detroit. The area was known as "The Potomac" because, it is said, the police had so much trouble there that when they were asked how things were going they hoped to report that "All's quiet on the Potomac." The area from Jefferson Avenue north, up to Fort Street East, bordering on Cadillac Square and Campus Martius, was known as "The Heights." Silas Farmer wrote in the late 1880s:

"The Heights is a name applied to a region near the westerly end of Fort Street East, occupied in part by former denizens of the Potomac quarter. This last region being on lower ground, a removal to Fort Street was spoken of as a removal to the 'Heights'; possibly the fact that 'high old times' have been frequent in this locality has also had something to do with the particular designation. These last localities have numbered among their inhabitants the worst classes of both sexes" (62, *p. 928*; 166, *p.44*).

Farmer's comment is supported by data in the Census of 1880, which listed houses of prostitution or prostitutes on the following streets: Beaubien in the vicinity of Monroe, Larned East, Jefferson, Franklin, Atwater and Brush (Figure 3).

Police records make it clear that more than sex was involved in the old Third Ward Red Light district.[2] Sex was often the bait to make petty thievery possible. For example, on 2 February 1897 a man "went into 421 Rivard Street—stayed the night with a woman named Lillie and she robbed him of $22.00 cash." On 6 February 1897 a man complained to the police that "while in a sporting house near the corner of Hastings and Clinton," he was robbed of a watch and chain. On 4 March 1897 a man took two girls to the Hotel Congress at 12–16 Congress Street East; he complained that they robbed him in the middle of the night. Police records report that the girls roomed at 148 Larned Street.

[2] M/S Police Department Complaints, Vols. 1 and 2, 9 May 1896 to 19 April 1897 and 19 April 1897 to 14 December 1897. [Burton Historical Collection, Detroit Public Library.]

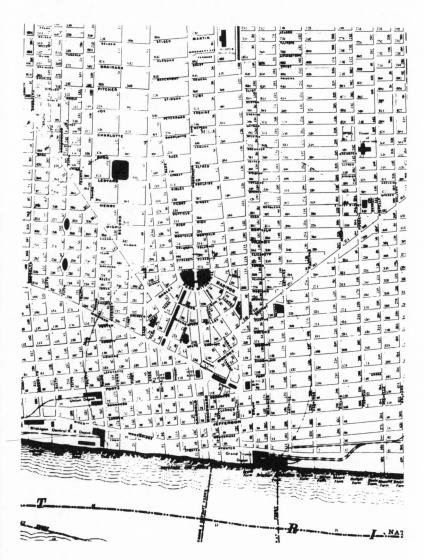

FIGURE 3.—*Portion of "The Official Map of the City of Detroit," Published by Silas Farmer & Co., 1898.* [In the collection of the Library of Congress.]

On 30 May 1897 a woman got drunk in a saloon and, while she "formed the acquaintance of a young man," her money and watch were stolen. Her home address is given as 143 Fort Street East. On 21 June 1897 two employees of the Griswold Hotel, located at Griswold and Grand River, went to bed together at the Jefferson House, located on Jefferson east of Bates; she awakened the next morning to find that he had stolen her money and disappeared. On 7 August 1897 a man complained of a diamond shirt stud that was stolen, apparently while he was drunk in a house of prostitution at Monroe Avenue east of Brush. Sometimes more than petty thievery was involved: on 12 January 1897 a man reported that he had been a victim of the "irate husband racket" at 222 Hastings Street.

While the area east of Woodward to Hastings became stereotyped as Detroit's "segregated vice district," there were also some of the same activities to the west of Woodward on the opposite side of the business district. The Matron's Register of the Central Police Station for 1901[3] notes that of the girls and women who were held during that time for sex-related offenses, 15 came from the East Side Red Light district, another 3 came from not far away, while 5 were from west of Woodward Avenue and 5 from elsewhere in the city.

There is reason to believe that, despite occasional arrests, Detroit was operating a de facto system of licensing by the turn of the century, as suggested by the comment of the Mayor of Chicago in his introductory remarks to the report of the Chicago Vice Commission in 1914: "I was informed that Detroit, Michigan, and New York City, have experimented along certain lines" (215, p. 3). Apparently the Detroit Red Light district was closed down in 1915, but the brothels soon reopened. In 1916 a visitor took sardonic delight in pointing out to Detroiters that they were deluded if they thought that the district had really closed down. He reported on a Sunday night trip to Detroit's Lower East Side.[4] After having been shown 10 places by his

[3] *Matron's Register*, Central Police Station, 21 December 1900 to 21 December 1901. [Burton Historical Collection.]

[4] East of Woodward Avenue: 65, 78, 79. Beaubien; 223, 232, 244, 257, 266 Brush; 102 Larned Street. West of Woodward Avenue: 67 First Street with an entrance at 147 Congress St. "Detroit's red lights." *Detroit Saturday Night*, p. 2, 22 July 1916. [Burton Historical Collection.]

helpful cabdriver, the author was assured that in the area bounded by Lafayette East, Hastings, Jefferson and Brush streets (a 12-square block area) there were at least 75 brothels operating with apparent impunity. These were places with White prostitutes; a few blocks away, on Madison Street, there were a number of brothels with Black prostitutes.

Detroit tended to "run wide open," according to a report of the American Social Health Association about conditions in the city in 1925.[5] Prostitution flourished flagrantly within a mile radius of Cadillac Square, in the transitional and working-class area surrounding the CBD. House after house was used exclusively by prostitutes. Ordinarily the houses would have rented for about $40 a month; when rented for purposes of prostitution, they brought $75 to $100 a month. The street corners were gathering places for solicitation; women sat in the windows of the houses, stood on the stoops or in the doorways and either tapped on the window pane or called loudly, inviting passersby to enter. Five blocks east and 5 blocks west of Adams and Charlotte streets (just north of Grand Circus Park) there was so much prostitution that respectable women did not want to be seen on or about the streets at any time. The prostitutes lounged about semiclad, receiving each customer in turn, i.e., there was a "line up" system in operation. In good seasons, the prostitutes reported that they averaged 10 to 15 customers a day; the only ones who complained about poor business were those who had lost their attractiveness. Within a half-mile radius of Cadillac Square, then, there was apparently a Red Light district; beyond that, there was an area of somewhat more expensive clandestine prostitution.

Soliciting also took place from automobiles. According to the report, women would drive in front of the leading hotels, blow their horns, shine their spotlights and slow down almost to a stop as they went by the entrances. The usual charge was $5 to $10; the women averaged between 10 to 15 men a day in the winter and as many as 20 in the summer. Also, according to the report, there were 269 places where prostitution was practiced

[5] AMERICAN SOCIAL HEALTH ASSOCIATION. Detroit, Michigan, general summary, undercover investigation of prostitution . . . 1926. . . . [University of Minnesota Libraries, Social Welfare History Archives Center.]

openly and, also presumably, within the one-mile circle of Grand Circus Park; there were also 134 places that were operating clandestinely and were presumably further out.

By the 1880s the East Side had begun to be an area of major charitable concern. Table A-5[6] presents data from a little over 50% of the cases of the Detroit Association of Charities during 1887 to 1888. The West Side wards accounted for 30% of the cases, while the East Side wards accounted for more than twice that proportion. Furthermore, not all the cases were evenly distributed: Wards Three and Five (both on the East Side) accounted for 35% of the cases. These wards had Beaubien Street as their western edge and Russell Street to the east. The area west of Chene to Beaubien Street was one of poverty, illness, dependency and alcoholism. This was a larger area than the Red Light district, of course, but the latter was on its edge and, to some extent, was the western part of it.

Michigan, as a frontier state in the early 19th Century, had its share of drifters. There were no jails at the time, and Friend Palmer, citing the Detroit *Gazette* of 23 November 1821, reported that the Territorial Legislature mandated that "any justice of the peace may sentence idle, vagrant, lewd, drunken or disorderly persons to be whipped not exceeding ten stripes or to be delivered over to any constable to be employed in labor not exceeding three months, by such constable to be hired out for the best wages that can be procured, the proceeds of which to be applied for the use of the poor of the County. The practice of selling–disposing of a vagrant's time was continued until way along into 1830. . . . It remains to state that the citizens of Detroit and the adjoining counties derived many benefits from the effect of sending from the territory very many drunkards and vagabonds that thronged into it from Canada, Ohio, and the state of New York."[7] At least of passing interest because of the racism, as well as the associated status anomalies (as sociologists would describe it), is the incident cited by Palmer (134) in which some White passengers on the steamer Walk-in-

---

[6] Table A-5, Ward Location of 306 cases of Detroit Association of Charities, 1887–1888, has been deposited with NAPS. To order, see Appendix A.

[7] "Reminiscences of Friend Palmer in Detroit." Detroit *Sunday Free Press*, 12 July 1903. [Burton Historical Collection.]

the-Water persuaded a Black member of the crew to buy the services of a presumably White "drunken vagrant" for 10 days for $1.

Whatever the law required, the whipping post and selling vagrants' labor fell into abeyance in 1826. For a while, drunkards were sent to the county poorhouse. This institution first opened in 1832 on the East Side at Gratiot and Mt. Elliott; in 1838 it was moved far out in the country to Nankin Township (Eloise), where in 1845 a building was constructed that had separate "cells" for "drunks" and for the "crazy" (31, *Vol. I, p. 427*). By 1860 vagrants were sent to the county jail which had been at Clinton and Beaubien streets since 1847 (it is still there). The Census enumerator for the old Third Ward commented in his 1860 report that "the fact that we have no city prison or workhouse has filled our county jail with a great number of vagrants which confuse a very great number of the present number." That is, the enumerator was saying that bona fide residents of the ward were less than the official number because of the presence of the County Prison. Such notations were unusual (and unauthorized) and this one should probably be interpreted as a manifestation of agitation for a workhouse. In fact the Detroit House of Correction opened in 1861 at the site of the city cemetery on Russell Street and Wilkins, well out on the outskirts of the town at the time. It continued there until 1931 when it was torn down and the Brewster Public Housing Project built on the site (31, *Vol. 1, p. 415*; 233, *p. 178*).

We have already noted the housing for seamen in the Potomac neighborhood. They were a noticeable element among the homeless men and it should not be surprising that there arose a demand for a more socially desirable and uplifting environment for seamen. Thus, N. W. Wells, Chaplain of the Western Seamen's Friend Society, wrote on 15 October 1851, "Permit me also to suggest the great want in this city, of a boarding house for sailors, in which there might be some accommodation for the sick, and to which there might be attached a library and reading room" (222, *p. 211–212*).

We do not know whether Wells's proposal was implemented, but an essentially similar idea was developed, probably after the Civil War, to aid the city's vagrants, especially young people. The Detroit *Free Press* of 24 January 1868 commented on a "Mission Lodging house" that "The lodging house for newsboys, bootblacks, etc., at the corner of Atwater and St. Antoine Streets, is gaining public favor, no less because of the great good resulting from it, than from the knowledge that charity expended in its behalf is made of practical use." During the week ending 22 January 1868, 381 meals were served and 180 persons were supplied lodgings; the mission also maintained a night school with a competent teacher from 7 to 9 PM.

There were several other facilities ostensibly for seamen that provided food and lodging to Detroit's vagrant and alcoholic population. There was, for example, a Seamen's Bethel Lodging House located at the corner of Griswold and Atwater Streets just west of Woodward Avenue; in December 1887 a mentally ill vagrant was referred to it for food and shelter. In January 1888 the case record of the Detroit Association of Charities also comments about a woman given tickets for meals and overnight lodging at the Bethel who had just been released from the House of Correction and was destitute.[8] The Seamen's Bethel continued at Griswold and Atwater until the early 20th Century. Known variously as the Detroit Bethel Mission and the Seamen's Bethel Home, by 1897 it was known as the Seamen's Home and by 1902 it was listed in the City Directory with the name of William F. Haynes, proprietor. Not long thereafter it apparently went out of existence, for it was no longer listed in the city directories.

A second seamen's institution was also located on the lower West Side. From the time when it opened in 1849 until 1926, however, the Mariner's Church functioned primarily as a religious and social service referral center for transient men and did not provide housing. In 1926 the Mariner's Inn, a 100-bed dormitory, opened at the corner of Woodward and Jefferson avenues in the 3 upper floors of the old Central Hotel, which was remodeled for the purpose. The 4th annual report (60) of the Detroit Episcopal Mission justified this new enterprise with the argument that "the cheap flop-houses are a disgrace to

---

[8] Detroit Association of Charities, case no. 7, 7 December 1887; case no. 133, 9 January 1888. [Archives of Labor History and Urban Affairs, Wayne State University.]

modern civilized society; the Y.M.C.A. caters to a different class of man socially from the usual type working in our industrial shops; McGregor Institute adequately cares for the restless drifting transient—it cares in part for the men of whom we are speaking, but denies them that freedom which is conducive to proper self-respect since the Institute is thought of in terms of a charitable organization." Men who lived at Mariner's Inn were, as the statement implies, expected to pay for their room and board, although a limited number of free beds were available for those who were "really destitute." In November 1934 a new Mariner's Inn was dedicated not far away at 300 Griswold Street, from which site it was relocated in the 1960s when the Civic Center redevelopment took place.

While the Mariner's Inn was on the edge of the CBD on the west side of Woodward, it was close to the homeless-man area that developed. We can document the existence of a lower East Side homeless-man area through the development of gospel rescue missions. The most important was the McGregor Mission or Institute (the founder called it "The Helping Hand Mission") begun by Thomas McGregor, a successful Toledo businessman. In 1888 he founded the Bethany Mission School in Toledo, and not long afterward he acquired the O'Connor Place at 69–71 Larned Street East in Detroit with the intention of establishing a mission there. "This building will be fitted up with all the improvements necessary for a work of this kind where the tramp, the criminal, the drunkard, and all other classes of men who have become outcasts from society, can have a Christian home, with food, shelter, and all the conveniences of cleansing the body and clothing, and have the Gospel of Jesus Christ preached to them twice a day . . . the only requirement for admission being their need" (111).[9]

McGregor arrived in Detroit on Thanksgiving Day, 1890, with three other men planning to open the following April. However, he found 150 men already in the building and, from that time until the mission "officially opened" in April 1891, 100 to 200 men were housed and fed daily. Thomas McGregor died less than a month later, and his son continued his work, merging his

[9] See also the Detroit McAuley Mission (239); Burton et al. (31, *Vol. 1, p. 421*); and McGregor (112).

efforts with another mission already located at 55 Cadillac Square. Liberally endowed with bequests and gifts, the Mc-Gregor Institute–Helping Hand Mission became the major Detroit institution for the care of the down-and-out. During 1894 it housed an average of 99 persons nightly; this probably fluctuated with the seasons, for, with a capacity of 150 beds, it reported that "at different seasons during the past year, it has been impossible to accommodate the destitute men who were willing to work for help received." All told, the McGregor Mission helped 6,736 men in 1894; from 1910 to 1915, it dealt with 23,508 men annually (110). In 1901 the mission was moved to Brush Street above Clinton on the lower East Side and adopted an industrial mission style. This involved a clothing and shoe salvage program, a tailor shop, shoe repair shop, employment bureau, and a 140-acre farm. In addition, the men who lived in the mission split 1000 cords of wood annually from logs shipped by contract from the northern parts of the state. The mission facilities were housed in a 3-story building with dormitory space for 300 to 350 beds, as well as 50 "small bedrooms" (cubicles?) which rented, along with board, for $3 a week (112). The similarities to the activities of the Philadelphia Society for Organizing Charity and the Sunday Breakfast Association are readily apparent.

Will Allen's Rescue Mission and Workingmen's Home at 34 Cadillac Square also operated a low-cost restaurant and soup line from early morning to midnight. The operators of the mission stressed that they were not oriented to tramps but to poor workingmen, and that they sold the food, although at less than cost, to those who came to the mission. "If a man has no means and is worthy, we give him work to enable him to earn his food and lodging for a time" (243). The following rates prevailed at Will Allen's Rescue Mission: "bed, bath and breakfast, five cents; 21 meals and lodgings, one dollar; bath and use of reading room, free; one good dinner, five cents."

The mission was unique in that its preachers went out onto the public street to preach and raise money; they had a horse-drawn wagon from which the preaching took place so that they could pull up to the curb wherever it was deemed appropriate. The mission did not last very long beyond 1900.

Finally, the Detroit City Mission started in 1909 on Randolph

Street near Clinton, on the Lower East Side, and continued there for a number of years. The location had once housed a notorious saloon and resort for prostitutes and criminals, it was said.[10] The Detroit *Free Press* of 4 June 1916, reporting on the early days, commented that "It was not always plain sailing. At first the proprietors of the resorts in the vicinity looked on the mission in mild amusement, and joked with their patrons about the nerve of the man who would start anything like that. . . . They later took it more seriously when it was reported that 'this or that one-time patron of the saloons had got religion,' and his accustomed place among the bar flies was filled by a stranger." Over the years, the location of the mission shifted. In 1928–29 it was at Rivard and Larned Street East, where it remained until urban renewal and expressway construction forced it to move. It then moved to Third Avenue in the Cass Corridor area, an area that is discussed in a later chapter.

There seems little doubt that Detroit's major homeless-man area was on the Lower East Side after 1889. This conclusion is supported by the comments in a Detroit Association of Charities case in 1888 of a man who lived in the Forester Hotel, 59 Cadillac Square. The investigator said that he was "very dissipated in his appearance . . . could easily secure work but does not like it . . . prefers to spend his time loitering around the many low saloons near the Central Market . . . has been frequently arrested and served time for disorderly conduct."[11]

The Detroit Skid Row, however, did not remain on the Lower East Side. After World War II, there was steady public pressure to eliminate the Skid Row area, but at the time it was located

[10] This was a common procedure in the period from the Civil War to World War I. Thus, the Water Street Home for Women at 273 Water Street, New York City, was located in what had been John [Van] Allen's saloon-house of prostitution. Allen rented his place for some preaching and prayer services (probably as a cynical gesture, initially), subsequently went to the Howard Mission and was converted; and then reopened his place sometime in 1868 or 1869 as a refuge for prostitutes who wished to reform. Kit Burns's place was notorious for its dog and rat fights; Burns also rented his place for services and was himself converted. At his suggestion, the place was rented at $1000 a year for 6 years to Rev. William H. Boole, of the Protestant Episcopal Church, and, in 1870, the place was dedicated by the Bishop as a mission (117, *ch. 36;* 163, *pp. 471–476*).

[11] Case Books, Detroit Association of Charities, 1887–1888. [Archives of Labor History and Urban Affairs, Wayne State University.]

along Michigan Avenue from Shelby west to perhaps Twelfth Street on the west side of Woodward Avenue. The Michigan Avenue area became stereotyped as "Detroit's Skid Row" and the Lower East Side area had largely faded from public awareness as a Skid Row area. To explain when the Michigan Avenue area became the principal residential area for Detroit's White homeless men we must stress the racial element, for racial segregation prevailed in Detroit on Skid row as elsewhere in the city, as it did in Philadelphia.

There were many hotels that clustered in the Lower East Side homeless-man area, but our data do not permit us to designate them as "Skid Row hotels." Another way to examine the problem is to note the increase in certain kinds of businesses on a selected block that might be used by Skid Row men. On Michigan Avenue, in 1896, there were no pawnshops between Cass and First, but there were two in 1912, six in 1923, and seven in 1935. Similarly, in the same block, there was one restaurant in 1896, two in 1912, eight in 1923, and four in 1935. This does not mean that there was a decline in the number of restaurants along Michigan Avenue, however, for between First and Second avenues there were two in 1923, and five in 1935; in the block between Second and Third, there was an increase from three in 1923 to nine in 1935. The data suggest that during the 1920s the Michigan Avenue Skid Row area grew relatively rapidly while moving westward (away from the CBD as it expanded) and much of this population lived on the streets to the south of Michigan, but above Fort Street, i.e., on Labrosse, Bagley, Porter and Abbott. (The homeless-man activities of the Mariner's Inn and the Seamen's Bethel are best considered an extension of the East Side because the new Skid Row was not contiguous and represented an "invasion" of a different segment of the Lower West Side.)

As in the Philadelphia case, our explanation of this series of events is to be regarded as tentative and as the basis for additional research. Detroit's growth from 1910 to 1920 was nothing short of phenomenal and there can be little doubt that one consequence was the expansion of the CBD. This expansion enveloped the Cadillac Square area and the homeless men were driven out of it, their housing preempted by the downtown expansion and their saloons closed by Prohibition.

In addition, even more so than in Philadelphia, a racial withdrawal theory may be offered. Until the 1910–1920 decade, the Detroit Black population was never large and it grew slowly in comparison with the White population. There were Blacks among the townspeople relatively early, as evidenced by the listing in the 1837 City Directory of an "African Church" on Fort Street (East). In the Directory of 1845 a Colored Methodist Episcopal Church is listed on Fort Street west of Beaubien and an African Baptist Church on Fort Street between Beaubien and St. Antoine. In 1850, there were three: St. Mark's (at Congress and St. Antoine), the Colored Methodist Episcopal (now at Brush and Beaubien), and a Colored American Baptist Church (apparently the same one as that listed in 1845 but with a different name). As the Black population grew, it clustered in the lower East Side racial enclave (95, *pp. 25–28*). In 1869, Blacks were settled in the old Third, Fourth, Sixth, and Seventh Wards; the riot in 1863 burned out the heart of the Black residential area from Monroe to Congress Street and from Brush to Beaubien (167, *p. 115*; 242). The competition of the expanding trade on the periphery of the CBD pushed Blacks out of the old Third Ward and they moved eastward and northward into the old Seventh and Sixth Wards, with the same movement into the old Tenth Ward. (The post-1880 Wards 1, 3, 5 and 7 approximate the same area.)

Although Detroit's Blacks were a small minority of the rapidly growing population, they were caught up in the drunkenness, petty crime, and vice of the Lower East Side. There are several sources of information for this in addition to Katzman (95, *pp. 28, 170–174*). The enumeration sheets of the 1860 Census list the inmates of the County Prison: 61 White men, 21 White women, and 10 Black women (no Black men were listed). By the next Census there was a Detroit House of Correction, and the enumeration sheet lists as inmates 244 White men, 110 White women, 19 Black men, 16 Black women and 2 mulatto men. Of course, no reason for their incarceration is given. Table 2 is based on 20% samples of manuscript registers of prisoners of the Detroit House of Correction. Police practices varied over the years, but the predominant reasons for imprisonment of Blacks and Whites of both sexes were alcohol-related disorderly conduct and drunkenness. Among Whites offenses such as larceny and burglary continued to be relatively important from 1862 to 1890, whereas assault and battery declined. While apparently never involving large numbers, White women were imprisoned for sex offenses proportionately more and more consistently over the years than were Black women.

Examples of Black involvement in the petty criminality of the area include an incident on 28 September 1896 when a man complained to the police that he had been "called into a house in the Booker Block by a colored woman, he was going to get

TABLE 2.—*Offenses of Detroit House of Correction Inmates, by Race and Sex, Selected Years, in Per Cent*[a]

	1862[b]		1870		1874		1880		1890	
	W	B	W	B	W	B	W	B	W	B
N male	40	5	182	8	344	25	267	11	412	22
N female	25	2	46	6	71	11	43	5	74	23
Disorderly (Intemperate)[c]										
Male	42	60	16	26	21	52	20	64	53	95
Female	48	50	28	34	15	46	14	0	79	69
Drunkenness										
Male	0	0	39	37	34	8	35	18	2	0
Female	0	0	33	33	42	9	59	80	0	0
Vagrancy										
Male	3	0	5	0	17	8	9	9	9	0
Female	12	0	7	0	13	0	0	0	4	0
Disorderly (Temperate)[c]										
Male	15	0	2	0	4	12	0	0	1	0
Female	8	0	13	33	14	18	9	20	3	9
Sex Offenses										
Male	0	0	0	0	1	0	0	0	0	0
Female	0	0	2	0	4	0	7	0	7	13
Other										
Male	40	40	38	37	23	20	34	9	35	5
Female	32	50	17	0	11	27	11	0	7	9

[a] 20% sample of the manuscript registers of prisoners, Detroit House of Correction. [Burton Historical Collection.]

[b] First full year of operation.

[c] The Register distinguishes between prisoners with "temperate habits" and those with "intemperate habits." We infer that the "intemperate" were jailed as disorderly while drunk.

into bed but the woman robbed him of $19.00 and ran away."[12] (Edward Booker had a saloon at 169 Beaubien Street and the house in question was probably in the vicinity.) On 28 August 1896 a man was robbed of $18 at the Booker Building, the girl was convicted and sentenced to $25 or 30 days in the Detroit House of Correction. The woman and the "irate husband" who have already been cited at 222 Hastings Street in 1896 were both "colored" according to the complaints to the police.

While Detroit's Black people on the Lower East Side were caught up in vice and the social problems of the area, the numbers were relatively small during the development and height of the Red Light district. Even after World War I, when the Red Light district was "closed down" (dispersed might be a better word), vice was predominantly a White phenomenon.

In brief, the Michigan Avenue Skid Row was not Detroit's "original" Skid Row. That was on the Lower East Side. Our explanation for the shift to Michigan Avenue involves a "squeeze" on the area. The expanding CBD, responding to the boom of the period roughly between 1915 and 1929, preempted the land and buildings in the vicinity of Cadillac Square. In addition, because of the substantial settlement of Blacks in the Lower East Side Wards, most of the migrant White population moved out. The area that offered the least resistance to their resettlement was across the CBD along Michigan Avenue. The most rigid racial segregation continued in Detroit through the 1940s, i.e., the Black migrant ghetto was on the east side and the White migrant ghetto on the west side of Woodward Avenue. This shift to Michigan Avenue, then, was the consequence of displacement by business interests in combination with White racial prejudice and segregation.

It seems evident that there was no Skid Row area in Detroit before the Civil War. However, there was an incipient Skid Row-like area in Detroit, especially after 1850, that was generally similar to the Lombard–Southwark–Moyamensing slum section of Philadelphia. In the post-Civil War period, the Potomac and Heights were undifferentiated with respect to slum housing conditions, prostitution, gambling, crime and homeless persons.

[12] M/S Police Department Complaints, Vols. 1 and 2, 9 May 1896 to 19 April 1897 and 19 April 1897 to 14 December 1897. [Burton Historical Collection.]

Exactly when the Red Light district developed in Detroit's old Third Ward is not clear, but it seems to have occurred during the mid-1880s and early 1890s.

While there are important differences between Philadelphia and Detroit with respect to the racial composition of the populations and the relationship of the two areas to the CBD, once the areas had become differentiated, there were important similarities. In both cities segregated vice districts were embedded within a larger low-income "social-problem population" residential area on those sides that did not abut the business and commercial section. The similarities were more than just in form; they were the consequences of the same generally accepted standards of behavior with respect to women and sex, alcohol, politics, and ways to deal with poverty.

As the Red Light district became differentiated in Detroit, the homeless-man area developed on its edge, centered around Cadillac Square. This was a somewhat different sequential pattern from that in Philadelphia where the homeless-man area came later. Nonetheless, the relationship between the Tenderloin of both cities and the Skid Row was similar: both Skid Rows were on the edge of the Tenderloin closest to the CBD. It seems reasonable to conclude that the reason was the same—that these were economically marginal areas undesirable as either residential or prime commercial areas. The higher concentration of public transportation, the availability of laboring jobs in and near the CBD, and the availability of the recreational resources of the Tenderloin–Red Light district would have all contributed to the location of the homeless-man area.

One major difference between Detroit and Philadelphia emerges: the Detroit Skid Row moved away from the Cadillac Square area to the Michigan Avenue area on the West Side. Insofar as there was a dispersion of prostitution to the West Side, especially to the north of where the Skid Row developed, we can say that the Tenderloin also moved, keeping in mind that it no longer had "official" police protection, although de facto police protection continued. This needs a further limitation, for it was the White homeless and the White Tenderloin men who moved (and not all of them either). The argument has been offered that this was a response to the rapid increase in Detroit's Black population. This sequence of events did not occur in Philadelphia; rather, the differentiation of the White homeless men from the Black was due to pressure from White social reformers who drove the White vagrants out of the area and thereby seem to have been a major factor in the relocation of vagrants into the Philadelphia homeless-man area. They left behind the Black vagrants as well as Black pimps and prostitutes, who simply "moved over" into the growing Black residential area; a residuum of White prostitutes also remained.

In the strictest sense, then, the "sociological" hypothesis has been demonstrated by these case studies of Philadelphia and Detroit.[13] In both cities, Skid Row was a post-Civil War phenomenon. At best, however, this is a gross simplification. Detroit was too small to have a Skid Row before the Civil War. In Philadelphia, the "classic" Skid Row developed subsequent to an earlier undifferentiated slum–vice–homeless-persons area and in a location different from the later stereotyped Skid Row. But there is no reason to believe that homeless persons living in the Lombard–Southwark–Moyamensing section in 1880 were substantially different from those living in the Skid Row section north of Market Street in Philadelphia in 1885 or 1890. Nor is there any reason to believe that those who lived in the Heights were very different from those who lived in and around Cadillac Square in Detroit. One of the consequences of this conclusion is to call into question the meaning and usefulness of the term "Skid Row." It is to such a reformulation that we turn in a later section of this monograph where attention is directed to "Skid Row-like people."

[13] This was also true in New York City. The Five Points area was the undifferentiated slum–Skid Row–vice area in the pre-Civil War period and for a few years thereafter. The movement of business and the use of some of the land for public buildings as well as insistent pressure from public health workers and various missionaries led to a shift of the population into the Bowery area. The vice district moved as well, so that what became known as the Tenderloin was well north of the Bowery; but vice continued to be characteristic of the slums surrounding the Bowery-Mulberry Bend section. According to Thomas Byrnes (32, *p. 646*), the Skid Row "cheap lodging house" was first developed in New York City in about 1877 in Park Row (Chatham Street); by 1892, there were 270 such places with a capacity of 12,317 rooms (cf. 171, *p. 200*; 27, *pp. 94–95, 195–196*; 123, *pp. 34, 49, 94*; 50, *pp. 44, 48–50*; 13, *pp. 7, 8, 12, 23, 41*; 117, *pp. 47–49, 189–190, 197, 303–305, 312, 315, 334, 337, 344–346, 356*; 164, *pp. 12–19, 33, 42–59, 66*; 126, *pp. 20–24, 36–42, 48–50, 74–75, 189, 194*; 228, *pp. 121–126*).

Part II

Where Will Skid Row Move?

Chapter 4

Approaches to Prediction: Philadelphia[1]

WE INITIALLY conceived of Skid Row as a distinctive area that was not difficult to recognize or to delineate. Bogue used a similar approach in his study of Chicago (25, *ch. 1*). This stereotypical quality was recognized by Griffith Edwards and his associates when they identified the areas of the Elephant and Castle and Waterloo (South London) and the Stepney and Aldgate sections (East End) as the chief haunts of "broken down inebriates" in London, England (58, *pp. 249–252*). While we have changed our concept of Skid Row substantially since 1959, the present chapter approaches the question of prediction from the initial frame of reference, if for no other reason than that concepts must be held reasonably steady while attention is given to a specific prediction problem (21).

In Philadelphia, there was a recognizable and stereotyped homelessman area which had such "Skid Row institutions" as cheap hotels, bars and restaurants, rescue missions and a park, day-labor offices, vaudeville houses that had become burlesque theaters and all-night movies, liquor stores, and blood banks not very far away. The Skid Row residents, as they were initially thought of, were the most conspicuous population in the area, that is, they "lived" there—it was their area. The other land-users "lived" elsewhere and, presumably, had "normal" family lives.

[1] We acknowledge our indebtedness to the following: Drs. Charles Blumstein and Herman Niebuhr of Temple University; the Warden and staff of the Philadelphia House of Correction; the Police Department of the City of Philadelphia; Drs. Michael Lalli and Lawrence Rosen, Department of Sociology, Temple University; Bernard Meltzer, Bernard Camins and Richard Cohen, formerly of A.M. Greenfield & Company; Sally Meisenhelder, Malcolm Bonner, Robert Beale, Steven Roche, Leonard Moore, Harvey McIntyre and Shelly Silverstein. In addition, we wish to express our appreciation to the *Journal of Studies on Alcohol* in which a part of this chapter has previously appeared. Bernard Meltzer, Bernard Camins and Richard Cohen were the authors of the analysis of the economics of Skid Row residential real estate that has been incorporated in this chapter.

The question of where Skid Row will recur is clearly dependent on public land-use policies and so it is important to review the possibilities. At least the following outcomes to the redevelopment process may be conceived as far as Skid Row is concerned:

Alternative 1: A new major Skid Row area may develop. This alternative assumes that the Skid Row area uniquely supplies services to its specific population, which has been segregated from the general population, and that specifically Skid Row institutions have developed to meet the needs of the Skid Row population. It assumes that as long as this kind of population exists, a Skid Row area will develop to meet its needs, given a sufficient number of men to support the complex of institutions. For example, Bogue (25, *p. 17*) concluded that American cities of 500,000 or more usually have a Skid Row neighborhood and that there are tendencies toward such a development in cities with a population of 175,000 or more. Dunham expresses the assumption differently when he says that "the Row is actually to be best explained in terms of a sociological theory of subcultures—that is, the society functions to create certain institutional forms that will meet the needs of those persons whose needs are not met by any of the existing institutional structures" (57, *p. 57*). Dunham argues that Skid Rows perform a socially significant activity and, from this point of view, as long as there are sufficient numbers of poor and homeless men, one can expect that a set of Skid Row institutions will develop in some area of the city to provide the services that they need (at a price, of course).

This policy alternative also assumes that there is a "natural process" involving competitive bidding for the use of land and buildings (as well as the abuse and neglect of buildings when their structures are no longer highly valued but the land on which they rest retains high value). Natural processes occur within a framework of assumptions about how land should be used, as well as the kind of people who should use it, i.e., who should benefit in other respects in the longer run. Put another way, these natural processes occur when "politicians" permit them to, either by explicit decisions or (more often) as a consequence of decisions about land-use elsewhere in the city.

It may be argued, of course, that the power and authority of politicians ultimately rest on the "will of the people" democratically expressed, but the history of big-city politics over many years suggests that politicians as a group are more subject to control by the courts than they are responsive to the general electorate when it comes to land-use decisions. This was especially true in the 19th and early 20th Centuries. Zoning is still relatively new and manipulable for economic and political advantage.

In terms of the clearance of the Skid Row area and the possibility of its subsequent recurrence elsewhere, the natural-process approach assumes at least the following: (1) That the city government will not use its police powers to drive poor and homeless men from the city. For example, Lovald (107) reported that there was no Skid Row in St. Paul, Minnesota, apparently because there was such a policy. Poor and homeless men were picked up by the police and taken to court, where they were given the option of a jail sentence or a "floater" if they would leave town. (2) That there are no substantial restrictions placed on the relocation of retail liquor establishments, rescue missions, blood banks, casual labor offices, pawn-shops, pool halls, and similar activities; that a political policy of laissez-faire prevails with respect to Skid Row institutions. We would expect in this alternative that, given a sufficient number of men to support Skid Row institutions, a new Skid Row area would develop not far from the center city or "loop" and would bear the same dependent relationship to the CBD as earlier Skid Rows.

Alternative 2: A number of smaller Skid Row areas may develop. This alternative also postulates that Skid Rows are natural areas that fill a need, but it assumes that there is either a moderately effective program of detection and prevention of a single large Skid Row area by public officials, or that the process of redevelopment of downtown areas has raised land values to the point where it would be unprofitable to oversupply low-rent housing downtown. One might still find a smaller Skid Row area that is marginal to the CBD, but such areas may also be marginal to the older commercial subcenters which have developed at the intersection of major lines of transportation in metropolitan areas. Small Skid Rows might be less efficient from the point of view of the homeless man but might still provide the necessary sources of income and services. Something of this sort seems to have been happening in Philadelphia.

Alternative 3: Skid Rows may be completely eliminated and the men dispersed into the general population. This alternative does not deny the argument that Skid Row men have important needs but argues that there is more than one way to meet them. Thus, cheap housing, cheap liquor, blood banks, casual labor offices, and so forth are already scattered in other Philadelphia slum areas. This alternative assumes that the highly decentralized and permissive land-use practices of the laissez-faire era will no longer prevail and may or may not be accompanied by rehabilitation programs to reduce the demand for services provided by Skid Row institutions. When the Philadelphia Skid Row program began in 1959, some of this sort of thinking was involved in its planning (24). However, Philadelphia has not developed a program of regulation of Skid Row institutions, preferring to place its bets on a program of rehabilitation for the residents.

Alternative 4: Skid Row may be replaced (212, 213). This alternative is similar to the planned development in Chicago, in which the main-stem West Madison Street Skid Row was to be replaced with a municipally sponsored but privately built residential facility for men displaced from West Madison Street. The facility's design was reminiscent of a ship, complete with porthole-style windows, and was to include a restaurant, barber college, liquor store and rescue mission in a high-rise structure. At this writing, West Madison Street is undergoing redevelopment, but the fate of its sponsored replacement is unknown.

In 1959 we predicted that Philadelphia's Skid Row was to move to the north of the existing area and still within Police District C (Table 3). The next most likely move was to the west of the existing area within District C and into District E. The third most likely move was to the south of the existing Skid Row on the other side of the CBD into District J. These predictions were consistent with the notion of marginal location drawn from Ernest Burgess's concentric zonal hypothesis of the growth of the city (30).

Drawing an analogy between plant and animal ecology and the spatial-economic behavior of human groups, Robert Park and his protégés, Roderick D. McKenzie and Ernest Burgess, developed the notion of "natural areas." In their view, human commercial and cultural competition in the city "naturally" produced several different kinds of areas: the CBD, ethnic communities, industrial zones, high-class apartment districts, and so on. One of these natural areas was Skid Row.

At the same time, they developed a theoretical model of the growth of the city (30, 113). The city grew outward from the center but, at any time during the growth process, several roughly concentric zones could be distinguished: the CBD, the "one in transition," the "zone of workingmen's homes," and so on. According to Burgess, the zone in transition was territory which was formerly the zone of workingmen's homes but would eventually become part of the CBD when the latter expanded. As such, the transition zone was characterized by high land values, but, since the buildings in the zone were probably worthless for CBD functions (offices, specialty and department stores, and the like), they bore low rents and were "naturally" the site of businesses and other functions which benefited from the high traffic levels generated by the CBD but were only marginally profitable. The functions found in the transition zone, thus, included small wholesalers and jobbers, immigrant housing (especially the area of first settlement), some light manufacturing (usually of clothing) and Skid Row.

Thus, when Skid Row moves (essentially being displaced as a consequence of the expansion of the CBD), it would be expected to move away from the CBD into the new zone of transition or into analogous parts not too far away, even though these might be on the opposite side of the CBD. Given a social and political policy of preventing a single new Skid Row, one might then regard major commercial subcenters within the city as analogous to the CBD and one would expect that the secondary Skid Rows would also form with respect to these inner-city commercial subcenters in a similar fashion.

There is at least one alternative to this theory of zonal marginal location that has been offered, as well as a number of major conceptual attacks which we have tried to take into account (203). The sector theory (220, 221) argues that business or populations in search of rehousing will tend to move outward from the CBD but retain the same general relationship to it. Presumably this is because the range of choice for a new location is limited, not only by cost, but by an inclination to look nearby or further out along already familiar lines of transportation (83, *ch. 19, 20*; 113). This sector approach need not be inconsistent with the marginal location approach if the move is to adjacent sections farther out in the same area.

When the initial predictions were made in 1959, it was with the full expectation that the site would be cleared and well on the way to redevelopment before 1973. A part of the area was indeed cleared, but several cubicle hotels and several missions providing "food and flop" were still in operation in the summer of 1973. As a consequence there was only minor pressure on the men to move out of the locality for, as a hotel closed, a number of men simply moved to those that remained (at increased prices, to be sure). Nor did all the core institutions move away. One cheap restaurant closed when its owner's hotel was taken for redevelopment and the site cleared, but others remained. This is an inadequate situation for a test of predictions and, in the last analysis, this chapter can only report trends. Nonetheless our problems and procedures, with respect to prediction, can be instructive to others.

A conceptual problem emerged as well. From the beginning, the phrase "potential and incipient Skid Rows" was used to suggest a series of progressions: a residentially and institutionally desirable area deteriorated until it became a "potential Skid Row"; when it deteriorated still further, it was ripe for "invasion"; and when the Skid Row area was cleared and the men moved, it would take little for the incipient Skid Row to become the "new Skid Row." When the research was planned, an all-or-nothing approach was used, i.e., either an area was or was not a Skid Row. In time it became apparent that this was naïve.

It was also assumed that the entire process would take place in something less than 10 years and, hence, relatively rapidly. Unbeknownst to us, Alan Schwartz (one-time chairman of the Mayor's Committee on Alcohol Problems in Detroit) had observed that, "It usually takes a neighborhood about thirty years to reach the danger point and then only a few years to make the complete transformation."[2] And, while it is doubtful that the final transformation takes place as quickly as Schwartz suggested, the historical research reported earlier in this book supports his conclusion that these changes do indeed take much longer than had originally been anticipated. This conclusion was a major factor in later efforts to develop a long-run indicator on the basis of real estate assessments that are discussed in this chapter.

Finally, it seems likely that discussions such as these may lead to a self-fulfilling prophecy with respect to the "new Skid Row." Our current position is that the location of a Skid Row area is compounded of (1) Skid Row-like people, (2) Skid Row institutions and (3) a public stereotype of the area as "Skid Row."[3] There are areas in Philadelphia which have some of the former two but are not yet designated as a "Skid Row"; and the final push into actually being a Skid Row area may occur when an area is labeled as The New Skid Row, and the press, the political leaders, the real estate operators and the general public respond to the area in terms of that label. We have already adopted the use of pseudonyms for areas of the city, although admittedly a knowledgeable and persistent person, such as a newspaper reporter, could undoubtedly make the identifications. If this eventuates in some effective prevention program, then perhaps it would be desirable, but it can more easily result in the consignment of the area into the perdition of "Skid Row" because the flood of anxiety and hostility might be generated in combination with the unlikelihood of effective legislation by the city council or effective enforcement by public agencies.

We attempted to detect a "pre-Skid Row condition" in other

[2] Detroit *News*, 10 February 1957.

[3] The matter of stereotyping was not systematically examined. However, 55 Philadelphia taxicab drivers were interviewed on the assumption that they best fit the criterion of knowledgeable informants whose perception of the situation might evidence the combination of fact and fiction that goes into the public's stereotype of where a Skid Row is located. The cab drivers, who were all questioned at the Philadelphia International Airport, had been driving for a median of 21 years: 98% were able to identify the Vine Street Skid Row that existed at that time. There was no clear agreement on the future location of Skid Row. This is taken to mean that no stereotype had yet developed on the matter among the general public of Philadelphia.

sections of the city by investigating the presence of "bottle gangs," the prevalence of Skid Row offenses, neighborhood real estate characteristics and long-run real estate trends.

Bottle Gangs

An obvious first effort to identify Skid Row-like conditions is to identify the location of bottle gangs. A bottle gang is a group of people who contribute to the cost of a bottle of wine and then pass the bottle from person to person. (To date, only male bottle gangs have been reported.) Usually the drinking is done in the park, on a curb, or in an alley; much depends on local police policy, for the men seek to avoid arrest. Some bottle-drinking groups are temporary, being assembled by a "captain" from those who have money and dispersing when the drinking rituals are completed. Other bottle gangs, located outside the Skid Row area, are relatively stable in membership and persist over a number of years, according to our informants. Rooney (169) has discussed the norms of Skid Row bottle gangs in detail and Rubington (175) has written of the bottle gangs off Skid Row. It seems reasonable to argue that since bottle gangs off Skid Row are composed of what we have called Skid Row-like men, their presence would be an indicator of a potential Skid Row area.

In the summer of 1959 informal interviews were conducted with members of the staff of the House of Correction, who had had a continuous experience with Skid Row-like persons over a period of years. They indicated a number of places in the city that might be designated "little Skid Rows." Their criteria, more limited than ours, were based on their knowledge of drinking groups in the areas where prisoners lived before jailing (and often between sentences). After those locations in which boundaries were not specific enough for our purposes were eliminated, there were 11 areas and street intersections in most of the older sections of the city. These included large shopping centers, junctures of a business street and a public park, "spottily" built-up industrial areas, stadium–sports arena areas and along railway rights-of-way which have been included into the street pattern for freight purposes. These sections of the city were briefly inspected for other evidences of a Skid Row-like character.

The location of bottle gangs was reexamined during 1963–

1965 by staff members of the Diagnostic and Rehabilitation Center/Philadelphia. These were "knowledgeable informants," for all of them were recovered alcoholics and most had lived in the Philadelphia Skid Row area for some time and had participated in bottle gangs both on and off the Row. Their information came from their own experience, from information given by Skid Row respondents at the Center and from field inspections of rumored bottle-gang locations. A final restudy was made in 1967–1969.

It would have been unusual to find a group actually in operation, but it was easy enough to find the accumulation of cheap wine bottles in alleys, empty lots, abandoned houses, neighborhood parks and parking lots behind stores. In the Skid Row area it was especially indicative when empty cans of "canned heat" were found. While in most places quart bottles were found, in one park there were half-gallon bottles of cheap port, sherry and muscatel.

The cumulative findings of these three investigations suggest that the presence of bottle gangs is not a useful indicator of an incipient major Skid Row because the bottle gangs were so widely scattered throughout Philadelphia. Almost every blighted commercial strip, small city park in a deteriorated neighborhood, and railway right-of-way seemed to have its bottle gang. There were too many to indicate that this was a case of smaller "secondary" Skid Rows. We can only conclude that bottle gangs are endemic in the areas of poverty as well as some declining working-class sections in Philadelphia, areas in which Skid Row-like men can readily be found. All are potential Skid Rows in the broadest sense, but for purposes of relatively short-run prediction the procedure could not be considered useful.

Skid Row Offenses

It seems reasonable to argue that incipient Skid Row areas will be characterized by the prevalence of "Skid Row offenses" at a higher rate than elsewhere in the city, albeit lower than would be found in Skid Row itself. If Skid Row is redeveloped, one might reasonably expect an increase in Skid Row-type offenses in the incipient Skid Row areas. That is, these areas already had more than their share of Skid Row behavior and it might be expected that they would be least resistant to, or even welcome, Skid Row men moving in. We examined rates of drunkenness, vagrancy and disorderly conduct, those offenses most closely associated with Skid Row behavior and with the process of turning prisoners into "urban nomads" (193, *ch. 3, 9*).

Philadelphia police data are aggregated annually by district (there are also subunits known as "car sectors," but a complete set was unavailable for 1970). District boundaries are relatively stable, although between 1958 and 1970 one district was completely eliminated and eight others were renumbered. No adequate data are available to establish a satisfactory population base for the calculation of crime rates, since the Police District boundaries are not coterminous with census tracts.

Table 3 presents the numbers of offenses reported to the police and arrests for the three categories of crime by selected police districts in 1958 and 1970. (The districts have been given pseudonymous letter designations.) The numbers of offenses reported and arrests differ not only because police do not always locate the person committing the offense but because, even if they have located the offenders, they do not always make an arrest. Furthermore, it is not uncommon for the police to arrest more than one person for what has been listed as a single reported offense; thus there may be a report of drunkenness and the investigating officers may arrest four or five persons. The districts chosen for examination in Table 3 were

TABLE 3.—*Reported Offenses and Arrests for Drunkenness, Vagrancy and Disorderly Conduct in Selected Police Districts of Philadelphia, 1958 and 1970, and Percentage Change*[a]

DRUNKENNESS

District	Offenses			Arrests		
	1958	1970	% Change	1958	1970	% Change
C	6971	7035	0.9	8972	8973	
J	3522			4127		
K	2802	1801	−35.7	3196	2024	−36.7
P	2443	1673	−31.5	2865	2135	−25.5
M	2237	2262	1.1	2645	2602	−1.6
E	2107	3039	30.7	2363	3567	33.8
I	1981	2065	4.1	2100	2334	10.0
H	1894	1274	−32.7	1995	1377	−31.0

[continued—

TABLE 3.—*continued*

	Offenses			Arrests		
District	1958	1970	% Change	1958	1970	% Change
U	1751	1246	−28.8	1559	1487	−4.6
N	1533	1544	0.7	1674	1963	14.7
V	1368	1435	4.7	1475	1647	10.4
R	1218	1145	−6.0	1295	1207	−6.7
O	953	1782	46.5	994	1957	49.2
L	711	1066	33.3	791	1231	34.9

VAGRANCY

District	1958	1970	% Change	1958	1970	% Change
C	452	923	51.0	621	1627	62.1
J	138			166		
K	29	9	−69.0	27	4	−85.2
P	31	15	−51.6	34	13	−61.8
M	50	23	−54.0	52	26	−50.0
E	273	100	−63.6	271	128	−52.8
I	27	28	3.6	22	13	−40.9
H	32	6	−81.2	27	7	−74.1
U	77	25	−67.5	40	30	−25.0
N	27	7	−74.0	25	8	−68.0
V	55	28	−49.1	13	43	69.8
R	18	6	−66.7	16	9	−43.8
O	12	20	28.6	16	22	27.3
L	11	16	31.2	12	16	25.0

DISORDERLY CONDUCT

District	1958	1970	% Change	1958	1970	% Change
C	282	212	−24.8	1468	312	−78.7
J	450			1490		
K	380	60	−82.4	2393	110	−95.4
P	349	144	−58.7	2214	156	−93.0
M	269	170	−36.8	1282	309	−75.9
E	188	124	−34.0	888	219	−75.3
I	223	149	−33.2	1999	289	−85.5
H	261	80	−69.3	1759	97	−94.5
U	176	191	7.9	601	255	−57.6
N	185	167	−9.7	790	277	−64.9
V	168	193	13.0	452	277	−38.7
R	224	120	−1.8	1216	241	−80.2
O	133	240	2.9	133	282	52.8
L	43	63	31.7	83	69	−16.9

[a] Data from the Philadelphia Police Department.

above the mean for either 1958 or 1970. They are rank ordered with respect to drunkenness offenses in 1958. District C is, in fact, Police District 6, the "Skid Row district." One special peculiarity of the table needs explanation. District J was a center-city district in 1958 in which it was common for men to panhandle and also where a potential and incipient Skid Row was located. The district was subsequently abolished and its territory distributed to Districts C and E. We are able to make some approximations, however, from car-sector data for 1958 by offenses reported to the police. Approximately 55% of the drunkenness, 61% of the vagrancy and 52% of the disorderly-conduct offenses were in the car sectors that were assigned to District C and the balance were in sectors assigned to District E.

Keeping in mind the allocation from District J for drunkenness and for disorderly conduct, there was a decline in both offenses reported and arrests. With respect to vagrancy, there was an increase in both offenses reported and arrests. It is probable that this is the consequence of changes in police practices that occurred as the result of a court decision which declared the arrest of an alcoholic illegal on the grounds that alcoholism was an illness and therefore not punishable (23, *ch. 4*). Neither Districts K nor P in 1958 would have been probable places for a new Skid Row, if by that term a "White" residential area is implied, for both these districts had a high percentage of Black residents. The percentage of Blacks on Philadelphia's Skid Row has increased since 1960, but until now a stereotyped Black Skid Row (as distinct from slum, or even Tenderloin) has not been evident in Philadelphia.

When drunkenness alone is considered (because the number of cases is so much larger than for vagrancy), the data suggest that a district (District E) to the west of the present Skid Row (District C) might be developing in the direction of another Skid Row. However, arrests for drunkenness are more likely to be made in this area to maintain its quality as the prime commercial area of the city rather than because it is a Skid Row residential area. In general, then, increased reports of drunkenness offenses and arrests should not be considered a positive finding with respect to the prediction. In general, the police-district data do not confirm the predictions. But neither do they conclusively upset them. The data do not tell us that a single Skid Row area has developed during the 12-year period, one which can be identified clearly as a "new Skid Row." The data are not detailed enough to tell us whether a number of smaller Skid Row areas may have developed, nor whether dispersal into the general population has been such that not even "secondary Skid Rows" have developed.

Neighborhood Housing

Another way to approach the question of an incipient Skid Row is through an evaluation of neighborhood housing and real estate quality. While it may be argued that the recurrence of another major Skid Row, or of secondary Skid Rows, might be detected by moves of the Skid Row institutions to which we have already alluded, few of these so-called Skid Row institutions are distinctive to Skid Row at the present time. This is not to deny that they may have had a greater Skid Row-relatedness in the past. What is most distinctive about Skid Row, not considering the characteristics of the population itself, is the housing. Attention was therefore given to housing and related neighborhood amenities. After some casting about, the following procedures were developed, derived from collaborative experience with the real estate consultants of the Urban Renewal Administration 314 Demonstration Grant Project that was conducted between 1963 and 1965 (121). They highlighted a number of important characteristics of the real estate market that were significant for the recurrence of a Skid Row area. These became background considerations for the actual real estate data that were collected.

1. The Skid Row housing market is a rental market. The owner of Skid Row-type property must be a specialist because of the hazards of the business. These hazards include dealing with alcoholics, guarding against theft and vandalism, holding down operating expenses, and very often dealing with public officials who seek to put him out of business. These conditions necessitate close supervision by the operator. If the operation is a rooming house, the operator may be expected to live on the premises or in the neighborhood (or to have a manager who does).

2. Property owners believe that there is a high investment risk inherent in Skid Row properties. The owner–operator of a Skid Row property anticipates an annual return of 50 to 100% on equity before he will venture into a deal.[4]

The hypothetical operating statement of a typical Skid Row cubicle hotel given in Chart 1 may help clarify the economics of

CHART 1.—*Hypothetical Operating Statement of a Skid Row Cubicle Hotel*[a]

Assume: 100 people at 75¢ a night ($5.25 a week) as unadjusted gross;
26 weeks (October through March), 90% full; and
26 weeks (April through September), 70% full.

Adjusted Gross: $21,840

Expenses		Operation	
Taxes	$1,000 yr	Cleaning	$1,800 yr
Permit	200	Personal furnishings	1,100
Heat and hot water	1,200	Laundry and linen	1,350
Insurance	600	Miscellaneous	
Repairs and		(Attorney, etc.)	1,000
maintenance	1,500	Total:	$5,250
Utilities	800		
Total:	$5,300		

Total Expenses and Operation: $10,550

Financing

$35,000

1st mortgage of 40% @ 6% interest with	
5-point discount, 15 years	$1,417
2nd mortgage of 25% @ 20% interest, 5-years	2,900
Total:	$4,317

Equity $13,250 + $1,400 (discount) = $14,650

	Gross Income:	$21,840
	Less:	14,867
		$ 6,973

Return on Equity: 48%

[a] Data from Meltzer et al. (121).

[4] This is as fast a turnover rate on invested capital as can be found anywhere in the real estate industry, as the following listing of expected annual rate of

Skid Row housing operations. This analysis assumes that the owner has not paid himself a salary for the work that he is doing. In addition, it is assumed that there are also many "free flops" (a night's lodging) in return for clean-up or other maintenance work performed by Skid Row men. If these were "priced-out" and included in the expense and operating statement, the rate of return would be lower.

Table 4 gives the assessed values of 8 of the largest and most important Skid Row hotels from 1920 to 1971. It is evident that, insofar as we can take assessed valuation as a measure of approximately 65 to 70% of market value, the above cost analysis is not far off for some Skid Row hotels. For others, the investment would have been much lower and, therefore, the return on equity would have been substantially higher.

3. The minimum size required for conversion of a building to Skid Row residential occupancy is influenced by the relative inflexibility of rooming-house expenses and operating costs and

TABLE 4.—*Assessed Values of the Most Important Philadelphia Skid Row Hotels, 1920–1971*[a]

Hotel	1920	1930	1940	1950	1960	1971
A	16,000	18,000	9,000	36,900	34,600	[b]
B	62,000	80,000	23,300	40,100	37,800	[b]
C	30,000	35,000	21,800	28,200	26,700	29,900
D	28,000	33,000	23,400	30,900	29,000	[b]
E	16,000	20,100	11,200	15,700	16,100	[b]
F	60,000	65,000	37,300	38,400	38,400	38,400
G	9,000	15,000	8,600	14,500	12,700	12,700
H	35,000	41,000	18,900	10,300	10,300	10,300

[a] Source: Philadelphia Tax Assessor's Office.
[b] Acquired for redevelopment and removed from tax rolls.

returns shows (estimates for June 1965): prime long-term leases (U.S. Government, prime AAA concerns, etc., all net), 7%; AAA companies (net), 7½%; gas stations, 7½–8%; good apartments, 9–10%; good to fair apartments, 12%; shopping center (excellent), 8–9%; shopping center (ordinary), 10%; office building (good), 9%; office building (old), 11%; motel (leased to national chain, net), 12%; motel (ordinary), 15%; hotel (sale leaseback to Hilton, etc.), 8%; hotel (ordinary), 12%; hotel (second and third class), 15–18%; slum property (absentee owner), 50%; Skid Row dwelling, 50–100%.

the inability or unwillingness of the Skid Row residents to pay more than the lowest possible housing costs. To illustrate the way in which market forces work out, Meltzer et al. (121, *pp. 19–24*) estimated the operating costs of rooming houses with different numbers of rooms for rent. For a building with three rooms for rent at $7 a week each (1965 prices), and the owner sleeping in, the property just breaks even disregarding any mortgage conditions. For a property with six rooms for rent, assuming three singles and three doubles, the return on equity would be 26%. Finally, for a property with nine rooms for rent, assuming four singles and five doubles, the return on equity would be 61%.[5] The analysis of rooming-house costs is especially relevant because cubicle hotels are now a nonconforming use under Philadelphia codes, and rooming houses are a most probable substitute.

In brief, neither the three- nor the six-room rooming house is economically feasible. There may always be some in existence, however, because some owners may be willing to trade the amenities of single-home occupancy for financial relief. On the other hand, the nine-room rooming house is economically feasible for Skid Row housing.

4. Skid Row properties generally have unfavorable mortgage terms because lending institutions are cautious about such a high-risk venture. Generally, too, owner–operators are financially marginal persons with low credit ratings. Further, there is a general "flavor" about a Skid Row property that makes it undesirable to the major lending institutions. The consequence is that most mortgage lenders will be private or one of the less conservative building and loan associations. Typical financing terms would be 33 to 50% of value (commonly referred to as "low ratio" of loan to purchase value), a 5- to 10-year period (short term), 6% interest on the first mortgage with no limit on the second mortgage (high interest), and a 10-point discount on loans of 8- to 10-years' duration.

5. Where the initial purchase price of the property or a high investment is required to put the business into operation, low rents are improbable. These are the conditions in "prime" real

[5] These estimates have been deposited with NAPS as Rooming House Cases I, II, and III. To order, see Appendix A.

estate areas, but increases in real estate values that may lead to prohibitive rentals can also occur in the blighted areas bordering the CBD. Thus an area may have extremely low-rent rooming houses, but there may be rumors that the area will be physically rehabilitated. There is a high probability that properties will then sell at prices that are out of proportion with current income as investors gamble on expected future profit rather than seek current income. There will be a tendency for rents to be forced up. Under circumstances of high or rising real estate values (a condition that increasingly prevails in the area east of center city), a Skid Row rooming-house area would be much less than the "highest and best" use of the land. Put another way, a Skid Row rooming-house situation can flourish only where real estate values are declining and where there is a continued expectation of low rentals.

6. Skid Row rooming-house operations are socially undesirable. Operators feel that adverse publicity may put them out of business through the application of public action, such as the strict enforcement of various zoning and housing codes. They seek areas of dilapidated housing. Often these areas are very heterogeneous with respect to land use. While the operation is getting under way, they can be relatively inconspicuous. Basically, the Skid Row operator wants to be anonymous and to be left alone. The deteriorated neighborhood is where he is most likely to have the conditions he wants (sociologists would call the area "anomic"—there is no code of social norms to which most of the residents conform on a voluntary basis).

7. Where there is a reasonably high prevalence of home ownership (50%, for instance), it is likely that there will be some pressure on owners and real estate operators from civic groups who express a desire to preserve the neighborhood status quo. Given some assistance and encouragement, many such groups will make considerable efforts to upgrade the area, although the larger changes in the urban society generally seem to operate to nullify many of their efforts. Homeowners will also attempt to organize the responsible tenants in the neighborhood. They will seek to apply the greatest possible political pressure on landlords who accept Skid Row-type renters.

It seemed evident that certain neighborhood real estate characteristics were related to whether an area was a potential

Skid Row, but, even though a large number of "sociological" reports on block frontages were collected, the procedure broke down because it required interviews with too many businessmen in the local real estate field. Experience during previous research indicated that even a whisper that an area was regarded as a potential Skid Row called forth strong local reactions. Residents and real estate professionals were likely to be much less detached than social investigators. Their response might alter land values and the kind of persons living in the area. That is, residents might "fight" what they perceived to be a harsh commentary about their neighborhood's becoming a Skid Row. Alternatively, real estate people and other property owners might react to the stereotype by further neglecting the maintenance of their buildings and by the encouragement of rooming houses and apartments which were adapted to Skid Row-like residents. The belief that an area was becoming a new Skid Row might then involve a self-fulfilling prophecy. This would defeat our major goal, which was to prevent the recurrence of a new Skid Row. Not only were there operational problems, therefore, but there were serious social policy questions as well.

In brief summary, some attempt was made to develop "objective" measures of relatively short-run changes in Philadelphia that might lead to the confirmation or denial of the predictions that were made in 1959. While in each case there were specific reasons why the procedure failed to be effective, there are some overarching considerations: (1) It now seems evident that the relatively small number of Skid Row men who were residents of the area at that time (only about 3000 in 1960) could easily be lost with hardly a trace in the cheap rooming-house areas of Philadelphia. As the Skid Row area has been cleared, something of this sort seems to have happened. Field work indicated that there were many Skid Row-like men living in inner-city areas which we had called "potential Skid Rows." That is, the "neighborhood bums" were not readily distinguishable from Skid Row men—rather than waiting for Skid Row men to move into a locality, the possibility was that they were already there, but that they had not been perceived as such. "Skid Row" was as much in the eye of the beholder as it was in the characteristics of the men and women to whom the appellation was applied.

It seems likely that there were larger social and political processes at work which were evidenced in the general decline in "Skid Row crimes." Perhaps it was as simple as a change in law-enforcement administrative policy, perhaps it was the increasing age of the residents of the Skid Row area who would be less likely to be drunk in public, less likely to be panhandling in the CBD and less likely to be out late at night, given the danger from muggers and jackrollers. Perhaps it was the increasing availability of alcoholism treatment facilities in the city (although more are needed) even though such treatment programs are not usually effective in reducing Skid Row crimes. Perhaps what we have is evidence of the decline of the White Skid Row and of the rise of the Black Skid Row; police practices with respect to Blacks tend to be somewhat harsher in some respects but somewhat more lenient in others.

Finally, it seems likely that still more comprehensive "urban trends" simply made the predictions naïve and unrealistic in the first place. It certainly is possible for the occupants of an urban area to change markedly in 5 years, especially when a change of racial composition is involved. Such a change took place in Atlanta during the Hartsfield administration, when an entire subdivision shifted from White to Black occupancy in an orderly fashion. The disruptive results of "block busting" are only too familiar in American cities. But such a rapid transition into a Skid Row, at least in Philadelphia, is highly unlikely. It is more likely that the development of Skid Row is a relatively long process. It seemed desirable, therefore, to seek an indicator of potential Skid Rows that would project over a relatively long period of time. We examined long-term real estate trends to see whether they would yield a measure of change that would indicate an area's becoming increasingly Skid Row-like. We also wanted to see whether an area could be found in which the long-run trends were similar to those which had occurred in the Philadelphia Skid Row.

Real Estate Trends

The job was too big to analyze trends for the entire city without the assistance of a massive computer program, but a pilot study would be indicative. Nor would interviews with real estate operators be satisfactory, despite the fact that they have a good idea of trends in their territories. Inquiry made clear that old real estate firms may be able to call on partners or records that go back over several generations. But this information on real estate values is almost always of a very general nature. Furthermore, finding the person most knowledgeable about a locality is almost as difficult as finding a needle in a haystack.

Attention was therefore turned to the official tax records of the City of Philadelphia. These records have an advantage in that they are retained for long periods of time. There was the additional advantage that the effective administrator of the real estate tax assessment procedures had been involved with them over a professional career of perhaps 50 years. Assessed real estate values are not necessarily "true market values" for both technical and political reasons. The assessment comes closest to true market values only when the property recently changed hands. Under ideal conditions, the assessor arrives at a judgment that is supposed to be based on what similar properties in the locality are selling for during the same period. Furthermore, taxes are not levied on the assessor's judgment of the market value, but on some fraction of the market value. The rationale for this involves a hedge against the uncertainties of the real estate market; that is, it can be argued that because one property on the block sold for a given amount, we cannot assume that they all will. Indeed there is a strong possibility that if a second one were put on the market, the demand would be less and the price obtained would be less; a third would attract still less demand and a still lower price in a regression series. Assessment, therefore, should be at less than the supposed market value. In Philadelphia, the officially stated aim is about 65% of market value.[6]

[6] We do not wish to appear entirely naïve in this. In point of fact, in the period from 1958 to 1969, a 12-year period, the ratios of assessed market value to actual market value generally declined from 61.5% to 51.4%. Furthermore, there were variations between wards; in 1969 Ward 20, largely inhabited by Blacks, was the highest at 66.3%, while Ward 26, racially mixed but largely Irish and Italian-American, was lowest at 39.5% (Philadelphia, Office of Finance Director, 1971). Leonard Goldenberger, a student at Temple University, in an unpublished paper (ca. 1971), examined the assessor's records for the 20th Ward and found "that many properties were sold at a nominal rate (under $5000) but on the books were still being assessed at up to twice and three times as much as their current sales price." He also found that the assessments sometimes had not been revised in excess of 5 years. He found that, especially

There are political considerations as well. Thus, public taxing authorities need a degree of stability in land values which they propose to assess to make proper predictions of future taxes and future indebtedness. Also, it is politically unwise to have the assessed valuation fluctuate from year to year because it invites considerable taxpayer protest. If there must be fluctuations, it would seem to be politically more expedient to permit the rate of taxation to fluctuate; the taxpayer is thus better able to make his own calculations and his own personal predictions than when both the assessed valuation and the tax rate fluctuate. The stated policy, then, is one of continuity and stability with slow changes in assessed valuations being the norm. Finally, there may be illegal considerations related to party politics. That is, we hear rumors from time to time that it was not uncommon for the political party representatives in power to adjust tax assessments in favor of persons registered in their own party. We have no direct evidence of this, however.

Four sections of Philadelphia were selected for study.[7] From the point of view of tracing a parallel process in the present Skid Row to trends in the potential Skid Row, it would have been desirable to trace property values from 1875, but Philadelphia's tax assessment records seem to be available only from 1913. Area A is a census tract just south of the existing Skid Row area involving 1370 properties. (It might have been better to select the northern edge of the Skid Row area, but this would have involved parts of four wards and thus seemed too complex to manage with limited resources.) Area B is a part of a potential Skid Row perhaps 2½ miles from the present Skid Row, involving approximately 2800 properties. Area C is in a mixed working- and middle-class area perhaps 6 miles from the present Skid Row and is a kind of "control" or comparison area. Area D,

---

during the appeals process, social class and racial considerations played a part in the sense that a "human element" is taken into consideration when assessing "desirable" neighborhoods where property values are rising. The reported motive, according to the Appeals Supervisor of the Board of Revision of Taxes, was to provide relief for "already highly-taxed middle-class citizens." While these considerations cast doubt on the value of the scheme that is discussed, it is hard to believe that the tax assessment system is so corrupt that it is of no value at all as a measure of long-run real estate trends in Philadelphia.

[7] The median assessed values of residential properties are reported in supplementary Table A-6 and those of commercial properties in Table A-7. To order, see Appendix A.

largely inhabited by Blacks, is a series of blocks in a blighted area that has had a long history of association with Skid Row-like people.

Data on all blocks were gathered in Areas A and B, but, when it became apparent that residential blocks in the same area were assessed at very similar values, the data collection in Areas C and D was limited to two commercial frontages on two blocks and residential frontages on three blocks. Assessments were determined for the years 1915, 1920, 1925, 1930, 1940, 1950, 1960 and 1971. All values for areas A and B were recalculated in terms of current dollar values, using 1957–1959 as the base (241, p. 76). This procedure was adopted to control for fluctuations in the value of the dollar between 1915 and 1971; during that time the value of the dollar fluctuated greatly and declined nearly one-third.

At the present time the four "commercial" blocks selected for study are predominantly commercial although there were more residences on these blocks 50 years ago and there continue to be some. The commercial block frontages in the vicinity of the Skid Row area were chosen to avoid the extreme values in some blocks on Arch Street, which is one block north of the principal business street (Market Street). The residential frontages in the vicinity of the Skid Row area were chosen so that one was generally southeast of it. The commercial blocks selected in the other areas were most Skid Row-like or typical of the commercial frontage in the census tract selected for study, and the other residential frontages were representative of all of the residential properties in the area. Since Philadelphia has a large amount of row housing, it is not atypical to find whole blocks with substantially the same assessed valuations.

The data on individual properties were aggregated for block frontages in Tracts A and B. Figure 4 shows both the median assessed value adjusted to the 1957–1959 dollar and as assessed in current dollars. The values clearly indicate the effect of the policy of assessment stability. The adjusted medians tend to be responsive to changes in the value of the dollar because the assessed values remain unchanged for long periods of time. This correspondence of changes in property values and the value of the dollar has been greater since 1940 than before. That is, the policy of assessment stability has been a guiding princi-

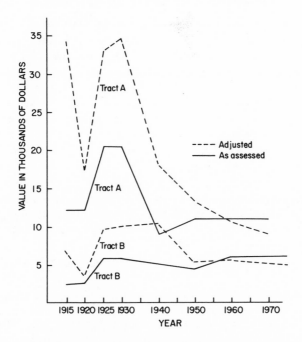

FIGURE 4.—*Median Assessed Values of Block Frontages in Tracts A and B, in Current and 1959 Dollars, by Year*

ple even more after that date. It should be noted that the sharp downward break in assessed valuations is a reflection of city-wide reassessments made in response to the Depression. Assessments were cut more or less across the board from 45 to 55%, but we cannot explain variations between individual properties from the bare bones of data that are available to us.

Commercial property adjacent to the Philadelphia Skid Row has slowly increased in assessed valuation since the low of 1940. We can attribute this partly to the expansion of the CBD so that the block is more desirable as a commercial location. In part, it may be due to commercial success of the Philadelphia Chinatown section, which is in parts of these blocks. Area B declined from the 1940 Depression adjustment in all but one case. One of the block frontages in Area B is a rooming-house area that houses Skid Row-like men; it seems likely that it has been such an area since at least several years before the 1960 assessment. There is some evidence that Skid Row housing is profitable, but the data suggest that this is a part of a large decline in housing quality of the area (as measured by assessed valuations).

In contrast, the values in Area C rose above the Depression adjustment (indeed, in one block there was no adjustment, and in the other the adjustment was proportionately not quite as great as in less prosperous sections of the city). In Area D valuations rose above the 1940 level somewhat and then stabilized or started to drop. The racial, ethnic and commercial trends are highly complex in these block frontages (which is not, of course, revealed in the statistics directly). It is perhaps enough to say that there have been Black Skid Row-like people living in poverty in the area for many years, but that only after 1960 has the area deteriorated badly as a commercial area, and this is reflected in the assessed values. While one might conclude that Area B is blighted and, therefore, possibly ripe for Skid Row tendencies, the data do not support that conclusion for Area D at the present time, although our knowledge suggests that if private or public renewal does not take place within the next few years, the assessed valuations will continue to fall. Should this be the case, it seems likely that Area D's assessed value will approximate the tendencies revealed in Area B.

Residential valuations in the four areas also changed from 1915 to 1971. The assessment of the 200 block of Ninth Street (east side) rose only $1000 from the 1940 low. The area is undesirable for residential purposes and few of the buildings are yet wanted for more than marginal uses. On the other hand, the 1000 block of Spring Street (south side) has appreciated substantially since 1940. This is because the street is occupied by Chinese American families and by rooming houses (one of several streets included in prediction area A). We have had a number of reports from men with alcohol problems, currently not on a spree, who were living in these rooming houses. In Area B, while the commercial frontages have declined, the workingmen's residential area behind it has maintained its value, with modest appreciation. In Area C the residential values appreciated since 1940; and in Area D the residential value of the selected block frontages has a mixed picture, somewhat like the commercial frontages in the same area.

This chapter has examined various approaches to the prediction of the next Skid Row. None was wholly satisfactory. We would not be able to recognize an incipient or pre-Skid Row area from the data alone. In a limited way, they do lend some support to the idea that the development of well-defined Skid Row areas takes place over many years and that the question of where the next Skid Row is going to be located is an inappropriate one. Rather, the issue would seem to be which areas of the city are deteriorating both commercially and residentially and which are likely to do so. These would seem to be incipient or potential Skid Rows. However, which of the areas will ultimately become the stereotyped Skid Row is not suggested by the data.

The data suggest a complex process of real estate trends in potential and incipient Skid Row areas. As an area deteriorates and becomes more blighted, land values decline, but there comes a time when conversion to cheap rooming houses for Skid Row-like residence leads to a rise in values in the midst of the blighted area. Bizarre as it may sound, in a sense Skid Row housing is a "higher and better use"; that is, it will pay for the site, presumably because it is more profitable.

Finally, the data suggest that a program of Skid Row prevention is a long-term process if it is to be more than a simple ejection of the stereotyped Skid Row people from land that is now about to be incorporated into the CBD. Attention must be given to long-run trends of blight and slum formation in inner-city commercial-residential sections if "secondary Skid Rows" are to be prevented. The process will require greater attention to what "natural processes" lead to their decline and to the concomitant development of concentrations of socially and economically marginal Skid Row-like people in low-quality rooming houses and apartments.

Chapter 5

The Redevelopment of Skid Row[1]

THE key to the prevention of Skid Row localities lies in the detection of incipient or pre-Skid Row areas, on the one hand, and in site clearance and prevention of the recurrence of Skid Row-like neighborhood conditions, on the other. But what does an incipient or pre-Skid Row area look like? This chapter discusses "Bathhurst" (a pseudonym for prediction area A referred to in Chapter 4). It also discusses Anglia (pseudonym), an area which was not predicted, but which was recognized early as pre-Skid Row. As in most large American cities, many sections of Philadelphia have distinctive racial, ethnic and socioeconomic characteristics. And, while Bathhurst and Anglia differ in their racial–ethnic mix, they are similar in the presence of Skid Row-like persons and the increasing use of the area by people who formerly lived in the Vine Street Skid Row locality. They are similar, too, in the presence of cheap rooming houses in the midst of family residences and blighted commercial activities.

Turning to site clearance and prevention through urban renewal, we must recognize that other cities besides Philadelphia have had "Skid Row projects." In general, the projects have sought to deal with the issue of Skid Row prevention either through the development of programs of social services for resi-

---

[1] We wish to express appreciation to the following for their assistance; their reports are the basis of our summary statements about Bathhurst and Anglia: Phyllis Richman, Harvey Shapiro, Eric Blumberg, Terry Blumberg, Leonard Moore, Richard Blackburn, Robert Beale, Sally Meisenhelder, Donald Wallace, M. Richard Cohen, Patricia Jacobs, Patricia Robinson, and William Hood. We especially wish to acknowledge the warm hospitality of Earl Dombros and Irene Miller of the Redevelopment Agency of the City of San Francisco; and Marjorie Montelius, Executive Director of the Travelers Aid Society of San Francisco. In Detroit, special thanks are due to the Honorable Melvin J. Ravitz, President of the Common Council of the City of Detroit; Richard Dakesian, Executive Director, Mayor's Committee on Alcohol Problems; Don Ball and Ruth Brown, *Detroit News*; and James H. Knack, Detroit City Planning Commission.

dents of the area as it was about to be demolished or those projects have sought to achieve the aim of Skid Row prevention through plans for land use and zoning control. This chapter considers Detroit and San Francisco as examples of each approach to Skid Row prevention.

In making an assessment of Bathhurst and Anglia as pre-Skid Row areas, a variety of methods were used that, taken together, can perhaps be described as "observational saturation." In addition to block frontage data for parts of Bathhurst and Anglia, the following procedures were used: From the time the Diagnostic and Rehabilitation Center/Philadelphia opened in 1963 until 1971, the research staff had continuous reports from Anchor Counselors of the agency on the presence of former Skid Row residents in other sections of the city (23, *ch. 1*). Most of the time follow-up interviews were conducted with men who had come to the Center for assistance; a substantial number of the interviews were done by men who had lived on Skid Row or who had had an alcohol problem. We had participant-observer reports from a social scientist who lived in Anglia for a short time. Considerable information was collected by our professional community organization worker. The program staff interviewed local residents; the interviews varied from a small-scale scheduled interview study in Anglia in 1964 to a relatively large number of unsystematic interviews with neighborhood residents, businessmen and landlords in Bathhurst in 1971 and 1972.

Bathhurst

From the beginning of fieldwork in 1963, it was apparent that Bathhurst had been physically deteriorating for a long time, as would be expected from the age of the dwelling units and its close-in location. The census tract of which the area is a part had only 35% of the units rated as sound with all plumbing facilities, compared with 85% in the city as a whole. Fieldworkers, some of whom had themselves formerly lived on Skid Row, knew former residents of the Skid Row area who were now living in Bathhurst rooming houses. They found men drinking in parked cars. They found vacant houses that were boarded up in the front but open in the rear with empty "canned heat" containers scattered about. There were empty gallon wine bottles and empty quarts, still in the bags in which they were sold by the State Liquor Store, near empty quart bottles of paint thinner on vacant lots. All of these are characteristic of the Skid Row drinking style.

At many of the minor street intersections in Bathhurst, there are small bars, usually in converted private residences. These have been typical in Philadelphia since colonial times. There are at least 16 bars and 2 State Liquor Stores in the area. The area is within easy walking distance of the same blood banks, parks, bars, employment agencies and gospel missions used by Skid Row men. The rooming houses and cheap apartments are relatively attractive to older men or men receiving retirement, public assistance or disability checks.

Housing costs are relatively cheap although they are more expensive than a Skid Row cubicle hotel or mission lodging. From 1965 to 1970 property turnover in the different block frontages varied from 10 to more than 50% of the units, with about 25% as the norm. Unvandalized buildings could be bought for between $500 and $2500, the average being about $1500. Rentals of small houses in Bathhurst could, therefore, be low and still achieve 50 to 100% return on investment. These low-rental properties could be, and indeed are, attractive to low-income people, most but not all of whom are Black or Puerto Rican. But the attractiveness of low rentals is more than offset by the general condition of the area. On most block frontages there are several abandoned buildings, most of which have been boarded up and subsequently vandalized. On a number of frontages between a third to a half of the houses have been cleared from the site and the lots lie vacant, weed-grown, collecting old tires, abandoned shells of automobiles and wine and whisky bottles.

Room rents in Bathhurst vary considerably, even in opposite frontages. In the summer of 1968 rentals on the south side of one block were about $9 a week, some $10; these rentals included furniture but not private bath and, in about half of the cases, the tenants were permitted to cook on a hot plate. Across the street the rents were $4.50 a week. (Twenty years ago rents in the same block frontage are said to have been $3 a week for a furnished room; landlords blame the rise in rents on higher taxes.) Not only is there variation in room rents from one side of

the street to the other, but there are differential rents paid by
Blacks and Whites. On the north side of one block frontage in
the summer of 1968 White tenants were paying from $8.25 to
$11 for a small furnished apartment (a sleeping room, cooking
facilities and semiprivate bath), while Blacks were expected to
pay up to $15 a week for the same conveniences. In another
block frontage on the same street, rents went as high as $18 a
week for Blacks. (That the landlord might be Black seems to be
irrelevant; one of the biggest real estate operators in Bathhurst
is Black.)

For those block frontages on which we have data, it would
seem that in more than half of the rooming houses and large
dwellings converted into small apartments the owners were also
the resident managers. In a large proportion of the remainder,
the owner or the agent lived in the locality and regularly supervised the premises and collected the rents. This did not really
make the landlords more reachable when it came to repairs,
however, for in 1971 tenants were complaining that landlords
refused to fix the place unless forced to do so.

Bathhurst is an area of changing racial and ethnic composition. The larger northern segment is almost completely Black in
its residential composition; the smaller southern part is predominantly White. Puerto Ricans are scattered in both areas but
tend to be more concentrated in the center of Bathhurst.

The White Skid Row-like residents say that Bathhurst is not a
particularly safe place to live. According to the police the crime
rate is higher in the northern section; the police believe that
this is caused by the prevalence of drug addicts in the area. This
affects the area to the south which has a higher percentage of
persons who are 45 years of age and older. The elderly residents on pensions, social security or public assistance are often
mugged for their checks. On the other hand, in the predominantly White southern area the police are alleged to run period-
ic "sweeps" through the area to "clean out" the bottle gangs.
The men are booked for vagrancy or disorderly conduct. This
lends credence to the conclusion that the area is perceived as
near-Skid Row by the police.

The older more stable residents see the encroachment of the
Redevelopment Authority as inevitable. They hate the idea of
leaving old friends, saying that poor people more often have to

depend on their friends to help them in times of emergency than people with higher incomes. Others, such as those who own their own homes, do not want to begin paying rent or making large mortgage payments. (These are common sentiments among persons in redevelopment project areas.) Some families are worried about children getting involved in adolescent gangs when they are forced to move to another neighborhood; but this shows a considerable degree of parental naïveté because their children probably are already involved if they are old enough.

While they are reluctant to move, this does not mean the residents have found the area comfortable and satisfying. During informal interviews, the problems mentioned most frequently by the residents included fighting by juvenile gangs, vandalism by children, poor housing, bottle gangs, widespread use of drugs, excessive number of bars and private houses where wine or whisky is sold (i.e., bootleggers). The residents perceive that a major problem in the area is medical and health care. These are virtually nonexistent, especially for the chronic conditions such as widespread use of drugs, alcoholism and the health problems of the elderly.

While Bathhurst is identifiable by outsiders as an incipient Skid Row, there is, nonetheless, a strong sense of community among the minority of stable residents in the area. However, they are ineffectively organized to resist further deterioration of the area and they are never likely to be effectively organized. Their efforts have been hampered by limited funds, inexperienced leadership and ignorance of the resources that might be available to them. There is little communication between the various levels of government and the stable residents of Bathhurst. One wonders whether they have already been stereotyped as near-Skid Row people and are victims of the opinion that the best that can be done for the area and its people is to clear the site and to remove the residents as quickly as is economically and politically feasible.

Anglia

Anglia is an old section of Philadelphia in which there are pockets of Skid Row-like residents. Anglia has always been a predominantly working-class home-ownership area, although in recent years the difference between the residential side streets and the commercial through streets has become stark. The modest brick row houses on the side streets are relatively well maintained, but the large former residences that have been converted or rebuilt, and are now located on commercial and through streets, have deteriorated badly.

As early as 1963 the area had a reputation among Skid Row men as a "vacation land." That is, the men would visit there on weekends or rent rooms in the vicinity when they were temporarily better off. Furthermore, there has been some movement between Anglia and prediction area C (see Chapter 4). By 1963 the presence of men who had formerly lived in the Skid Row area was readily recognizable to fieldworkers from the Center, who identified 150 to 200 known former Skid Row men although some were daytime spot-job workers and others were weekend visitors.

Also by 1963 there was reported acceleration in the rate of conversions from single-family dwelling units to rooming houses and very small apartments. There were 50 bars and, after the first stages of the Skid Row clearance were completed, local community workers believed that even more had been established. Bars are commonly found at major intersections and are known throughout the city for their "roughness" as well as their local pride. There are also neighborhood bars located at side-street intersections in a pattern that was common before the Revolutionary War. These bars are characterized by substantial sales of cheap wine that is poured directly from gallon jugs into "juice" glasses at prices no more than a nickel or a dime above those prevailing on Skid Row. In these bars drunkenness is common, and the conversation of both men and women is loud, boisterous and profane.

By 1963 the bars in Anglia had begun to lower their prices in the face of competition and to cater to Skid Row-like persons. Panhandling by Skid Row-like persons on the main commercial streets of Anglia was more common than it had been in the past. Small neighborhood parks ("squares") had been taken over by male loiterers and bottle gangs, and children no longer went there to play. Families stopped sitting on their front doorsteps (a common practice in workingmen's neighborhoods in Philadelphia). On the other hand, the residents of the cheap rooming houses, who did most of their drinking either in the local bars or in their rooms, continued this drinking pattern and were thereby conspicuous.

Sections of the commercial through streets are, at this writing, blighted. The number of vacant stores in badly maintained buildings is increasing. At least one circular-distribution firm has located its permanent office in the area, and several distribution subpoints are now located near bars; the bars are filled with Skid Row-like men early in the morning hours when the "muzzlers" drink up their advance pay from the foreman. A blood bank and spot job agency are located close to the most important intersection in the area. In the most blighted parts of the commercial and through streets, there are now a substantial number of cheap lodging houses (the difference between a room and an "apartment" is sometimes a cheap refrigerator).

There are also a number of bar-hotels, i.e., cheap bars with rooms for rent in the upper stories. The quality of these rooms varies considerably. Moreover, while the bar-hotel operators have shown by their behavior that they prefer stable men who receive a social security, pension or public assistance check ("check men"), the rooming house operators are less able to encourage stability, and they rent rooms by the week or for 2-week periods principally to unattached men and women who apparently have an alcohol problem or may be on parole from the local mental hospital. As is typical of such rooming houses, there is a good deal of anonymity, although if a man has lived in the locality for a period of time (even if he has drifted from one rooming house or apartment to another), he builds up a circle of acquaintances. Not all Skid Row-like men had this sort of housing; there were several who normally slept in cars that were parked in marginal used-car lots in the area, spending most of their money for alcohol. Finally, there are now at least three gospel missions in the area and another not far away. The missions attract Skid Row men to their programs, which vary a little, but all provide some kind of food along with their worship service; one also has a salvage program.

Skid Row has not arrived in all of Anglia, for Anglia covers a much larger area than the Skid Row conditions that we have discussed. Rather, there are little "pockets" of pre-Skid Row and Skid Row-like activity. These pockets are in parts of police districts L, M and O listed in Table 3. The fact that they exist in several police districts may partly explain the findings in those districts. The police would have a tendency to let matters ride whenever possible rather than resorting to systematic round-ups of Skid Row-like people; each pocket being somewhat small, the police would perceive the situation as local and as something that they could easily keep under control. Furthermore, Anglia is out of the limelight of public opinion, in contrast to the Franklin–Independence Square area, so that the police are under relatively little pressure to "do something" about the situation. Local community activists would be more likely to perceive a problem as a responsibility of the Department of Licenses and Inspections, which has charge over rooming houses, or of the Pennsylvania Liquor Control Commission, which licenses the bars. (The latter seems primarily interested in maintaining decorum in the bars.)

Anglia is a relatively close-knit area; that is, the residents are suspicious and moderately hostile to outsiders. Public comment in the press is likely to occasion defensive attacks from residents and former residents who grew up there. Professionals, who do not live in the area, although identified with it by virtue of their jobs, are also prone to come to Anglia's defense.

It is well recognized that the edge of the area is in transition from mixed British–German White to Black and Puerto Rican occupancy. The core of Anglia continues to be strongly British in origin, working class in character and strongly anti-Black. Any minority racial family moving into the heart of Anglia would be burned out.

Aside from the commercial streets and parts of the through streets, the area is predominantly a family residential area. Furthermore, the rooming houses and transient apartments are occupied by both men and women, sometimes as couples and sometimes singly. Participant-observer reports suggest that a large number of the men and women drink excessively; i.e., it is not uncommon for them to be drunk almost every night. While some of the older men are on public assistance or social security retirement benefits, the middle-aged men are often employed steadily at temporary jobs or only intermittently as a consequence of their heavy drinking. They are long-time residents and are recognized as such in the locality. Many have lived and may continue to live with their mothers or their sisters, some-times with wives, while they drink in the cheapest of the local bars and participate actively in local bottle gangs.

The common drinking sequence over the years is "boiler-makers" (whisky with a beer "chaser") and, when they no longer can afford that, to drink a substantial number of quarts of beer each night, and finally cheap wine when they can no longer afford the beer. This correlation between money avail-able and quality of drink is found among alcoholics as well. Middle-class alcoholics describe their binges as beginning with mixed drinks, passing through straight drinks, and ending with wine as their money runs out.

Drinking generally starts at age 15 or 16. The young people get a neighborhood "wino" to buy cheap wine for them at the local State monopoly liquor store. By the time a young man is in his mid-20s drunkenness is no longer a new experience and by his mid-30s or early 40s he may have progressed from having an alcohol problem to being in a marginal social and economic situation. It is often the sister or mother who keeps a man stable; when she dies or moves away, he then drifts into the Skid Row or into the Skid Row-like rooming houses that have developed in Anglia.

The staff of the Diagnostic and Rehabilitation Center have had a substantial number of conferences with professionals (such as ministers, health workers, community organization so-cial workers and social welfare workers) and community repre-sentatives (such as leaders of the various antipoverty organiza-tions and private drug programs and youth workers). In general, the professionals have a greater awareness of alcohol problems in Anglia and say that they would like to be involved with helping others do something about it. However, they are being pushed by the urgency of other approaches to the urban prob-lems of the day. Most salient at the present time is the emphasis on expansion of drug treatment programs, in recognition that there is not only heroin use in the area but that glue sniffing is common among children still in school.

There are also those who are committed to what might be described as a "big picture" (or at least a middle-sized picture) in their emphasis on the organization and management of anti-poverty organizations, such as the local units of the Philadel-

phia Anti-Poverty Action Committee, or community mental
health, or neighborhood renewal. These programs tend to see
the excessive use of alcohol as derivative—change the slum and
blight, get people jobs, help them with their deep emotional
problems and there won't be any alcohol problems.

Insofar as we limit the discussion of the recurrence of Skid
Rows to White residential areas, then Anglia is the nearest
White residential area beyond the interstitial Black residential
area that is adjacent to the present Skid Row. In saying this, we
must recognize that racial segregation has made a significant
difference in the distribution of activities in Philadelphia, but
we should also recognize that there are many residential streets
between the old Skid Row and Anglia which are not very much
different from Anglia, except for the racial segregation that has
been forced on the area. Anglia and these Black residential sections are similar in that they are both working-class areas and
have a number of marginal residents with alcohol problems. In
terms of the zonal versus sector theories of urban location and
growth, Anglia fits the sector concept. But in a broader sense
Anglia is analogous to the marginal zones around the Skid Row.
American racial prejudices as much as anything else have led to
this "jump" of several miles from the old Skid Row to Anglia by
Skid Row men. In a sense, then, it fits the zonal theory as well.

In brief summary, it seems evident that while logically we
would not expect "The New Skid Row" until the old one has, in
fact, been cleared, the evidence indicates otherwise. In fact,
Skid Row-like "pockets" are already evident elsewhere in
Philadelphia, but they do not have public recognition and
stereotyping.

On the other hand, it is to the long-run decline of the area that
we attribute the emergence of Skid Row-like men, who, having
lost their family and employment ties, continue to live in the
area rather than drifting out to Skid Row. It may be that this is a
normal process that happens in most deteriorating White working-class neighborhoods and that only a remnant may ever be
expected to drift to a distinctively stereotyped Skid Row which
exists elsewhere in the city. This needs further, and long-term,
investigation.

We briefly turn now to the site removal and social welfare
approaches to Skid Row prevention as evidenced in San Fran-

cisco and Detroit. Pseudonyms are not used here because the areas have either been discussed by public officials, referred to in the press or are so evident that the use of pseudonyms would be an empty gesture.

San Francisco

San Francisco's program was established after the City's officials visited other programs, such as those located in St. Louis and Philadelphia. It is not accidental, therefore, that the San Francisco program strongly resembles that of the Philadelphia Diagnostic Center and, because there is such a close resemblance, a detailed description of the San Francisco New Start Program is not given here. On the other hand, authorities in San Francisco apparently found it politically inexpedient or philosophically inappropriate to adopt measures directed at controlling the possible recurrence of Skid Row institutions outside the redevelopment area.[2]

The San Francisco Skid Row is a part of the Yerba Buena Redevelopment Project, in the district south of Market Street. Alvin Averbach (3) points out that there have been homeless men living in the district from the earliest days of the city, but it "emerged as a predominantly single men's quarter only after the earthquake and fire of 1906." Mission Street, which was the northern edge of the Skid Row area, is historically a major thoroughfare from downtown to Mission Dolores and then south on the peninsula. It continues to be important for local traffic. In general, Folsom Street several blocks to the south of Mission Street, was the boundary of the old Skid Row area. Howard Street lies between Mission and Folsom streets. Up until the time of redevelopment, Howard Street to the west of Third Street was the heart of the San Francisco Skid Row.

In 1967 the New Start Center began to work in the area (179, 180, 181). Most of those who accepted assistance in relocation were referred to public housing; a cheap hotel at Third and Howard was partly converted to a domiciliary for Skid Row men. Meanwhile, pressure to relocate was generated by actual

[2] In addition to interviews with Earl Dombros, Director of the New Start Center, Yerba Buena Project, 40 Holland Court, San Francisco, and Marjorie Montelius, Executive Director of the Travelers Aid Society of San Francisco, extensive on-the-spot observations were made in May 1969.

clearance of almost all buildings on Howard Street and many of those nearby on Third and Fourth streets.

About 50% of the men were "self-relocated," to use the appropriate jargon. A large portion must have simply moved west several blocks, because inspection indicates that the Skid Row area is now along Sixth Street between Mission and Folsom, just beyond the boundaries of the Yerba Buena Redevelopment Project. There can be little doubt that the area was already well on the way toward becoming an incipient Skid Row before the Yerba Buena Project began. But, apparently, there was no effort on the part of the city government to prevent this or the final conversion of the area outside the project boundaries into the city's "new" Skid Row area.

Detroit

Detroit is an example of efforts to develop restrictions on land use that are aimed at the prevention of a new Skid Row in combination with a weak service program for "Skid Row alcoholics."[3] For many years, the generally recognized Skid Row was along Michigan Avenue and several adjacent streets, with Fort Street as the southern boundary. The area and its residents were perceived as highly objectionable, especially since World War II. The city's highest priced hotels were only several blocks away; the route from the airport to these hotels in the pre-freeway era went right by the Row; the complex of saloons, dormitory hotels, missions and temporary employment offices was believed to have a blighting effect on the CBD; and, finally, the amount of taxes taken from the Skid Row area was consider-

---

[3] The data for this discussion are based on interviews with Don Ball, *Detroit News*; Hon. Melvin J. Ravitz, President, The Common Council of the City of Detroit; Richard Dakesian, Director, Mayor's Committee on Alcohol Problems; Frank Imbriaco, Detroit Housing Commission; Alan Schwartz, Esq.; Carl Amblad and James Knack, Detroit City Planning Commission; H. Warren Dunham, Department of Sociology, Wayne State University; Msgr. Clement Kern, Pastor, Most Holy Trinity Roman Catholic Church; Mrs. Diane Edgecomb, Central Business District Association; Richard Weston, Men's Social Service Center, Salvation Army, Detroit; Armin Roemer, formerly of the Detroit City Planning Commission; Fr. Vaughan Quinn, Director, Sacred Heart Treatment Center. These interviews took place from 4 October to 8 November 1971. In addition, extensive on-the-spot observations were made during the same periods. Extensive use was made of the files of the *Detroit News*.

ably less than that from nearby lands.[4] But the Skid Row area had been there for many years. What had happened to change the situation, basically, was that the growth of the city made the Michigan Avenue Skid Row no longer peripheral to the CBD but a part of it.

As early as the late 1940s, there was a steady anti-Skid Row drum beat.[5] While it is admittedly hard to prove, it seems probable that this was privately stimulated by the Central Businessmen's Association. It was publicly led by political leaders who were perceived in the rhetoric of the time as "liberal," as well as by those who were "conservative," for all were highly responsive to the expectations of the "business community."[6] The moral indignation of the political leaders ultimately led to the designation of "the" Skid Row for redevelopment under the label of "Central Business District Project Number 1."[7]

As the time for site clearance came near, and the discussion of what to do about the relocation of the men and the Skid Row institutions intensified, city planners discovered a number of "secondary Skid Rows": on Third Street north of Grand River and below Cass Park (a part of the Cass Corridor discussed below); a few blocks on Jefferson Avenue just east of the new City–County Building; and Gratiot Avenue near Beaubien Street, also on the East Side, and a few blocks north of the Jefferson Avenue area.[8] The former of these two areas was identified as a "White" Skid Row area while the latter was identified as "Black." In fact, aside from racial segregation that largely prevailed in the cheap hotels, a better way to conceptualize the situation is as a single somewhat dispersed Skid Row population in an area from Jefferson Avenue north for about eight short blocks and east for perhaps three. Historically, it was the stabilized remnant of an older Skid Row–Tenderloin.

In addition, city planners also identified a number of "poten-

[4] *Detroit News*, 24, 29 September 1953; 14 April 1954.
[5] *Detroit News*, 11 July, 12 September 1948; 11, 16 November, 14 December 1949; 7, 10 February, 3, 6 June, 9 July 1950; 4 March 1951; 12, 23, 27, 29 August 1953; 27 June 1954.
[6] *Detroit News*, 23 April, 19 June 1953; 4 February 1954.
[7] *Detroit News*, 8 January, 10, 13 February, 13 August, 14 December 1954; 17 November 1955; 12 February 1956.
[8] RAVITZ, M. J. Notes of problems of Skid Row. Presented at a meeting of the City Planning Commission, 15 October 1956; revised 14 March 1962.

tial" Skid Rows: Michigan Avenue from the John Lodge Expressway to 18th Street; Fort Street from 3d to 12th streets; the west side of Woodward Avenue from Vernor Highway to Canfield Street; Grand River Avenue, six blocks east and west of Van Dyke Avenue; Jefferson Avenue, east near St. Jean Street; John R. and Brush streets north and south of Vernor Highway; and Gratiot Avenue near Chene Street.[9]

Since Michigan Avenue and Fort Street were the north and south boundaries of Skid Row, the first two potential Skid Rows were predictions that Skid Row would move further out on the same side of the city ("sector") into areas that were already slumlike residential areas mixed with commercial–industrial use. The Woodward Avenue and Grand River Avenue locations were, in fact, two edges of the Cass Corridor. They represent a move due north from the old Michigan Avenue Skid Row and peripheral to the expanded CBD. The Mack Avenue area, adjacent to what had become a working-class Black residential area to the north and racially mixed middle-class residential area to the south, was rapidly deteriorating. (We cannot here go into the peculiarities of Detroit as a consequence of overzoning commercial strips along main streets.)[10] It perhaps should have been more accurately characterized as a Tenderloin than as a stereotypical Skid Row, but this distinction was not made by Detroit's planners.[11] The Gratiot Avenue strip and the Mack Avenue strip were the consequences of clearance for the freeway system of an extensive redevelopment program just to the west and closer to the CBD. Finally, the Jefferson Avenue–St. Jean area has a number of cheap hotels and bars in a declining commercial strip and is a considerable distance east of the downtown area. To the extent that these potential Skid Rows became areas in which people with discernible Skid Row characteristics came to live, especially if they had moved from either the Michigan Avenue Skid Row or the East Side Skid Row area, we would have a situation approximating the Alternative 2 discussed in Chapter 4.

After World War II the agitation about the Michigan Avenue

[9] *Detroit News*, 21 July 1962; 13 May 1963.
[10] BALL, D. H. Neighborhood political action to alter land-use patterns in the City of Detroit. Unpublished manuscript; 1970.
[11] *Detroit News*, 11 July 1963.

Skid Row eventuated in the formation of a Mayor's Rehabilitation Committee of Skid Row Problems in 1950 (which continues its work as a part of the present Mayor's Committee on Alcohol Problems). The activities of this group of concerned citizens and professionals from various city agencies went in several directions. They recommended that the city develop a program of rehabilitation for alcoholics, initially in a minimal walk-in day-care center. Over the years, the program came under attack by local businessmen and the center was closed. The current program of the Committee centers on training alcoholism counselors and encouragement of private agencies, such as the Sacred Heart Center, located on Mt. Eliot Avenue.[12]

It was also recommended that the city try to prevent new Skid Rows by the control of the concentration of bars. Eventually this led to the passage of the Regulated Uses ("Skid Row") Ordinance as a part of the Official Zoning Code.[13] This provided that no more than two "Skid Row-related" business activities could be located within a thousand feet of each other and covered the following: (1) establishments for the sale of beer or intoxicating liquor for consumption on the premises, (2) hotels or motels, (3) pawnshops, (4) pool or billiard halls, (5) public lodging houses ("flop houses"), (6) secondhand stores, (7) shoeshine parlors, (8) taxi-dance halls. Finally, it was recommended that an effort be made to scatter the residents of the Skid Row area in a mile radius around the CBD, also with an eye to keeping the concentration of Skid Row institutions low.[14] This policy was never explicitly implemented, although the move by the Salvation Army Men's Social Service Center from 12th and Lafayette to Fort Street west of Trumbull into the old Detroit Central Warehouse is consistent with the scheme.

[12] *Detroit News*, 14 December 1949; 3, 6 June 1950; 5 August 1951; 2 October, 17 December 1952; 29 September 1953; 19 September, 1, 19 November 1963. Cf. Sacred Heart Center for the Treatment of Alcoholism (176) and Radice (158).

[13] *Detroit News*, 25 August 1952; 15 December 1961; 19 January, 10 November 1962. Cf. Official Zoning Code of the City of Detroit, Section 66.0000, Regulated Uses, pp. 55–56; and letter of 15 October 1962 from Robert S. Aikenhead to John Hathaway, Assistant Corporation Counsel, in files on CBD Project No. 1, Detroit Housing Commission.

[14] First draft of a memorandum, 20 June 1963, in files on CBD Project No. 1, Detroit Housing Commission; Application for Loan and Grant, Final Project Report, Relocation Plan, October 58, in files on CBD Project No. 1.

The site of Detroit's CBD Project No. 1 has been cleared and redevelopment is slowly proceeding. If we consider the planner's statements of "incipient Skid Rows" as predictions, we are then in a position to ask whether the intervention in the "natural processes" through the "Skid Row Ordinance" was successful. The basis for reaching a conclusion rests on actual inspection of the areas in question and from conferences with knowledgeable informants rather than on an analysis of statistical materials.

With one exception, the incipient Skid Rows named above continue to exist with little evidence of physical expansion, and several additional areas in blighted commercial areas are now also perceived as incipient Skid Rows. As we have noted before, the distinction between a Tenderloin (an area of vice and crime) and a Skid Row is not clearly drawn in Detroit at the present time and these new areas seem to be more Tenderloin than Skid Row. They have been invaded by noisy and gaudy bars and late-hour short-order food establishments; the residents of the adjacent areas perceive heavy and disorderly drinking and possibly solicitation for prostitution as well as drugs. That is, the areas are blighted commercial strips in otherwise working-class residential districts and seem not to provide housing for homeless people, although it may not be unusual to see drunken persons on the street or small groups of men drinking from bottles from time to time.

The one major exception is the Cass Corridor. The boundaries of this large area are Grand River Avenue, John Lodge Expressway, Woodward Avenue and the Edsel Ford Expressway. The area includes Wayne State University. Within that large area, Detroit's Skid Row has become reestablished in roughly the southern half—Henry Street, Grand River, Third, Selden and Woodward Avenue.

The "natural processes" of urban land use had long before made this an area of initial settlement for White southerners and it had long had a reputation for "tough bars," prostitution and cheap rooming houses and apartment houses that had seen better days. While the Skid Row hotels were not permitted to relocate in the area, there was enough low-cost housing available or old apartment buildings and rooming houses that could be easily downgraded for the use of Skid Row people.

A second factor of major importance was that, even before site clearance actually took place, missions had begun to move into the area. Thus the Mariner's Inn, an old institution that initially provided housing and other services for merchant seamen on the Great Lakes and had come to provide housing for other transients as well, relocated in the Corridor when its site was taken for the Civic Center in downtown Detroit.[15] The Salvation Army and the Howard Street Mission initially moved into the area to provide housing for elderly men who had been living in Skid Row housing.[16] Once there, the Salvation Army expanded its services to younger Skid Row-like residents—it argued that the area was already a Skid Row and the services were needed. The City Rescue Mission, which had begun operation in the Old East Side Tenderloin–Skid Row and had subsequently moved to the Michigan Avenue area on the West Side, acquired a site in the area and constructed a building with the express approval of the Mayor and over the opposition of local residents.[17]

Finally, the Regulated Uses Ordinance seemed to be most effective in limiting the location of bars (most of which really could be more advantageously located elsewhere; licenses were reputedly worth as much as $18,000). Most of the other regulated uses that located in the area were able to do so either with the express permission of Common Council or were able to move into buildings that had previously been put to the same use. Knack (96) reported that "Although the Zoning Ordinance restricted the number of regulated uses relocating to other Skid Row areas, a considerable number did relocate to those areas despite the provisions of the Zoning Ordinance. The primary reason for this is that the provisions of the Zoning Ordinance controls do not apply to all districts, nor do they control a business relocating to a building that has been used previously for the same purpose" (p. 126). And he concludes, "The similarity of the relocation experience of Skid Row uses [but unregulated by ordinance] and [regulated] Skid Row related uses indicates

[15] Detroit News, 15 September, 23 October 1960.
[16] Detroit News, 15, 19 September 1961. Cf. Memorandum of meeting, 26 September 1960, initialed W. Joseph Starrs, in file on CBD Project No. 1, Detroit Housing Commission.
[17] Detroit News, 15 September 1961.

that effective business relocation must include control of all businesses which comprise Skid Row. When it is not desirable to control all businesses which comprise Skid Row, then it is more important to regulate the location of Skid Row uses such as employment agencies, handbill distributors, and missions than it is to regulate the location of Skid Row related uses such as pool rooms, shoestring parlors, and bars, if the objective is to regulate Skid Row relocation through controlling business relocation" (96, *p. 128*). Put another way, Detroit's planners yielded to certain stereotypes about undesirable uses and the Regulated Uses Ordinance failed to regulate those which were most important for the recurrence of a Skid Row complex of residents and related institutions. Furthermore, it seems clear that, in the Detroit case, the application of even these controls came relatively late and it may be that they would not have been effective even if the planners had correctly perceived the situation.

In summary, both the San Francisco and the Detroit examples show that "natural processes" have real consequences when we think about the prevention of Skid Rows during urban redevelopment. If a new Skid Row is to be prevented it will require an improved ability to predict. It will require considerable legal ingenuity as well. Much that happened in Detroit could not be controlled by the Regulated Uses Ordinance, either because the wrong factors were associated in a scheme of causality, or because the uses were already in the Cass Corridor area in sufficient density to provide a base for the Skid Row population, or because no significant control was adopted to limit the location of the missions in the Cass Corridor. But we should recognize that Detroit's efforts to develop a counter to the long-run or "natural" process are something of a first. For the scheme to succeed, Detroit would now need to redevelop the Cass Corridor and remove the Skid Row-like conditions that have developed there while, at the same time, modifying its Regulated Uses Ordinance to make it more effective as a preventive procedure.

Finally, it should be clear that if the policy alternative is the complete prevention of a Skid Row concentration either in a single stereotyped Skid Row close to the downtown area or in a series of smaller "secondary" Skid Rows, then it will take a drastic interruption of the long-run "natural processes" of land use in our cities. The pre-Skid Row condition of Bathhurst and Anglia supports this conclusion. Put in its simplest terms, this will mean a program to prevent blighted commercial areas, as well as the regulation of rooming houses and lodging houses to prevent their deterioration to the Skid Row level. It will also require a program of prevention directed at people who use alcohol heavily and who also have other personal problems that become exacerbated by their degradation through jail, poverty and chronic illness.

Part III

Skid Row-Like People

Chapter 6

Two Neglected Skid Row Populations: Blacks and Women[1]

THE residential Skid Rows of both Philadelphia and Detroit are disappearing while the Skid Row populations are beginning to become less differentiated from other poor residents. In a curious way the present transformation resembles a much earlier pattern, that of a time before the distinctive Skid Row and Red Light district emerged. At that time, Black and White vagrants of both sexes, especially alcoholic derelicts, were to be found living in slum areas intermingled with other poor people.

In light of this new transformation, we find it appropriate to examine two hitherto unexplored populations: Skid Row-like Blacks and Skid Row-like women. There is almost no literature on these topics; they seem to have been invisible to social scientists as well as to journalists and policy makers until very recently. In much the same spirit as Michael Harrington's *The Other America* (80) dealt with the "invisible poor," we examine in this chapter the "invisible Skid Row."

The present approach is clearly different from those used in the past and represents a development in conceptualization since *Skid Row and Its Alternatives* (23). To try to identify residential Skid Rows—White or Black—and to limit research and ameliorative efforts to only the residential Skid Rows is to be shortsighted and to miss the point which has become so evident: that "Skid Row" is not just a residential area with a characteristic collection of agencies within and surrounding it. Skid Row is a characteristic of people within our society. It is a complex of poverty, powerlessness, alienation, homelessness, and, perhaps, alcohol or drug addiction, for which we are all

[1] Leonard Moore was a junior author of the section that discusses Blacks and Skid Row. For their assistance we express our appreciation to J. Donald Porter, Paul Miller, Shelly Silverstein, Bonnie Greenfield, Greg Wilcox, Nancy Conway, Harvey McIntyre, Barbara Harper, and Marilyn Whitt.

121

eligible to a greater or lesser degree. And, in a society in which minority racial status and poverty are closely related, we expect that there is a larger proportion of Blacks than Whites who are more "eligible" for Skid Row.

The question of Blacks and Skid Row has been a blind spot for social investigators. Thus, Nels Anderson (1, *p.* 8), in his discussion of the Chicago homeless workingmen's area ("hobohemia") in 1923, pointed out that the White hobos lived on State Street north of 12th Street and that from 12th Street south to about 30th Street, State Street was occupied by Blacks; if there were any homeless men in the "Black Belt," they would probably have been found along State Street between 12th and 30th streets, although Anderson did not suggest this. He did briefly refer to the Douglas Hotel, located in the area, as a "colored men's lodging house."

Later, Anderson (2, *pp. 134, 137*) was quite explicit in calling attention to Blacks on the Bowery and elsewhere. In a sample of 4196 homeless transients who received welfare services in Philadelphia during the winter of 1932–33, 1000 were Blacks. In New York City in 1931, of 19,861 men studied at the Central Registration Bureau (which coordinated private charitable relief), 6% were Blacks, but of 1000 homeless who were examined by physicians in June 1931 at the Municipal Shelter (available only to legal residents), 15% were Blacks. While Blacks constituted 9% of the population of Pittsburgh in 1930, they constituted 22% of the 7918 homeless men registered in the Central Appalachian Bureau during February, March and April 1932.

Anderson's data on homeless men were largely obtained from the caseload records of welfare agencies. He commented that there was little information about homeless Blacks because many cities, especially in the South, had no shelter facilities; furthermore, many cities did not issue reports on the subject. "Generally," he observed, "the homeless Negro does not fare well, and this observation applies especially for New York City where resources for the colored homeless are far from adequate." Unfortunately, Anderson's *The Homeless In New York City* (2) was issued in mimeographed form, was stamped "confidential" and, apparently, was not widely circulated, so it had no conceptual consequences for social scientists.

Writing in the early 1960s, Donald Bogue (25) presented

some limited statistical information about Blacks, as well as Whites, on Chicago's Skid Rows. In 1963 Blacks constituted only 1.4% of Chicago's Skid Row population (*p. 14*). However, we learn little more about Black Skid Row residents and their characteristics. Bogue implied that the Blacks had been assimilated into the White Skid Rows; we believe that this has not, in fact, occurred. Furthermore, Bogue did not seem to recognize the possibility that there might even be a distinctively Black Skid Row-like population living outside the classic Skid Row areas of Chicago.

A few years later research derived from a New York City Welfare Department program, designed to improve living conditions and to provide more effective welfare services to Bowery residents, reported that Blacks constituted 29% of the population of the Bowery (9, *pp. 31–35*). The authors only briefly discuss this population.

Finally, it must be pointed out that Blumberg et al.'s *Skid Row and Its Alternatives* (23) also neglects consideration of Black Skid Row-like people. Research on the Philadelphia Skid Row began with an approach that generally followed the literature about the more important variables defining Skid Row. That is, Skid Row was seen as a "natural area" within an urban complex and the inhabitants of these localities were primarily men, unattached, suffering from pathological conditions and White.

There is evidence to support the notion that there is a population of Black Skid Row-like people, even though research on this group is very limited. Du Bois's 1899 study, *The Philadelphia Negro* (55), pointed out that Blacks were overrepresented among those arrested by Philadelphia's Vagrant Detectives. Through the last 100 years of Philadelphia's history, there has been a substantial population of Blacks who have been arrested for such typical Skid Row offenses as drunkenness, vagrancy, breach of the peace, and the like.

Two more recent studies can also be mentioned. Skolnick (184) investigated the relationship between the Black and White arrest rates for "inebriety" in New Haven in 1951 and found that lower-class position accounted for most of the difference found between the two. Finally, Levinson (102) examined differences in the characteristics of Black homeless men in the U.S. South and North in the mid-1960s.

We believe that the neglect of Black Skid Row-like people was a consequence of the fact that they were largely hidden in the Black slum. That is, the development of the stereotyped Skid Row area separated the homeless White workingmen and the homeless Black workingmen while it also separated the homeless White workingmen from the larger White slum. Furthermore, the general conditions of life in the slums were such that homeless Black people were not stigmatized as strongly by other Black residents as White homeless men were stigmatized in White residential areas.

Sterne (196, *pp.* 7–8) concluded from a review of the recent literature that alcoholism rates are higher among Blacks than among Whites, although other studies suggest that there is some disagreement (4, 90, 91, 116). A study (236) of the prevalence of alcoholism in Monroe County, New York, in 1961 lends some support to Sterne's conclusion, but is hardly conclusive. Zax et al. (236) compiled information from public agencies and private practitioners and found that Blacks had a higher alcoholism rate than Whites at most age levels in both sexes, especially in those under 50 years of age.

Insofar as alcoholism is a major contributing factor in a person's adoption of a Skid Row-like lifestyle, it may be that there are relatively more "hidden" Skid Row-like people in the Black slums at the present time than there are in the White slums. It seems reasonable to suppose that relatives and friends of Black alcoholics are less willing, or less able, to help with cash and other innumerable "protections" than are the relatives and friends of White alcoholics, albeit more willing or able to share their room and board. Black homeless men may or may not live in the (White) Skid Row; of greater importance is that they can readily be missed by the unknowing (White) sociologist, journalist or policy maker.

This is not to suggest that making the differentiation between slum and Skid Row was ever easy, for it probably was not. The personal, community and social problems that prevail in the Black slum are so pervasive that the task of differentiating a more specific Black Skid Row from the more general Black slum is extremely difficult. Indeed it may be that the existing operational definitions of Skid Row are not very useful for this problem. A tentative explanation for this is that (possibly excepting

Seattle and similar places where the term apparently originated) the term Skid Row is defined in a negative manner, i.e., it is defined in contrast terms—"Skid Row" is as much what it is not as what it is. In the past, the contrast terminology worked relatively well when viewed in terms of the activities of the "White community" or of the metropolitan community. Given the pervasive slum conditions in which poor Black people live and from which flight is difficult, however, the slum–Skid Row contrast is not easily achieved.

But to make that observation is not to accept the opposite position that no differentiation has occurred within the vast Black slums of the American cities. Some parts of the Black slum are apparently more receptive to Skid Row-like persons than others. In Detroit, for example, there is a flop-house on Macomb Street on the lower East Side that is used almost exclusively by Black men. In addition, there is an area to the north of the business district for about three blocks east of Woodward Avenue in which there are a number of Skid Row-like men living. In the John R.–Brush Street corridor there are blocks of low-rent housing, including at least one house which, in November 1971, reportedly permitted men alcoholics to pay 80 cents a night just to sleep on the floor. There are several other blocks in the area where almost every house has been converted into a hotel oriented to single Black men on public assistance, V.A. checks, and old-age retirement or disability pensions. The entire area is reminiscent of a Skid Row but has not been stereotyped as such by Detroiters.

There is at least one similar area in Philadelphia. Oakville (pseudonym) is about eight square blocks south of a redeveloping center-city residential community. The area has a very old commercial section, some blighted properties and deteriorated housing; much of the deterioration has taken place in the midst of a 10-year off-again, on-again, off-again highway construction project and, predictably, owners allowed their properties to fall into disrepair.

Oakville has become a Black Skid Row. There are a number of bars whose profits are apparently derived from the sale of cheap wine, a characteristic of Skid Row bars. One bar has no name; we call it "The Wine Shop." Almost all the liquor on display is gallon jugs of cheap wine. The place is filthy. It is a hangout for "winos" and serves as a pickup point for prostitutes (this last is reminiscent of the stereotyped down-and-out bar).

Those who need liquor when it cannot be legally bought can get it in the local speakeasies. There are at least two operating in Oakville. Admission is controlled and limited to those who are known or are vouched for. Beer is said to sell for 50 cents a can and cheap whisky at the same price per "shot." It is not unusual for 35 to 40 men and women to be present in each place at any one time.

Residential facilities include the "Good Ship Lafayette," a huge empty house in which squatters live; the "Community Kitchen," a rooming house; and two hotels, the Dewey and the Freedom (these are all pseudonyms). One of the hotels was condemned but was permitted to remain open pending relocation of its residents—a status similar to that of a number of hotels in the main Skid Row.

There are other Skid Row indicators. A commercial blood bank is nearby. The local State Employment Service office gives special attention to casual labor. There is a farm-labor pickup point. And panhandling and bottle-gang activity are very common. Thus, Oakville has become a residential Black Skid Row.

There are other areas of Philadelphia very much like Oakville in that they have not become reputationally distinguished from the slums in which they are located. Throughout the areas there are bad housing, commercial blight, a relatively large number of bars and substantial numbers of Blacks who appear to be "homeless." We know about Oakville because we identified the area as "looking like Skid Row" and then we discovered the collections of people and agencies which were similar to those in the stereotyped (White) Skid Row. One of the reasons why Black Skid Rows have been hidden is that no one has heretofore conceptualized Skid Row as being anything but the stereotyped segregated central area of homeless men.

It seems highly probable that the proportion of visible Black Skid Row men will increase over the next 10 to 15 years, i.e., the Black Skid Row-like men will more readily be perceived and stereotyped as "Skid Row bums." While there is considerable discontent over the speed at which citizens of the United

States are now able to secure jobs and housing without respect to race, it seems probable that the amount of housing and the number of job opportunities for Blacks will progressively increase in the next several decades. If this is so, as this process takes place an increasing proportion of the more vigorous and talented will leave the slum and the near slum, although some may continue to live in close proximity to other Blacks, because they feel more comfortable in Black neighborhoods (analogous to the Jewish "gilded ghetto"). The long-term consequence will be that those Blacks who are living a Skid Row-like lifestyle will become more visible.

Skid Row-like Women

Is the conceptual separation of designated areas of unattached women (Tenderloin, Red Light district) and of unattached men (Skid Row, Hobohemia) appropriate? Reckless (159, *pp. 167, 176, 178, 193, 209*) argues that the commercialized vice area (Red Light district) was characteristic of the central business district (CBD) and of the "womanless slum" (Skid Row). On the other hand, he said that the rooming house–apartment house area of the city was the world of homeless women and the natural region of clandestine sex. Anderson (2, *p. 13*) took a slightly different position: "The brothels so often mentioned in the descriptions of the districts of the homeless men were filled with women who were homeless when not plying their trade, and they became permanently homeless when at last they were unable to secure engagements in the brothels." The present position is not to deny Reckless's conclusion about clandestine sexual activities and is slightly more "radical" than Anderson's. Streetwalkers, women who used "cribs," parlor houses and houses of assignation should have been included in any consideration of "homeless women." Both the Tenderloin and the Skid Row were city-wide service areas and thus "natural areas" for Reckless and the sociologists of the University of Chicago during that period. It is this concentration on the natural-area approach to the city that led researchers such as Reckless and Bogue to ignore homelessness and Skid Row-like people elsewhere in the city.

Available data suggest that women have always been associated with Skid Row, although the evidence is scattered.

Long before the Civil War, for example, arrests for Skid Row-type offenses, such as vagrancy, public drunkenness, idleness and disorderly conduct, were common in Philadelphia.[2] White men and women were the predominant occupants of the prisons for Skid Row-type offenses and White women constituted a substantial minority of those committed in the period from 1790 to 1870. By 1880 the proportion of White women had begun to decline, so that by 1920 they constituted less than 10% of the Whites who were incarcerated for Skid Row-like offenses.

It is noteworthy that the arrests of women for Skid Row-type offenses declined as the Tenderloin became established as a quasi-official area of the city. This is not to say that all the drunken women were absorbed in prostitution and other activities of the Tenderloin. Rather, as Appendix D suggests, a number of social institutions arose which focused especially on women (and children) and which were relatively effective in their work. Men were treated in a much more severe manner. While Skid Row-like women and children came to be treated as victims, the men were treated as recalcitrants and malingerers who needed to be disciplined through work and prison.

What lies behind the decline in arrests, therefore, seems to be the social reform movement of the late 19th and the early 20th Centuries, which was antialcohol, antiprostitution, antitramp, anti-"political corruption," and xenophobic. The social reform movement was also the origin of the private social welfare system that dominated American charity before the Depression of

[2] Various dockets are available in the Archives of the City of Philadelphia. The series is consistent up to 1850. The 1850 and 1860 dockets list only vagrancy with no further breakdown, although the number of cases suggests that this total is comparable with the more elaborately recorded earlier dockets. A 20% sample of the 480 names listed in the 1850 Vagrant Docket yielded the following: males, 73% White, 2% Black; females, 25% White (no Black). Of the 2166 persons listed in the 1860 Vagrant Docket, the following were the proportions in a 20% sample: male, 63.8% White, 3.6% Black; female, 29.3% White, 3.3% Black. The relative insignificance of the Black population throughout the series is noteworthy. Data from 1874 and 1875 are included to give some idea of the importance of the House of Correction. It seems evident that the distribution of charges and convictions altered with the opening of the House of Correction. Whether the reality "out on the street" changed is problematical. Tables A-8–A-18, deposited with NAPS, report Skid Row offenses of inmates of Philadelphia County Prisons by sex and race for the years 1790, 1810, 1820, 1830, 1840, 1870, 1874, 1875, 1890, 1900 and 1920. To order, see Appendix A.

the 1930s. Women have continued to be more acceptable to social welfare agencies as objects of charitable giving, and church organizations are more willing and able to provide them with a protected environment. Social Security legislation of the 1930s, a product of the reform, made it possible for women to draw benefits at a younger age than men, although they have a longer life expectancy. These protective and preventive activities in some undetermined way reduced the probable prevalence of women moving into Skid Row or adopting a Skid Row-like lifestyle. In addition, the traditionally female occupational skills, such as housekeeper and wife, are in constant demand. These services may or may not be combined with sexual availability in the specific case. The consequence of this combination of greater availability of institutional protection, occupational demand, and sex-related characteristics is to reduce sharply the prevalence of Skid Row women and the visibility of Skid Row-like women.

Occasional references indicate, however, that Skid Row-like women did not completely disappear. Ben Reitman's (160, *pp.* 68–69) anonymous young woman deftly describes New York's Skid Row-like women 40 years ago. And Ann Geracimos,[3] writing about New York City in 1972, brings us up to date when she describes "female drifters—homeless, hapless, eccentric, women who are unable to cope . . . [who] stumble around with shopping bags, panhandling occasionally; sit dazedly in subways and train stations; comb Bowery bars."

Not much attention has been given to homeless women by social scientists. Possible male biases aside, perhaps it is because the proportion of such women to the total residential Skid Row population is low, just as the proportion of residential Skid Row men to the total metropolitan male population is low despite their conspicuousness. A national census of homeless women was taken on 22 March 1933, but it was done in terms of agencies helping the homeless. Nels Anderson (2) suggested that it was therefore not very helpful as a source of estimates, because destitute women are less likely to apply for assistance to agencies than are the homeless.

[3] GERACIMOS, A. The homeless women among us. *New York Sunday News*, 23 April 1972.

Furthermore, when women apply for help it is likely to be to agencies that are unlikely to be reported in a census of the homeless. Before the Depression, the number of women in the municipal lodging house of New York City rarely was more than 3% of the number of men, although it was about 20% of those sheltered in the New York City police stations when they provided such housing. Anderson (2, *pp. 123–133*) pointed out that until 1909, when larger facilities were developed and the policy changed, women were not admitted to the municipal lodging house in New York and, perforce, the police stations were where they went; but the conditions in the police stations were abominable, thereby encouraging alternative private shelters for women (126, *pp. 85–86; 192, p. 126*).

The best data now available on Skid Row women are those reported by Garrett and Bahr (71) in New York City, and they showed that the number of women is not important there. They secured a list of all the women admitted to the municipal Shelter for Women over a period of 2 months. The list was updated at the beginning of each day. Over the 2 months only 61 clients were admitted to the Shelter, of whom they interviewed 52 (71, *pp. 1231–1232*).

Our approach differs from that of Garrett and Bahr. We examined the differences between Skid Row women, Skid Row-like women, and non-Skid Row women with alcohol problems who came to the Diagnostic and Rehabilitation Center from 1963 to 1972. The numbers are too small for suitable statistical analysis: only 4 definitely Skid Row, about 20 Skid Row-like, and 60 non-Skid Row women came to the Center during that period. The descriptive statements that follow may be regarded as tentative, designed to provide a basis for future more detailed investigation. Because there are so few Skid Row women, and because many women leading a Skid Row-like lifestyle lived in other sections of the city, we examined non-Skid Row areas and the socially marginal women who live in them. We have gone beyond survey data and case records and drawn on informal interviews with the officials and women guests of agencies in Philadelphia and the House of Detention for Women. In addition, we rely on ex-Skid Row staff members of the Center for comments and anecdotal material. A case history of a Skid Row woman is included in the hope that it will clarify the term.

Philadelphia has no housing facility for women analogous to the Skid Row cubicle hotel; there is no need. Nor does it have a municipal facility for either women or men. At most there seem to be only a half dozen or so women who live in the Skid Row area itself. A few of the women seem to be alcoholics, all are best described as "inadequate persons"; i.e., they have a long-standing inability to cope with their life problems that seems to predate any problems they have with alcohol. Most of the women are 50 years of age or over and look older. They are derelicts, no longer having families that are helpful or significant for the solution of their everyday problems; and they live temporarily with whoever will have them. They are "beat up," "broken down" and slovenly in appearance and lack sufficient confidence to hold a job. They are truly homeless. There is an occasional possibility of bunking with a woman friend in the marginal Skid Row-slum area nearby, but often they sleep in the doorways and alleyways; "to carry the stick" is the local term that men use for this behavior.

While some of the women are apparently sexually promiscuous, such behavior is most reasonably interpreted as a part of their minimal survival pattern rather than as an occupation. In a few cases the present lifestyle may be the end of a long prostitution–alcoholism sequence, but one ought not to generalize that Skid Row women are ex-prostitutes. Nels Anderson (2), writing at a time when the Tenderloin was more actively associated with the Hobohemia, found it necessary to state the matter with caution: "Women and girls among the homeless have never been numerous and frequently such women were prostitutes, or had been identified with prostitution" (p. 12).

Skid Row is a dangerous place for women, perhaps more so than for the men. The men are beaten up and jackrolled and the women are too; but in addition, it is our impression that the Skid Row women have been raped three or four times over the course of their years. Their damaged faces and broken noses show the effects of beatings. They have a history of recurrent commitment to jail on charges of public drunkenness, vagrancy and sodomy (illegal sexual activities in which money is not exchanged). They have used the blood banks and, occasionally, they panhandle along the street. All in all, Skid Row women and men are similar in many of their characteristics.

The difference between Skid Row-like women and Skid Row women is a matter of degree. The Skid Row-like women live in cheap rooms in Oldtowne (pseudonym), in the Black slum near the Skid Row area, or in rooming houses not very far away. All have an alcohol problem; most of them are spree drinkers. The Black Skid Row-like women are younger (median age 39 years) than the White (48 years); they tend also to be addicted to drugs, while the White women are not. Both Black and White Skid Row-like women reported unstable relationships with men. Whether their relationships with men were legally sanctioned or not, in most cases they had long since been broken off; indeed, it was not unusual for the women to have been through several liaisons in the previous few years. The women usually attributed their heavy drinking to these relationships, for they said that they usually began drinking to keep the man company and that when the men left or they broke up they could not stop drinking. Their principal source of current income was public assistance, but in recent years they tended to have been employed as waitresses, chambermaids in hotels and motels and as domestic servants. Because of the disruptive effects of spree drinking on employment, their recent job histories had been unstable. Some of the women "hustled" (solicited for purposes of prostitution) to supplement their public assistance checks. A number had been jailed for prostitution as well as on charges of drunk and disorderly conduct. Of those who had children, the instability had been so great that the children had been placed in other homes because the mothers were no longer able to care for them.

The non-Skid Row women alcoholics who came to the Center were generally referred by some other agency. Most of them were drinking daily and a large number were spree drinkers as well. Many had been hospitalized for their alcohol problems, but once having left the hospital they recommenced drinking. Most of their drinking was done in the home, however, rather than in public places.

These women had stronger family ties than the others we have discussed; their parents, brothers and sisters were helping them financially and emotionally. Although a large proportion were divorced or separated, they still had their children; they had emotional defenses in depth against the loneliness, isolation and defeat that seem to have been common with Skid Row-like and Skid Row women.

Many of the non-Skid Row women alcoholics were house-wives who had not worked regularly and some had never worked outside the home. None were employed when they came to the Center. Those who had been recently employed had lost jobs as waitresses, secretaries, office clerks, factory operatives and hospital aides. Most of them had had some high-school education, several had been to college.

A major difference between the non-Skid Row women al-coholics and those discussed earlier is suggested in their rela-tionship to the law enforcement agencies. Most of the women had no prison experience, only a few had ever been arrested on "drunk and disorderly" charges, and none had been arrested for sex-related offenses. Thus, arrest or incarceration may serve as an entry into a new status for non-Skid Row women. If this is true, there are important implications in the way our society treats alcoholics who have become hopelessly ill. The U.S. Su-preme Court's decision in *Powell v. Texas*[4] upheld the constitu-tionality of arrest and imprisonment of alcohol addicts in the absence of treatment facilities. In the continued absence of free and nonpunitive treatment facilities, the consequences of arrest may help to produce Skid Row and Skid Row-like women.

Almost all of the non-Skid Row women alcoholics were cur-rently living in the working-class sections of Philadelphia. While the White women tended to be supported by relatives, the Black women tended to be on public assistance, but in both groups the family relationships were intact. This seems to be the most important difference between the Skid Row and the Skid Row-like women and the non-Skid Row women: the latter could still draw on the support of their friends and relatives, while the former could not. Except for the disruptions related to drinking, the non-Skid Row women alcoholics were not easily distinguishable from the other citizens of Philadelphia in their lifestyle which had not yet come to approximate the Skid Row lifestyle.

There are also a number of other kinds of women who are marginal to the Skid Row residential area and its lifestyle. A

[4] *Powell v. Texas* 392 U.S. 514, 88 S. Ct. 2145, 20 L. Ed. 1254, 1967.

number of apparently alcoholic Skid Row-like women live in the slum area marginal to the Philadelphia Skid Row. They seem to be in the 35- to 55-year age range, live with men as "housekeepers" and are rarely seen or arrested. They seem to have developed a closeness and neighborly protectiveness among themselves. Many have been previously married and some have adult children living elsewhere in Philadelphia from whom they seem to be estranged.

There are also a number of older women living alone on the periphery of the Vine Street Skid Row area. Some may be living on the charity of real estate owners, while others apparently moved into the area to secure the cheap rents and cheap food. They live on savings and social security. They drink sparingly, if at all. In most respects, they seem similar to the older residentially stable men who were found living in some of the cubicle hotels and rooming houses in the Skid Row area.

There are also rooming houses in the low-income sections of the city that are managed by women. The conditions of management vary. Some women are owner-operators and others rent the building and sublease rooms. Their marital arrangements vary also: some were never married, some are widows and some are living with their husbands. Some have outside jobs at semiskilled occupations, such as in a clothing factory. They seem to be between 50 and 55 years of age. The income from the properties is apparently just enough to maintain service and support the rooming-house operators, i.e., these rooming houses are apparently economically marginal enterprises and, in that respect, they are hardly different from similar ones found in marginal working-class sections elsewhere in the city. Of all those who are associated with the Skid Row lifestyle, they have the greatest degree of control over their own lives. This control is somewhat reduced, of course, if they also have an alcohol problem. It is not uncommon for landladies of Skid Row-like tenants to have an alcohol problem and some are often not very far removed from a Skid Row-like lifestyle themselves.

One of the areas in which these landladies are found is Oldtowne. The area is not far from Center City and the Vine Street Skid Row area and has many Skid Row-like characteristics. There are cheap hotels and rooming houses in which former residents of the Vine Street area now live. Oldtowne is divided in local opinion into "lower" and "upper" sections. The lower section has become "tougher" in the last few years. It is reported that sailors come into Oldtowne looking for prostitutes on weekends; younger, heavy-drinking prostitutes are said to be out on the streets looking for pickups. The residents believe that in recent years the chances have increased that one will be strong-armed and robbed in the lower section. The upper part of the area is in transition so that one is less likely to find middle-aged Skid Row men and more likely to find younger bohemians, including a colony of homosexuals.

Oldtowne apparently has a comparatively large number of women with alcohol problems. Indeed, some informants referred to the area as the "Skid Row for women." These women live in rooming houses and apartments and most seem to be over 45 years of age. Many have been married; a substantial number are apparently living as housekeepers for older men with relatively stable incomes. They are usually able to keep out of the hands of the police because most do their drinking in private. However, some end up in the House of Correction after going on a spree; arrest under these circumstances is likely to be for indecent exposure, public drunkenness or disorderly conduct.

Oldtowne is visited occasionally by women who live elsewhere in the city. (There are also a number of men who are "visitors" in much the same sense as the women.) Both women and men use the Skid Row neighborhood and Oldtowne as a service facility; that is, they come to Skid Row bars to drink and to the rooms of their Skid Row-like women friends to visit and drink. These people rarely get into official difficulty. They arrive by public transportation and are taken home by cab. Most of the visitors apparently are spree drinkers and some are former heavy drinkers who have become moderate over time. Unsystematic interview data suggest that most of the spree drinkers and former problem drinkers live in working-class–lower-middle-class residential areas in West and Upper North Philadelphia. Most have maintained family ties, although divorced or separated from their husbands; many apparently have adult children. They do not seem dependent financially and come back to Oldtowne and the area peripheral to Skid Row to visit friends.

Charlotte Steiber, a Skid Row Woman

Mrs. Steiber (pseudonym) was born in 1919 and raised in a small town in Central Pennsylvania. She married shortly after graduation from high school and had four children during the next 9 years. She left her husband at this point and she and her children went to live with her parents. She said that she had made the move so that she could "devote more time to drinking."

From her drinking history it appears that she was a "full-blown" alcoholic by the time she was 19 or 20 years of age. (She told an interesting story of having tasted some home-made wine one evening and continuing to drink until her family found her sprawled drunk on the kitchen floor.) From her mid-teens, she seems to have been drunk on every possible occasion, and by the time she was 18 she was going on "benders," drinking in the morning, protecting her liquor supply and drinking alone. When she was 21 she began to have blackouts— alcohol-related losses of memory about recent events (91). She said that by the age of 26 she felt defeated by alcohol and was never able to stop drinking thereafter. Her subsequent life history lends support to this although there were occasional 4- to 6-month periods of abstinence.

Her first known experience with law enforcement agencies was in 1945 when she was 26 years old. At that time she was arrested at least 10 times and served sentences in upstate Pennsylvania, Delaware and South Jersey. Most convictions were on alcohol-related charges. In 1950 she gave birth to her fifth and last child, born of a paramour relationship.

When she was out of jail she stayed with her parents until she was 33. Then her older brother became completely disgusted with her behavior, packed all her belongings in a suitcase, drove her to Philadelphia, and abandoned her there. Her children stayed with her parents. She had exhausted her "social credit" with her family; that is, her relatives were no longer willing to invest time and money in her in the expectation that her behavior might change.

Steiber moved into the Skid Row area shortly after coming to Philadelphia in 1952. During the next 14 years she lived as best she could, "bumming around" without contact with any of her relatives or her children. In 1966 she walked into the Diagnostic and Rehabilitation Center and caseworkers there encouraged her to seek help from her daughters (two of whom were living in Philadelphia). The daughters refused to have much to do with her.

By 1972 Steiber had been arrested more than 70 times, usually being sentenced to terms of 1 to 3 months at the House of Correction. On several occasions she was seen panhandling in the Vine Street area or on the fringes of the CBD and police would arrest her for vagrancy. There were also arrests on charges of prostitution, although we find this charge hard to believe in view of her usually drunken physical condition and her general physical deterioration in the late 1960s and early 1970s. For example, during this period, she was hospitalized with a broken jaw from a particularly vicious mugging.

Steiber was in and out of rehabilitation and alcoholism programs at Norristown State Hospital, Eagleville Hospital, Pennsylvania Hospital, Alcoholics Anonymous and the Diagnostic Center several times each from 1966 through 1972. By 1970 she had developed emphysema, complicated by pneumonia. Charlotte Steiber dropped from sight in the spring of 1972 and was found dead that summer.

The career of Charlotte Steiber is generally similar to that of other Skid Row people. Her drinking began in adolescence and, by her mid-20s, alcohol was a major part of her lifestyle. Her experience with the revolving doors of prison and clinic apparently began somewhat earlier than for most, but otherwise seems typical for Skid Row people. She exhausted her "social credit" with her family and kinsmen; she was totally rejected. This often happens to a Skid Row man somewhat later in life, after his mother or a protective sister dies or gives up in complete disgust. The sporadic pattern of "drying out" with the assistance of Alcoholics Anonymous or with the help of agencies such as the Diagnostic and Rehabilitation Center is not unusual for Skid Row men; it is difficult to separate "conning" from "sincere" behavior, and it is not clear that such a separation is either desirable or useful.

What makes this case different from the usual descriptions of Skid Row people is that we are dealing with a woman. Charlotte Steiber's sexuality is significant because it had consequences for her relationships and for her career. While we do not have confirmatory evidence at hand, it is quite probable that her family gave up on her and that her brother abandoned her in Philadelphia somewhat earlier than most families give up on men or other women. Her unrespectability was more grievous than a man's unrespectability would have been because there is every likelihood that while in a drunken condition she was sexually promiscuous. She was neither a "good mother" nor a "good woman"; she was a "lay," and her family was ashamed. She acquired a police and jail record for prostitution as well as for the usual Skid Row offenses. We do not doubt that there were times that she did prostitute; it was the only resource that she had for surviving in the lifestyle that she had adopted.

Charlotte Steiber was the mother of five children from whom she was subsequently separated. Her pariah status was compounded, therefore, by the special poignancy of her parenthood.

It is difficult to say whether in later years she tried to use her children as another kind of survival resource. That may be. But there also seems to have been some hope on her part that her children would "accept" her and would help relieve the social isolation which oppressed her. Whenever "rehabilitation" took place, however, it moved Mrs. Steiber from alcoholic friendships to sober social isolation. These were the circumstances which led Wiseman's anonymous Skid Row informant to say "And I decided to hell with it, and I started drinking" (231, *p. 219*).

In view of the relationships that existed between the Tenderloin–Red Light district, the Skid Row and the surrounding slum, we need to consider why the White Skid Row man has been so obvious while women and Black Skid Row-like people are so invisible.

It is a curious fact that the populations that have been studied as Skid Rows have been so defined and labeled by the general public rather than by social scientists. This is probably at the heart of the answer. Thus, with respect to Blacks, one of the variables influencing the label may be racial prejudice. It just may be that the larger dominant White population may simply not have expected anything else from the Black population. Perhaps Whites did not notice the distinctive "problem" until it happened to "their own." There is some suggestion of this sort of thing in the sudden attention to drug addiction when it assumed "epidemic" proportions among White youth in the United States in the 1960s, although it had apparently been common in the Black slum for a number of years and had gone more or less unnoticed.

Clearly this is speculative and not supported by specific data. But there is a vast array of readily available material which shows that Blacks have been residentially segregated for many years. Almost all Skid Row-like Black people were buried in the Black slums. They simply would not come within the purview of the White general public nor that of the White social scientist. While it is true that social science is a frame of reference that leads to ways of perceiving the society that are different from those which are commonly held, the data and the problems that social science deals with are rooted in the general community. "Institutional racism" is the currently popular terminology for the phenomenon and social scientists are no less influenced by it than is the general public.

There are analogies between Skid Row men and Tenderloin women that are important and should not be ignored. The Tenderloin may be conceptualized as a female counterpart of the male Skid Row, with obvious and important functional differences. The recruitment into the homeless workingmen's life rested on the general conditions in the economy, specific employment practices, the work ethic of the time and the related attitudes with respect to social welfare as they were applied to men. The recruitment into the life of the Tenderloin rested on the general conditions of the economy, attitudes toward the employment of women outside the home, the definitions of sexuality and erotic differences between men and women and the unavailability of a safe and legal technology of birth control. Women in the Tenderloin came to the life in various ways, but once they adopted it, it was difficult although not impossible to escape. Similarly, once a man adopted a Skid Row style of life, it was hard to leave it, although there is no doubt that this did occur as it does today. The Tenderloin prostitute's work served a recreational function for men; the Skid Row had not only a recreational function but also served as a major labor recruitment center for the metropolitan area and, frequently, for the region. The Tenderloin and the Skid Row were also similar in their marginal location on the fringes of the CBD in low-quality boarding and lodging houses, frequently so inadequate that they deserve the appellation of "slum dwellings." The homeless workingmen and the majority of prostitutes existed at the lowest levels of community power and prestige, whatever their origins. They often lived behind nicknames and aliases, and thereby erected a barrier between their more respectable past and present status.

For reasons that are obscure to us, this analogy has not been drawn. It is surprising because its elements are so apparent. Their status could be considered a consequence of powerlessness and helplessness. The powerless are relegated to nothingness; they become social ciphers, existing only for fleeting moments when their services are needed and, even then, concealed in an almost impenetrable impersonality. Both the homeless workingmen and the prostitutes of the Tenderloin were relatively powerless in our society and this was specified in terms of gender. They were powerless not only with respect to police and the courts, but also in the sense that they had relatively few options concerning residential areas, occupation or companionship. Poverty and helplessness were characteristic of both. Despite the highlife of the Tenderloin, it is a lasting impression that especially the streetwalkers and the residents of those brothels that catered to the working classes lived poorly despite the amount of money they took in for their services. Helplessness can come about through many different routes, although a prominent one can probably be identified in drugs (including alcohol) and these figured in the lives of both the homeless men of Skid Row and the homeless women of the Tenderloin. Powerlessness and helplessness continue to be important considerations for Skid Row-like people.

In closing, the proposed reconceptualization of "Skid Row" to include Blacks and women removes it from the realm of esoterica and brings it back into the mainstream of urban theory, social science and social action. It suggests that value-biased definitions of pathology have produced social research, social agencies and social policies and programs which tend to ignore important relationships with respect to race, gender and power status.

Chapter 7

Skid Row and the Urban Poor[1]

PROBABLY the most familiar first element in a definition of Skid Row is that it is a specific area of homeless people who "live alone" outside what are generally regarded in the community as "normal family relationships." But homelessness by itself is an inadequate criterion, for it ignores the "homeless" men and women who "live alone" in rooms and apartments outside the area that is generally conceived to be "Skid Row." The Census refers to these people as "primary individuals"; there were almost 4 million male and 8 million female primary individuals in the United States in 1970 (210, *p. 40, Table 5*). If we take two-thirds of the median income of families and unrelated individuals to mean "low income," there were 45,489 primary individuals in low-income census tracts in Philadelphia in 1970; in Philadelphia as a whole the median income of unrelated individuals in 1970 was $2788. In the low-income census tracts, many Black primary individuals live in the large slum sections. Some of the low-income tracts in which White primary individuals live are Skid Row tracts and areas of cheap hotels and rooming houses. Others are university-related tracts which provide housing for young people not currently in school, as well as older men, some of whom are alcoholics.

The Census statistics suggest that "homelessness" by itself is an inadequate criterion, and this should also be evident from our descriptions of "Bathhurst" and "Anglia." According to the Census, these sections, taken as a whole, have relatively low proportions of primary individuals. Nonetheless there are

[1] This chapter draws on "The Skid Row Man and the Skid Row Status Community" by L. U. Blumberg, T. E. Shipley, Jr. and J. O. Moor, Jr., which appeared in the *Quarterly Journal of Studies on Alcohol* (21). We express our appreciation to the editors of the *Journal* for permission to use the article in its present form. We also acknowledge the assistance of William Hood, Donald B. Wallace, Edmund Sullivan, and Leonard Moore, all of whom were on the staff of the Diagnostic/Rehabilitation Center of Philadelphia. At Temple University, we express appreciation for the advice of Leonard Savitz, Department of Sociology.

people living there who apparently never lived in any Skid Row area, but who are not very different in their lifestyle from men who live on Skid Row. There are also men who formerly lived in the Skid Row locality who continue a lifestyle substantially similar to men still living in the Skid Row area. Finally, there are men and women living together who in other respects are Skid Row-like, but they have "normal family lives" in the sense that they are not "living alone." Does having a "home" under circumstances of poverty and drunkenness make a difference? The approach taken in this monograph is that the differences are slight and such people have been designated as Skid Row-like. In this conclusion we do not differ greatly from Bahr and Caplow, although we draw different conceptual consequences (8, *pp. 27–28*; 9, *ch. 15*).

An alternative to the concept of homelessness is to emphasize the extent to which Skid Row institutions are interdependent with the larger society. Examples of this interdependence are sustenance relations, including what seem to be the essentials of food, clothing, shelter, medical care, work, alcohol and sex. Like Bogue (25), we take the position that Skid Row is a part of the larger society in this regard; and we believe that Skid Row men are searching, along with the rest of the metropolitan community, for these scarce commodities (83). Moreover, they are dependent on the rest of the community for most of the success they have in getting these goods and services. The approach differs from those who stress the autonomy and isolation of Skid Row residents from the metropolis of which Skid Row is a part (33; 193, *ch. 19*; 217, *ch. 11*; 231, *ch. 1*).

It seems obvious that the distinctive Skid Row institutions such as gospel missions, bars and restaurants are interdependent with those of the larger community and that it is through these institutions that the Skid Row residents live out much of their interdependence with that larger community. This is more obvious when we consider employment agencies, circular-distribution agencies, and hotel, resort and institutional employment. Of course, not all Skid Row residents are equally interdependent with the larger community. Those who "panhandle," who steal from other Skid Row men, who work for missions, and those who are most active participants in Skid Row bottle gangs have, perhaps, a more attenuated relationship to the community than others. Even they, however, ultimately derive their funds from outside and use services that are economically tied to the larger community.

But over and beyond this interdependence, there is the question of whether Skid Row institutions—restaurants, housing, and drinking relationships—are unique in the extent to which they differ from those outside Skid Row.

Restaurants. The difference between Skid Row and non-Skid Row restaurants is in the stereotyped clientele rather than in the restaurants. A cheap restaurant that is used mostly by Skid Row men is a "Skid Row restaurant," while a cheap restaurant used by poor people who are not so stereotyped is not. Most Skid Row restaurants serve a nondescript American workingman's menu. Admittedly, prices are slightly higher in shabby restaurants located in other impoverished areas, but not much higher and the food is not very much different. Furthermore, destitute residents of the surrounding slum also eat in Skid Row restaurants.

Housing. Some Skid Row men sleep out, but this is a general symptom of poverty—not all those who sleep in subways are Skid Row men. Yet, while mission dormitories are not always restricted to Skid Row areas, it is rare when anybody except a Skid Row man will use them. Then, too, gospel rescue missions work outside the Skid Row area and their essential message is the same; there are even some mission feeding programs outside the stereotyped Skid Row area. The critical difference seems to be that, outside the Skid Row locality, the mission welfare programs are oriented to women and children, reminiscent of missions before World War I. That missions are more flexible in their clientele, while not changing their message, is witnessed by the fact that one mission in Philadelphia changed its location several years ago and redirected its efforts toward university students. In sum, it seems that it is not the gospel rescue mission, as such, that is to be closely identified with Skid Row, but the gospel rescue mission dormitories.

Cubicle hotels are restricted to Skid Row areas. However, the cubicle hotel question is largely a matter of room size and whether the room has an outside window. In Philadelphia there are other cheap hotels outside the Skid Row area which have rooms about 10-ft square and in which destitute and unattached men and women live. The residents usually receive social security benefits or public assistance payments and have developed stable friendships and patterns of caring for one another even though they are ostensibly strangers to each other (183). Mutual help among the poor and maritally unattached is not especially Skid Row-like behavior.

Drinking Behavior. Alcohol is pervasive on Skid Row. It is central to the way Skid Row institutions operate as well as to the stereotype of the general community about Skid Row. It dominates life: the smell of vomit in the cubicle hotel, the gospel mission's call to abandon drink and accept Christ, the wine bottles in the empty lots or where the doorstoop meets the building, the police round-ups, and the wine before work, at lunch and after work that are integral to the day of the laborer's and circular distributor's jobs. Skid Row drinking activities have been described in terms of the etiquette of bottle gangs, the anonymity of relationships and the presence of bar-girls in Skid Row bars (169; 193, *pp. 255–256*; 217, *ch. 5*).

However, some of these drinking patterns are not necessarily particular to Skid Row. Evidence of bottle-gang drinking has been found in widely dispersed areas of Philadelphia far from the Row. Rubington observed that in Maple City the "indigent unattached men" were virtually indistinguishable in their drinking behavior from men who lived in Skid Row localities in other cities, but that there was no discernible Skid Row neighborhood in Maple City (175). If there was any important distinction, it was that the drinking behavior of the Maple City Skid Row-like men was less well defined and less well controlled by the group. Cavan (38) reported on the etiquette in American drinking establishments in terms of seating, reciprocities in buying and accepting drinks, and anonymity. But such findings would need modification for the bars and drinking behavior of poor people. In the very poorest bars in this country, there may be some seating, but customers usually stand, and not all of these are in stereotypical Skid Row localities. Skid Row men also reciprocate in buying drinks when they can afford it; but generally, they cannot and so they form bottle gangs. Cavan reports that anonymity is also characteristic of drinking places off Skid Row; bar patrons tacitly understand that each may cut himself off from his "rightful biography" and invent a new one. A person is not unknown; rather, he is known superficially and in terms of his situation. Finally, B-girls, who, along with bartenders, try to mulct customers of their money, are hardly characteristic of Skid Row; rather, they are associated with the Tenderloin areas and the big city "bright lights" or nightclub sections. In brief, the drinking behavior stereotypically associated with Skid Row seems to be only slightly different from that of poor people elsewhere in our metropolitan cities.

In addition to Skid Row institutions, another approach to the meaning of "Skid Row" is to observe that Skid Row people are relatively powerless people. Bahr (8, *pp. 28–31*) comments that "organizations are the instruments by which men control the world, and their own destinies" and that "power is control over environment," and goes on to argue that the affiliation–disaffiliation of social relationships is the primary dimension along which to measure powerlessness. But Bahr's approach is too indirect and there is no great advance in it when the powerlessness of Skid Row people is so blatantly evident. This powerlessness is evidenced in the relationship of Skid Row people to the police and the courts, job exploitation, and in their victimization in other respects.

Police and Courts. These have been given attention by Bogue (25, *pp. 281–282, 414–418, 443*), Wallace (217, *ch. 8, 9*), Lovald (107, *pp. 310–336*), Lovald and Stub (108), Giffen (72) and Pittman and Gordon (153). Especially good in this regard have been the discussions of Wiseman (231, *pt. II*) and Spradley (193, *ch. 3–7*). Generally, local jails have continued as control agencies and as temporary rehabilitation centers. In Philadelphia there are still a considerable number of arrests for drunkenness, although there is some evidence of a shift in emphasis to arrest for vagrancy. Both of these criminal categories are now in transition from a philosophy of punishment to one of rehabilitation or of citizen rights in American jurisprudence. The policy in St. Louis, where the police department is one of the sponsors of a hospital detoxication ward for those found intoxicated in public

(151, 219), also calls attention to the powerlessness of Skid Row men, for the man who leaves against medical advice is threatened with jail. (In pointing this out, however, we are not commenting on the efficacy of the therapy program.)

But in what respect do the other poor peoples of the metropolis differ in the relationship to the police and the courts? The ethnic and racial identity of the poor varies from city to city and has varied over time; e.g., the Irish were once prominent on the criminal list (78, 79). "Police brutality" with the poor has been common in American society for many years (18; 40, *pp. 13–262*). As rough as the police may be with Skid Row persons, they are probably rougher with other types of citizens. Historically, perceived race appears to have been the initial criterion involved in "police brutality"; perceived foreignness was second; and, last, perceived class and status (or wealth and esteem). These are subject to change and regional variation.

Job Exploitation. Skid Row men are predominantly employed in service or unskilled-labor occupations. They wash the dishes in the hotels, restaurants and mountain resorts of Pennsylvania, New Jersey and New York; they work on trucks and in warehouses either through the intermediate hiring of a labor contractor or through street recruitment from the "slave market"; they do porter and janitorial work in the resorts and on live-in jobs; and they distribute circulars ("muzzle") in the high-density residential areas of the cities where it is cheaper to hire Skid Row men than it is to send "junk mail." Skid Row men generally work on a spot- or day-labor basis; and their drinking behavior is conducive to such an arrangement. In all of these situations the Skid Row man is likely to find himself with a short pay: his foreman advances him money so he can have his wine before he goes out muzzling; the hours of work turn out to be much longer than the job assignment sheet had led him to believe so that his effective hourly rate is much lower than it is supposed to be. The employment agency takes its percentage first so that the unstable Skid Row man finds himself with virtually no money after working several weeks. The spot-employment agency holds back a day's pay until the end of the week, but the man is either too drunk or in jail so he doesn't collect it. And the day-labor agency may require that its pay check be cashed in a

taproom where the worker is expected to buy a drink. Day labor
is a prime example of the victimization and exploitation of Skid
Row men.

Many non-Skid Row persons who use the casual labor offices
are Black, Puerto Rican, Chicano, and southern White migrants
living under Skid Row-like conditions (such as Chicago's Uptown). Indeed, the casual labor market no longer depends on
Skid Row people and would probably continue much as it has
been operating in the last few years even if the Skid Row areas
are physically eliminated. This is equally probable in the resort
industry. In the Catskill–Sullivan County (NY) area the employment offices were used by Skid Row men, Puerto Ricans,
Black adults and White young adults. If anything, we have
noted that, given an opportunity to hire a Black man or a White
Skid Row man for a spot job or a kitchen job in the Pocono
Mountains of Pennsylvania, there seems to be some preference
for the White Skid Row man. Hutter (88), in his discussion of
the small cheap resorts in the Catskills, observed that "the
non-houseman, non-prestigious staff is composed of socio-
economically deprived Negroes, Puerto Ricans and a small
number of Whites who are recruited from New York's Bowery
by employment agencies . . . who often stay at a hotel just long
enough to pick up one or two paychecks and then move on."

Victimization. Loan sharking is common among Skid Row
residents. The men borrow from hotel owners at rates that vary
from 25 to 100% (the time unit is usually until the next check
comes in, i.e., 2 weeks or 1 month). There is one rooming-house
operator in Philadelphia who has wine available at a mark-up of
125%. Strong-arm robbery and stealing from drunken men are
common, especially during the first several days after pension
and welfare checks arrive. Skid Row men believe that bartenders are often accomplices to muggings. There are some
bar–hotel operators and some hotel–restaurant operators who
prefer men receiving social security, public assistance or disability checks. It is common for the operator to hold a man's
check when it comes through the mail and to insist that he
"cash" it with the hotel operator. At that time, "accounts" are
cleared on expenses incurred during the check period just gone
by, and rent is paid in advance. A man rarely gets a receipt

(accounting is minimal) and he generally receives only a small amount of the check (essentially pocket money) when the process is completed. In short, Skid Row is a victim community, but too powerless to organize and demand better police protection, the last home of free enterprise in which, rather than "let the buyer beware," the more appropriate expression might be "woe to the vanquished."

But Skid Row men are not alone in being victimized. Such experiences are relatively common among the poor and powerless people of the big cities. The likelihood of mugging or jackrolling is probably higher for Skid Row men, however, because they are more likely to be drunk on the streets and, being middle-aged or elderly, they are more vulnerable. Loan sharking is common, too. Exploitative landlords are common in the slums of all big cities, but the ability of the landlord to get direct control of a social security or public assistance check is probably specific to Skid Row and develops because the mail is first delivered to his office. On the other hand, stealing such checks from mail delivery boxes is common in the poor sections of the cities.

The Skid Row concept can also be considered as a status relationship (107, *p. 50*; 118, *pp. 442, 455–456*). That is, Skid Row people are extremely low in terms of the degree of esteem and honor accorded to them by the larger community. Indeed, along a positive–negative axis, we would say that Skid Row persons are dis-esteemed and dis-honored. Indicators of this dimension are likely to be difficult to find when the differences are more subtle, but not for Skid Row people. They are stereotypically dirty, unkempt and unshaven; and, when they are drunk, or after they have been on a spree, they often smell from sweat, urine, vomit and alcohol; they may be lousy; they often wear no socks; they may have no laces in their shoes. Not infrequently they show scratches and scabs on their faces and hands; they are emaciated; even though their physical appearance is repellent, in an era of organized charity their panhandling does not call forth the pity and sympathy of an earlier era. They are perceived as the unsalvageable remnant of the larger community. From that viewpoint the function of the gospel missions is to make a final effort to locate the last salvageable person—the gospel missions are scavengers of men as well as of material such as old furniture, clothing and whatnots. If a Skid Row person goes to a hospital emergency ward when he is drunk, he is shuffled aside. When he is admitted to a hospital (usually on the basis of some other diagnosis), he is expected to sit long hours on clinic benches, passively, until he is called; then, like a child, he is addressed by his given name and directed "down the hall" or "over there." When a Skid Row person applies for public assistance, there is a long wait, the careful questioning about eligibility, the rejection masked in efforts to show the man that he must accept the fact that he has an alcohol problem and that he should agree to do something about it, and the great chance that, while his "alcoholism" will be defined as an "illness," he will not be considered eligible for public assistance on the basis of this particular disability. When a Skid Row man applies for a job in one of the expensive hotels in the Pocono Mountains of Pennsylvania, he is fingerprinted and photographed; it is not uncommon to look into his criminal history (arranged through a tie with the local police). When he applies for a job at some Pocono resorts, the wise Skid Row man will go to the local "Sally" and ask for a suitcase—it apparently changes the way he is perceived and raises the likelihood of getting the job. When an agency sends a man out on a job, it usually sees to it that he is shaved and "cleaned up" so that he does not present himself as a bum. In few, if any, of the social welfare agencies that offer services to Skid Row people are the men more than recipients of service—they are not participants in decisions about the kinds of service to be dispensed nor the priorities for service to be offered. They are not considered competent enough to be involved to that degree.

Lastly, Skid Row people are popular models of the extreme of what not to be—from Happy Hooligan, the petty thieving and irresponsible tramp, to newspaper and magazine cartoons that regularly appear in the press of our own day. Bahr (8, *pp. 67–80*) summarized a pilot study of cartoons illustrating the way that Skid Row persons are perceived by contributors to the mass media and the attitudes that are being suggested to readers. The "Freddy the Freeloader" role of Red Skelton, the television comedian, is an example of the same sort of cartooning in a different medium. Bahr concludes: "Certainly the dominant theme of the cartoonists that Skid Row men are recognizably 'human' and not basically different from other men is a positive contribution" (8, *p. 80*). Skid Row people are not the only ones who have been disesteemed and dishonored in our society. The rising storm of criticism and controversy over the treatment accorded migratory workers is a clear example. In our cities, the impoverished and relatively powerless are accorded a low degree of honor and esteem. They, too, are perceived as dirty, unkempt and irresponsible, even though so many exceptions are readily available. There are exceptions in the Skid Row area too, but they are not as easily seen as such as long as they live in the locality. It seems to be a matter of density of those who are otherwise very comparable, rather than the presence or absence of a characteristic or behavior. We can look at panhandling as a species of entrepreneurship; and we should recognize that other poor people practice welfare entrepreneurship differently, for example, when the "man in the house" becomes invisible so that welfare payments will continue. Current "job readiness" programs which are, in turn, elements of the "feeder programs" for the Opportunities Industrialization Center are similar in their scavenging functions to the gospel missions, in that the clients were regarded as "unemployable" in the past. The way the program is presented to the client and to the public is different, of course. However, there is no difference between the way Skid Row men and destitute non-Skid Row people are treated with disesteem in our hospitals and public welfare offices and when it comes to the job market. There are the same kinds of disrespect and the same kinds of attacks on personal dignity directed to Blacks, Puerto Ricans and Chicanos. The activities of the Welfare Rights Organization and Community Legal Services, as well as changes in organizational style by the Urban League, suggest that the poor, especially the ethnic and racial poor, are beginning to participate actively in social service agency planning. Finally, destitute racial–ethnic minority persons are no longer acceptable as butts for comic cartoons in the mass media. There are status differences, then, between Skid Row and non-Skid Row people even though the indicators are difficult to conceptualize and even more difficult to operationalize. In the past, except for some possible color–class considerations, there were minor differences between Skid Row and other destitute, powerless persons in our metropolitan cities. It seems probable that, as racial and ethnic minority people in the United States move away from destitution (and this change will be facilitated by emergent changes in power relationships that are now taking place), they will be accorded greater esteem and honor. It is in this respect that Skid Row and non-Skid Row people differ most significantly. Skid Row people, generally, have moved or are moving rapidly to the negative extreme of status in our society, while non-Skid Row people are moving to a less negative situation and an increasingly positive one in terms of sustenance, power and status.

"Skid Row" as a human condition is found in populations all over the poorer sections of the metropolitan cities, but there is a heavier concentration in the Skid Row locality. That is, homelessness, poverty, powerlessness, disesteem and, to some substantial extent, alcoholism are concentrated in that small section of the city known as Skid Row, an area usually peripheral to the CBD. But to a considerable degree this is a question of perception and labeling, for, as this chapter has pointed out, many of the so-called Skid Row institutions are just as easily identified with other impoverished city dwellers as they are with Skid Row as such. We took a field trip to Chicago some years ago. We had examined the four Skid Row areas in the vicinity of the Loop and were in the Uptown section speculating on whether it might also be considered a Skid Row-like section. Acting on the dictum that cabdrivers know where things are in their own city, we got into a taxicab and asked the driver to take us to some of the other Skid Row-like areas. Without hesitation, he said, "You're there already, Uptown is the hillbilly Skid Row." If we had questioned him carefully, using the method of "respects" that has been used in this chapter, we probably would have come to understand that a more accurate statement would have been that "Uptown is analogous to Skid Row; Uptown is where the poor southern White migrants have become concentrated in Chicago." The cabdriver had some kind of reputational map of the city "in his head" that he used for ready reference. This map is carried in some degree by most or all city dwellers, and the existence of this map has consequences for city dwellers' actions. To some extent, the map is based on a sort of "objective reality" derived from actual observations of the stereotyped

Skid Row locality, of its recent history, and of the institutionalization of that history in the mass media. They are further objectified when the press or influential public figures label an area as "The New Skid Row," for they, in turn, influence real estate practices and thereby may intensify tendencies that already exist. Thus rescue missions, commercial blood banks, day-labor employment agencies and other Skid Row institutions may use this definition in deciding where to relocate during urban redevelopment. These will be areas which will be least capable of resistance to invasion by such real estate uses. The public may begin to think of the identified area in a new way, thus influencing public policy affecting the area. The mass media may continue to "cover" the story of the area, and the residents begin to be uneasy. Public definition of an area as "deviant" or notable has predictable consequences which may have only a tenuous connection with "objective reality" (14, 201).

The position taken here is that Skid Row is considerably more than a state of mind, as Bahr (8, *p. 35*) suggests. Skid Row areas in the United States are changing radically; there are those who report that they are gradually disappearing (6). This monograph offers a different interpretation: Skid Row areas are not disappearing but being transformed either through site clearance and redevelopment or through long-term trends in our society. Furthermore, it is likely that the very way that the term was conceptualized in the past was myopic with respect to race and gender. If that is so, then a reconceptualization of what we mean by "Skid Row" seems indicated. Definitions in social science, as well as in social welfare policy, are not arbitrary, although it is clear that some definitions may be more helpful in one context than in another. Some of the defining criteria of Skid Row, such as poverty or status, are continuous variables, whereas others, such as community labels or stereotypes, are categorical—you are either on Skid Row or not. The meaning of Skid Row needs to be conceptualized in terms of both categorical and continuous variables; admittedly, this approach flows counter to popular practice. There are probably strong and pervasive emotional reasons for the popular stereotype of Skid Row as an area of the city. Perhaps one reason involves the emotional need of the general community to stereotype alcoholics, the need to be able to say, an "alcoholic" lives on Skid Row.

This stereotype is probably self-serving for many heavy drinkers; they may thereby more easily continue their denial of their own condition. In the past, existence of the stereotype most certainly was a part of the rhetoric of the Prohibition movement and its allied moral reformers.

Our analysis and experience suggest that housing is the one characteristic that is unique to the Skid Row area. The other Skid Row institutions exist in a symbiotic, or dependent, relationship to the housing. But under conditions of urban redevelopment, if this is accompanied by even modest upgrading of the housing code, Skid Row-type housing is likely to be sufficiently transformed to be relatively indistinguishable from the cheap housing for other poor people that exists elsewhere in the city. Does that mean that Skid Row will have disappeared? If one means the stereotyped, "traditional" Skid Row that developed in the last quarter of the 19th Century, then the answer may be yes. But if one recognizes that a Skid Row lifestyle has existed elsewhere in the city for many years, then the prevalence of the Skid Row lifestyle is the important issue, rather than Skid Row as a unique area of the city.[2] The sociological

[2] Long after this chapter was written, we came across George Nash's exploratory study (127). Nash postulated that homeless men lack family contact and have limited resources. In a preliminary fashion, he characterized homeless men as "responsibilityless." Using the characteristics of dead men whose bodies were turned over to the Mortuary Division of the New York City Department of Hospitals (because there was no one willing to pay burial costs), Nash found that about 80% came from elsewhere in Manhattan outside the Bowery. In comparison of the Bowery and non-Bowery population of those who received city burials, Nash found them similar with respect to marital status information (mostly "unknown"), age at death and cause of death; the Bowery population was 84% White and 14% Black, while the non-Bowery Manhattan men were 69% White and 31% Black. Nash made a special study of 19 non-Bowery Manhattan city burial cases and concluded that they were, indeed, homeless people. Extrapolating the ratio of Bowery men to non-Bowery men among the city burial cases, Nash suggested that there were 30,000 homeless men in sections of Manhattan other than the Bowery; most of these were in the Lower West Side (West 38th St. to West 14th St.), Upper West Side (West 104th St. to West 74th St.), and Central Harlem (Harlem River to 118th St.). Nash concluded that the outstanding characteristic of a Skid Row in comparison with a slum was that there was a relatively high concentration of homeless men in the Skid Row area with Skid Row institutions to serve them. The homeless men are in a majority in the Skid Row area, while elsewhere, they are not; "most make less long range commitment to their living facilities than homeless men in other concentration areas. Proportionately, more of the homeless men in the Skid Row are behavioral problems" (127, pp. D-28–29).

questions of why such specialized areas came into existence and whether a feeling develops among the residents that they belong to a separate community are well worth investigation. However, they are dependent on the larger conceptual issue. If "Skid Row" refers to a human condition wherever it is found in the metropolis, then, from the point of view of social science, we will want to know more about people living a Skid Row lifestyle. A comparison of those living in the Skid Row area with those living the lifestyle elsewhere is a valid enterprise. Bahr and Caplow (9) and Garrett and Bahr (71) have made significant contributions although they have used a different conceptual approach. In terms of social welfare policy, the view of Skid Row as a human condition means that programs and services need to be conceived differently than in the past: offering "rehabilitation services" to people as they move from the Skid Row area is a very minor part of the social welfare policy problem.

With these thoughts in mind, then, it seems that the differences between Skid Row and non-Skid Row persons are quite small. Many of the characteristics of the residents of Skid Row areas of Philadelphia are also the characteristics of residents of Bathhurst and Anglia and many of the residents of the Cass Corridor in Detroit. There are differences between Skid Row, Skid Row-like and other persons among the urban poor, but in many ways "they are differences that don't make a difference." People with a Skid Row lifestyle are not necessarily isolated from the larger community. To be a Skid Row person characteristically is (1) to be poor, often destitute; (2) to live outside the context of "normal" family relationships; (3) to live in extremely low-cost housing; (4) to have a greater probability of coming to police attention and "protective custody" for behavior that is somehow related to the use of alcohol; (5) to be more vulnerable to victimization than other destitute people, especially when social security, retirement or welfare checks are involved; (6) to have a superficial style of social relations; and (7) to have not only low status but a high probability of movement to the lowest level of esteem in our society, even in a period when other formerly disesteemed people are rising in the status accorded to them.

Chapter 8

The Wanderers[1]

ANY EXAMINATION of the future of Skid Row must consider the possible sources of new Skid Row-like populations. We argue that Skid Row is a human condition and not necessarily a place in the city: the life cycle, employment and addiction elements which help define the Skid Row population are found, but to lesser degrees or in different combinations, among non-Skid Row residents. Hence, the Skid Row locality houses a population that has "skidded" to the bottom of our society, lacking sufficient social ties to keep out of the Skid Row status. The search for future Skid Row residents must concentrate on apparently Skid Row-eligible populations: persons who are susceptible to those combinations of life cycle, employment and addiction which are likely, if exacerbated, to force them to the Row area or into Skid Row-like status elsewhere.

A possible source of Skid Row-like people may be the "street people" and other rootless intercity migrant populations in this country. This chapter begins with a historical look at a more or less traditional street-people area, continues with an examination of street people in a university area, and concludes with data derived from one agency which has attempted to deal with wanderers since its inception in the first decade of this century.

[1] We express appreciation to the following: Jeanne E. Bader, John Newmeyer, Stephen Pittel, Henry Miller, Jim Baumohl, Carroll Estes, Marjorie Montelius, Martin Goldberg, M.D., Catherine Kerner, Grace A. Yocum, Sarah Rosenthal, Rebe Maimowitz, Earl Wajdyk, Anthony M. Salvatore, Alan De-Wolfe and Irving W. Shandler. The discussion of the Travelers Aid Society and "people in flight" is based on: BLUMBERG, L. U., SHIPLEY, T. E., JR. and DeWOLFE, A. People in flight; a comparative study of migrants without plans. Presented at the National Conference on Social Welfare, Chicago, 1 June 1970. Goldberg (73) has another discussion. For the discussion of "people in flight," we acknowledge assistance from the Office of Mental Health, Department of Public Welfare of the Commonwealth of Pennsylvania, Project No. 01-21-84-3–429, and from the National Institute of Mental Health, grant No. RO 1-MH-14949, "A Project on Mental Health of Persons in Flight." Responsibility for the data and their interpretation remain with the authors.

The Haight

One of the first areas in the country which drew young unattached people in large numbers was the Haight–Ashbury section of San Francisco.[2] Beginning about 1965 streams of young
people, many of whom used amphetamines and other drugs,
came to the Haight and other blighted areas of large cities to try
to define their own "communities" and live lifestyles alien to
most of the rest of the country. Most of the areas where this
influx occurred were near universities and the "street people"
interacted with the university personnel, but conditions were
different in the Haight.

The history of the Haight begins with the establishment of
Golden Gate Park in the 1870s. The Park and the housing built
near it attracted residents from the dense and expanding city to
the area now known as Haight–Ashbury. The development of
the Park brought with it the establishment of cable car lines and
railroads converging on the Haight, stimulating social and
commercial activity and encouraging building. An amusement
center, bars, hotels and restaurants, as well as the Park, brought
thousands of people to the Haight on weekends. All these factors made the area attractive to the middle and upper-middle
classes. For a time, mansions were built which rivaled those of
the older wealthy area of Nob Hill.

The 1906 earthquake and fire encouraged further building in
the Haight and in surrounding areas by refugees from near the
Bay. The nearby Fillmore area became the substitute for a central business district (CBD) while the fire-destroyed downtown
was being rebuilt. During this period, multi-unit residential
structures were built in the Haight area and some of the single-
family houses were converted into apartments. Most of the
structures currently found in the Haight were built during the
two booms of the 1880s and 1906–1920.

The Haight's growth was tied to its nearness to Golden Gate
Park, its centrality in terms of public transportation, and its
commercial hegemony over surrounding areas (which itself was
based on high traffic volume, the Park and transportation). The
Haight was seen as a desirable place to live—as "unique"—

[2] Adapted from San Francisco Department of City Planning (178, *pp. 1–11*).

because of its transportation facilities, its educational opportunities, its theaters and its proximity to important institutions.
But the Depression produced a high vacancy rate, a heavy concentration of tenants living in absentee-owned apartment buildings and a deterioration in maintenance. The size of the apartments and the roominess of the mansions allowed two or more
families to live in the same building, and the proportion of
single-family houses fell to about 10% by 1939.

During World War II the housing shortage produced still
more doubling up in dwellings. The roomy mansions and flats
were subdivided into as many as six or seven units, increasing
the deterioration of buildings which were designed as single-
family dwellings and exacerbating the problem of maintenance
in the face of rapid tenant turnover.

From the end of the second boom in 1919 until 1950, with
almost no increase in the number of buildings, the number of
dwelling units in the Haight increased by 85%—from 4750 to
8770. The growing density and blight encouraged the flight of
older, more stable residents and simultaneously encouraged the
relocation into the Haight of non-Whites during the 1950s. The
proportion of Blacks in the Haight rose from 2 to 17% from 1950
to 1960, and income fell even further below the citywide average than it had been earlier. In the late 1950s and early 1960s
the increasing rents in the North Beach area forced artists,
writers and other "Beatniks" to migrate to the Haight in a
search for lower rents, large apartments and tolerance for cultural diversity. The attractive elements of Park and transportation continued to make the area desirable.

At the same time, the development of commercial centers
elsewhere in the western part of the city ended the Haight's
commercial hegemony. The late 1940s saw the increasingly
heavy use of the automobile for transportation to and from Gold-
en Gate Park, reducing the importance of the Haight as a
transportation nexus. The auto also allowed residents to shop
elsewhere. Thus the commercial base of the Haight was increasingly undermined at the same time as its residential density was increasing and the income received by its residents
was decreasing. The small merchants faced an increasingly difficult time attracting the volume of sales which would permit
them to match the prices offered by the more attractive shop-

ping centers elsewhere in the western part of the city. Even at that, the Haight's stores (limited in floor space) could not support the volume of trade necessary to permit them to continue, and the lack of truck docks and off-street parking meant that major purchases were less likely to be made there.

Deteriorating housing, lower rents, the commercial decline and the general malaise of the Haight contributed to the emergence of the "hippie" colony. The hippies emerged from the Beatnik movement of the late 1950s and early 1960s. Thousands of young people, encouraged by media coverage of the Haight hippies, began a pilgrimage to the Haight. The hippie movement generated a resurgence of commercial activity in the Haight, as not only they but the tourists they attracted used local merchants. As the hippies faded away, they were replaced by "street people," who came from significantly poorer families than did hippies and were thus less able to support commercial enterprises. Street people do not attract tourists and so, after the hippies faded from the scene, the commercial hippie- and tourist-oriented facilities went out of business. The housing stock continued to decline even as housing shortages increased.

The influx of low-income Blacks into the Haight has continued from the 1950s to the present day. The proportion of non-White residents in the central census tract in the Haight increased from 3 to more than 41% from 1950 to 1970. This influx meant an increase in racial and class-based conflicts.

Recently the Haight has been the site of continuing urban renewal with the aim of preventing further deterioration of the area and, since its location and transportation access to the CBD and its proximity to Golden Gate Park and the hospitals and universities remain, upgrading the quality of the neighborhood. Houses are being reconverted into single-family dwelling units, repaired and repainted. The Department of City Planning is concentrating redevelopment efforts, especially in the areas of transportation, commercial development, housing and community services.

These efforts seem to have encouraged the formation of community organizations through which the city can deal with the Haight citizenry—or at least those who are "represented" by the organizations. The Haight–Ashbury Neighborhood Council·takes as its boundaries those of the Department of City

Planning: 1970 U.S. Census Tracts 165, 166 and 171. The designation of community names and boundaries has political consequences for those "represented" and can fragment or consolidate a grassroots neighborhood (14, *ch. 8*). In the case of the Haight, the city's aim seems to be to foster consolidation; but, as Grogan (76, *pp. 238 ff.*) shows, organizations which claim to represent the "community" sometimes represent only their own members.

Clearly the Haight is too important and valuable an area to be allowed to deteriorate completely. The city is attempting to stabilize the community's "diversity" at present levels while encouraging rehabilitation of housing, increasing the proportion of owner-occupied housing units, guiding the direction of the nearby University of California campus, preserving open space, improving the delivery of city services, upgrading the commercial facilities of the area, and altering the present intrusiveness of automobile traffic in the Haight. Recently there has been some local community opposition to further rehabilitation efforts in the Haight, and it is impossible to predict in a politically aware city like San Francisco and in a politically astute neighborhood like the Haight what the outcome of the city's renewal efforts will be. Nevertheless, homeowners in the Haight are proceeding with several kinds of private renewal.

As both public and private renewal have continued in the Haight, most of the street people have left. According to a local informant, there are so few left that one begins to recognize faces very soon; and the era of the Haight as a haven for street people has ended.[3]

A visit to the Haight in early 1974 revealed more evidence of the congregation of heavy drinkers than of street people. There are places which could be identified as hangouts for "winos." The panhandlers in the area were older White men who appeared to be very similar to those in Skid Row. But community service facilities seemed to be ready for unemployed drifters. A printed poster in the psychiatric facility of the Haight–Ashbury Free Medical Clinic entitled "Job Resources in San Francisco, August 1973" included day-labor agencies, circular distributors, a blood bank, and a farm labor camp, i.e., typical Skid Row

[3] Interview with John Newmeyer, 10 January 1974, San Francisco.

resources. These job resources do not match the predominantly middle-class population of the Haight and seem to be aimed at whatever residual street people might be left. The poster was published by the Haight–Ashbury Switchboard, a facility established during the hippie era to help parents and wanderers who wanted to find each other.

A newsprint four-page handout, "San Francisco Survival Manual 1974," also published by the Switchboard, notified readers of missions and barber colleges and places to get free "food and flop." There has clearly been an intermixture of the Skid Row-eligible population with the "underground" population.

Thus the pattern of development of the Haight parallels that of Philadelphia's area north of Market. Both areas began as desirable places in which to live because of their convenience to the CBD and their housing possibilities. As the environment changed both areas declined in attractiveness for middle-class residents and served as living space for Skid Row and Skid Row-like people. Both areas are currently undergoing urban renewal because the land is so valuable. One of the most important differences between the Haight and Philadelphia's area north of Market is the contrast between the political savvy of the Haight people and the powerlessness of Skid Row men. There are still a few street people living in the Haight similar to Skid Row residents in health, economic status and powerlessness, but the Haight contains a large residential population which can appeal to City authorities and other interest groups for recognition and assistance. There are no community organizations in Skid Row.

Street People

This history of the Haight reveals a steady decline in the quality of the housing and population characteristics, ending with the influx of young, deviant, drug-using middle-class and (later) working-class drifters. A few working-class drifters can still be found in the Haight and in larger numbers in university communities and towns throughout the country. We refer to these working-class drifters as "street people."

Street people should not be confused with the earlier hippies. The hippies were similar to street people in age, drug involvement and migratory characteristics. But the two groups are markedly different on other measures:

"Left behind were the uneducated, the unskilled, the disoriented, lame and addicted. The Haight–Ashbury, in particular, became a sleazy no-man's-land of abandoned storefronts and empty streets, haunted by junkies, speed freaks, and other spectres of the psychedelic bowery. The characteristics of homelessness had changed; these were 'street people,' not 'hippies.' It was 1970, not 1966" (15, *p. 17*).

The transition began in 1967. During that spring, amphetamine use became widespread among the young people in the Haight, especially among those who were of a lower social-class background than most of the hippies. Pittel (150) claims that the patterns of "speed" use parallel those of heroin use and that users of amphetamines were similar to the traditional lower-class heroin users. Even though users were warned by the street subculture that "Speed Kills," three-quarters of the "bad trips" admitted to San Francisco General Hospital were due to overdoses of amphetamines during the summer of 1967. After the end of that summer, the Haight became the site of an increasingly amphetamine-using street culture, including significant numbers of runaways for whom "Haight–Ashbury" was a community in which no questions were asked and in which they can lose themselves (150). This observation by Pittel is of significance because it sounds so much like a statement about a Skid Row area.

The street people were able to exist in the Haight because they were in a quasi-symbiotic (almost parasitic) relationship with the rest of the youth ghetto of the Haight. The hippies and street people attracted the attention of tourists, and the street people panhandled the hippies and the tourists who were drawn by them. When the bulk of the hippies moved to the more viable youth ghetto in Berkeley, the street people could not "make it" on their own. As a result, the street people, except for a few, also tended to move across the bay to Berkeley.

Baumohl and Miller (16) conducted a study of street people in Berkeley under a grant from the University of California at Berkeley and the City of Berkeley. They chose as a survey site the Berkeley Emergency Food Project, a formerly free service which had wide word-of-mouth publicity. The survey was conducted during the winter so as not to catch too many "tourists" but, rather, to include a cross-section of the hard-core nomadic population. The Emergency Food Project feeds 150 to 200 persons each night for 35 cents each; if the client does not have the money, he is fed free. The hungry form a breadline-like lineup outside the Project facility as early as an hour before feeding time begins. The analogy to a secularized Skid Row mission is readily apparent.

The study was an interview and questionnaire survey of 295 clients of the Emergency Food Project. Of those studied 19% were White women, a much higher proportion of women than is usually found among Skid Row populations. This finding may reflect their youth: 64% were 20 years of age or less, compared with fewer than 20% of the men. Thus, the women may not yet have fallen into the protected status that United States society seems to accord to White females.

Most of the non-White street people in Berkeley were Black men (33 out of 50). Most of the remaining were American Indians from reservations in Oklahoma and North Dakota, coming to the West Coast for "the scene," but returning when they get confused by the city. Generally, they do not have marketable skills and are "really inept" at street survival, but the reservation is boring and so they travel back and forth from the city to the reservation. Among the Black street people there are some discernible subtypes: the first consists of recent migrants from the South, who tend to be from strong Christian fundamentalist backgrounds; these may be "Jesus freaks." The second group are children of not-so-recent migrants whose parents live in nearby cities (in this case, Richmond and Oakland) and have better jobs than the parents of the Black street people in the first group. Finally, there are Black hippies from eastern and midwestern cities who are "into music" and counterculture activities. Over-all, however, the street-people population is White (16).[4]

Baumohl and Miller's data suggest that street people are somewhat better off educationally than Skid Row residents. More than 45% of the White men and about one-third of the Black men have had some college experience; about 22% of the women have been to college, but, in view of their youth, this

---

[4] Interview with Jim Baumohl, 11 January 1974.

low proportion is understandable. Baumohl and Miller's most striking finding is that the educational attainment of street people is exceeded by that of their fathers: 53% of the fathers had had at least some college training, compared with only a little more than 40% of the Berkeley street people. Again, some of the disparity is due to the young age of the women, but even taking that into account there has been downward educational mobility. In view of American society's expectation of upward educational mobility, this intergenerational slippage is of interest. The origins of the Black street people are also striking; fully one-third of their fathers had some education beyond high school.

The data on social origins are a key to understanding the differences between hippies and street people. As Baumohl and Miller (16) note, according to their questionnaire responses almost half of a sample of Haight–Ashbury hippies and a quarter of the Berkeley street people had upper-middle class origins.

The street population is nomadic. Table 5 shows that among their street-people respondents, Baumohl and Miller found that the White women tended to be the most migratory and Black men the least, although the entire population must be considered highly transient. Further, Henry Miller[5] states that the young "speed-involved" wanderers follow a route from Van-

TABLE 5.—*Transience Patterns of Street People, by Race and Sex, in Per Cent*[a]

	Black Men (N=27)	White Men (156)	White Women (46)	Total[e] (243)
"Rooters"[b]	18.5	12.2	15.2	14.4
"Nesters"[c]	25.9	19.9	2.2	16.9
"Chronics"[d]	55.6	67.9	82.6	68.7

[a] Adapted from Baumohl and Miller (16, *p. 41*).

[b] Persons who have lived primarily in one city since leaving home.

[c] Persons who have spent most of their time in only two or three cities, i.e., those who show a tendency to settle into a city for six months or more at a time.

[d] Persons who have never spent an appreciable length of time in any one place, but who move about—either in a discernible pattern, or seemingly at whim.

[e] Includes small numbers of Black women.

[5] Interview with Henry Miller, 8 January 1974, Berkeley.

couver to Tijuana, stopping in the youth ghettos in university towns and in university areas of larger cities. Lofland (106) and Mason (119, 120) also describe the street people as nomads through the country, traveling from university settlement to university settlement in such places as Cambridge, Madison, Boulder, Ithaca, Chapel Hill and Ann Arbor. Baumohl (15, *p. 13*) states that they are found in traditional Skid Row areas as well.[6] It is of some interest that Baumohl and Miller (16, *p. 17*) report that about 37% of the Berkeley street-people respondents were born in the heavily urbanized and industrialized Middle Atlantic–East North Central states.

As would be expected from a sample of respondents studied in a free-food establishment, the Berkeley sample was over-whelmingly unemployed. Only 13% reported that they had had a job in the last month: they worked at odd jobs, performed fine arts, sold craftwork, or worked in domestic service. Three in five of those who worked had done so less than 20 hours a week during the month prior to the survey (16, *pp. 30–31*). Their skills are very limited at best, and thus they are eligible for Skid Row-like day-labor jobs, but day labor is almost impossible to find in university communities. This problem, coupled with the chronic unemployment and low-level employment characteristic of the street population, means that the population may be doomed to a lifetime of economic marginality. The striking poverty was exacerbated by the mass of more or less restrictive welfare regulations found at the time of the research in the Bay Area (16, *pp. 32–33*).

In summary, it should be noted that street people are not simply "worse-off hippies." They congregate in university areas and interact with the same institutions as university-related residents of the youth ghetto, but they are not friendly with the university descendants of the "flower children" (in fact, the students seem to be afraid of the street population) and seem rather to be pre-Skid Row people. One of the major dissimilarities between the two populations is the large portion of women on the street as compared with those associated with

[6] Baumohl also states that the West Coast nomad area extends from Seattle to San Diego, and that very few street people can get across the Mexican border and fewer still into Canada.

Skid Row. But, as we suggested earlier, perhaps the age difference (a second major dissimilarity) between the two populations is related to the overrepresentation of women on the street. Given the relative powerlessness of women in the United States, especially among lower-class populations, it seems likely that the street women will eventually attach themselves to men. Whether they will thereby be removed from the Skid Row-eligible population or will continue to live in marginal Skid Row-like residential areas remains to be seen.

Several tours of street-people areas in January 1974 revealed a high prevalence of panhandling for "spare change," "a smoke," and, once, for "a penny." Most of the identifiable street people were Whites, and all of the non-Whites were American Indians. Clothing was worn and bedraggled and needed patching; whereas the students' clothing was brightly patched, the street-people's clothing had holes. Most of the men were more or less clean-shaven, but all had very long (and dirty) hair. Shoes were very run-down, similar to those worn by Skid Row men. Both men and women were very thin; their faces were reminiscent of those in the classic "Okie" and "Arkie" photographs of the Depression and dustbowl era (15).[7] In sum, their poverty and degradation were clearly evident.

It appears that the street population is a Skid Row population of the future. The two groups have in common their educational and employment background, parents' social status, transiency, the inability to keep jobs, minimal employment skills, ineptitude, powerlessness, history of mental illness (23% of those surveyed in Berkeley had been patients in mental hospitals), apparent friendlessness, rootlessness and social ostracism. Even their military experiences were similar: 51% of those released from the military had less-than-honorable discharges (16, *p. 44*). Finally, alcohol is increasingly the drug most commonly ingested by street people. Miller says that liquor is not the drug of choice but that it is cheaper than other drugs and it is legal.

The street people are not a trivial phenomenon, much as Skid Row is not trivial. Baumohl, during our interview with him, estimated that 5000 street people pass through the Bay Area in a

[7] JOFFEE, R. Down, out, flat busted, desperate; the bloom is off the "flower era." *Washington Post*, B-1, B-6, 24 May 1974.

year and that there may be as many as a million disaffiliated street people in the United States.

People in Flight

The phenomenon of mobility is not new. As the country industrialized, variations in local employment conditions encouraged migration from the rural hinterland to the big cities. The pattern was a continuation of a transience which had existed from the beginnings of recorded history. But, in the United States, the study of migrations of unattached people during times of depression and panic became increasingly important for understanding some of the effects of industrialization. Social workers, too, became interested in the problems attendant upon migration and mobility, because they were so deeply involved in giving aid. Over the years the Travelers Aid Society has been particularly concerned; it was founded specifically to assist travelers to big cities (especially women) and continues to do so. We now turn to an examination of a sample of people who came to the Travelers Aid Society of Philadelphia (TAS) and who can be categorized as pre-Skid Row persons.

TAS gives individualized professional casework services to locally mobile people as well as to migrants. The program is directed to helping the client find a way to deal with his or her immediate difficulties and with his more basic problems as they are related to his movement around the country. The most difficult to work with are those migrants who are fleeing from situations they consider undesirable or intolerable and who express dependency needs, anxiety, fantasy and conflicts within themselves and their relations with others through their migration. Acting on impulse, these persons (often entire families) usually start out without adequate plans and seek help only at a point of crisis. We refer to this kind of migration as "flight," which seems to be similar to the "chronic transience" referred to by Baumohl and Miller (16), although Baumohl[8] says that the TAS is not seen by street people as being sympathetic to their problems.

TAS is specifically organized to serve an uprooted and highly

[8] Jim Baumohl, personal communication, 8 November 1974.

mobile population and, nationally, the TAS "chain of service" provides help to many persons in flight.[9] The agency has a staff trained to act quickly on client emergencies by providing material aid and daily interviews to stimulate the client's ability and willingness to discuss problems and needs. It is in this context, if they "perch" long enough, that clients in flight begin to reveal that they are caught in a web of problems. Their initial request for help usually cloaks a complex set of difficulties (they, like Skid Row men, are multiproblem clients). These multiple problems are usually of long standing. What is more relevant to our present interest is that their problem syndrome is associated with flight behavior. It is not uncommon for the same individual or family to turn up at 8 or 10 different local TAS offices over the years; their flight behavior may recur over a period of 20 years or more.

The client population was classified into those apparently in flight and not in flight (the "nonflight"). To facilitate further analysis, a further categorization of clients in flight was made according to the number of unplanned, or poorly planned, geographic movements in the last 5 years (F1 clients had made one such move, F2 two, and F3 three or more). An unplanned or poorly planned movement was one in which some or all of the following elements were involved: no job here or at "destination"; no provision for lodgings, no funds, no family or friends or resources in the new location; no prior communication with family or friends or other resources before coming. Clearly, these matters involved a subjective judgment on the part of the intake workers and reliability was achieved through discussion, an instruction manual, and a research assistant who fulfilled a "watchdog" function. Flight status was coded at the time the case was closed, permitting a shift from preliminary judgments as further information became available during the casework process. This procedure was followed because it is common for clients to change facts and their personal reactions to their problems as the relationship with the worker evolves. In addition, collateral sources may provide further or different information. This is particularly likely with clients in flight.

[9] The combined local agencies and affiliates reported 15,355 cases of flight in 1967.

The "structured interview" (in distinction to the usual interview procedure of the agency) was based on one developed at the Diagnostic and Rehabilitation Center/Philadelphia for Skid Row men. The revised interview was pretested with the TAS client population and subjected to critical examination by TAS executives and staff. After interviewers had become familiar with the items that were required, they were permitted some flexibility to weave the interview items into the context of the application interview, provided the central intent of the question was not altered. Data were collected on clients from 1 June 1965 to 24 October 1967. Study data were collected from about 25% of the approximately 3425 clients. The balance were excluded for the following reasons: 5% were runaways under 15 years of age; 13% were mentally ill or retarded, physically handicapped or too aged to be included; 3% did not speak English sufficiently; 21% involved a request primarily related to evaluating travel service requests, safeguarding children traveling alone, assisting the handicapped, and so forth; 12% were travel emergencies at the airport or came too late in the evening to make an interview feasible; 21% did not eventuate in a case because there was no client interview or the client withdrew from service very shortly after contact; less than 0.1% refused to complete structured interviews while service to the client continued. Of the clients who received the structured interview, 240 received intensive casework services.

Of the 826 clients for whom satisfactory data were available, 69% were men. In comparison, Table 5 shows that 76% of the "chronics" among the Berkeley street people respondents were men. It is unfortunate that further data about the latter are not available because it seems probable that there is a reasonably close resemblance between the 2 groups.

The TAS study clients were relatively young (53% were under 30 years of age), although not as young as the Berkeley street people. There were some differences in the proportions of men and women from one age bracket to another, but they were small. Similarly, while 60% of the clients were White there was no significant difference between Blacks and Whites with respect to the number of men and women.

There were important differences when marital status was examined, however. Of course, the proportion of clients who had never married was relatively high at the lower-age ranges; thus 85% of the clients under 20 years and 53% of those aged 20 to 25 had never married. On the other hand, about 40% of the clients aged 40 to 45 years and about 50% of those aged 50 to 54 were divorced or separated, quite high compared with the general population. Further, the comparison of marital status (ever vs never married) and sex was statistically significant ($p < .001$): men tended more often to remain single, while women tended more often to be married and still living with spouse or to report themselves as separated but not divorced. While not quite such a strong relationship was found between race and marital status, nonetheless, again on the basis of ever vs never married, the distribution was statistically significant ($p < .01$): 47% of the Whites reported that they had never married compared with 37% of the Blacks. While more Whites reported that they were divorced, more Blacks were still living with their spouse or were separated.

About 70% of the persons who completed the structured interview were in flight to some degree. Nonetheless, there were some limitations in their movements: 38% were born in the Middle Atlantic region and 26% in the South Atlantic; 42% reported that the city in which they lived the longest was in the Middle Atlantic region and for 23% it was in the South Atlantic; almost similar percentages were reported for where the client had lived before coming to Philadelphia. In general, therefore, the migrants tended to live and to move along the East Coast of the country in the same stream of migration that has been apparent for many years. In this they differ from the Berkeley street people.

With respect to flight status, there was a disproportionately large number of White males in the F3 category (chi square, $p < .001$). F1 clients were significantly younger than the F3 clients ($p = .05$). The data thus suggest that the TAS clients who completed the structured interviews may be categorized as (1) young Whites early in a possible "career of flight," (2) older White men well into a "career" of flight, and (3) Blacks of all ages who generally were not in flight and who used the TAS services to accomplish relatively well-conceived goals.

Clients were asked about the sources of income in the period immediately before they came to TAS. Table 6 shows the recent

TABLE 6.—*Recent Sources of Income of Travelers Aid Society Clients, by Flight Status, in Per Cent*[a]

| | NUMBER OF FLIGHTS | | | |
	1	2	3+	None
Employment	65	72	69	58
Spouse or parents	15	15	14	28
Other relatives or friends	12	6	6	7
Public assistance	4	4	6	9
Pension, savings, social security	14	16	13	9
Other	4	0	12	5
None	6	5	6	5

[a] Totals are more than 100% because of multiple responses.

TABLE 7.—*Sources of Income of Street People, by Race and Sex, in Per Cent*[a]

	Black Men (N=29)	White Men (181)	White Women (50)	Total (278)
Job	10.3	14.9	10.0	13.3
Savings	6.9	19.9	28.0	19.4
Unemployment insurance	0	3.3	0	2.5
Welfare	31.0	13.3	20.0	15.8
Food stamps	6.9	7.2	12.0	7.9
Social security	0	2.2	2.0	1.8
Parents or relatives	13.8	19.9	34.0	22.7
Husband, wife, girl- or boyfriend[b]	10.3	6.1	26.0	10.4
Friends	41.4	32.0	30.0	33.1
Panhandling	37.9	39.0	58.0	41.9
Drug dealing	37.9	20.3	16.0	20.8
Selling stolen property	13.8	1.7	0	2.9
Stealing	10.3	15.5	4.0	11.9

[a] Adapted from Baumohl and Miller (16, *p. 31*). The question put to respondents was: "Please check any of the following sources you have obtained money from in the last month." The percentages total more than 100 because most subjects checked more than one source of income.

[b] Few street people—4.4%—are married, although more (16.7%) have been through unsuccessful marriage relationships.

source of income by the number of flights. Employment was mentioned as the principal source of recent income. The entire distribution differs markedly from that of the Berkeley street people, as a comparison between Tables 6 and 7 shows. Table

7 also indicates that the Berkeley street people had hardly begun to make a place for themselves in the labor market. On the
whole, possibly because of their youth, they were more dependent on the charity and good graces of others in the larger community than the TAS clients seemed to have been. On the other
hand, the TAS clients may simply have been more agency-wise
and may have learned that it was more expedient to report that
one had previously been employed than that one had been on
public assistance or receiving support from friends in some
other city. At the very least, we see two patterns of social dependency in the two populations.

In the responses to a number of questions there were systematic differences between the nonflight and the F3 clients.
These differences will be referred to in terms of "flightness,"
and should have value in the identification and possible prediction of people in flight. In general, the greater the degree of
flightness, the less likely the client will have a permanent address or will use the address of a relative as a drop-box, and the
greater the number of towns or places the client reportedly
lived in during the past 5 years. This suggests that migration
accompanied by flight readily becomes a pattern of life. What is
further suggested is that such migrants become less and less
accessible through personal communications (e.g., the postal
service and the telephone); they are more likely to rely either
on direct conversation or on the mass media. In this respect,
they resemble the "mass man" often discussed in critiques of
modern organized society. We do not mean to imply that they
have lost all social ties, because they evidently have not, but
that their social connections may not be as "primary" as those of
more settled persons. Thus, among those clients who reported
that they had been married sometime during their lives, a
higher degree of flightness is associated with a reduced likelihood that the client was still living with his spouse. With the
greater flightness, also, it is less likely that relatives will be
solicited for support in a personal or financial crisis and more
likely that persons described as "friends" will be drawn on for
help. Because the flight pattern is so pervasive a part of life, one
may raise a question about the degree of intimacy that the term
"friend" connotes.

There were similar patterns in other crises besides financial.

In general, the higher the degree of flightness, the more likely they are to say that they are sick or ill at the time that they come to the TAS for assistance. Further, this is likely to be associated with reports of chronic ailments. Of considerable importance is the heavy use of alcoholic beverages. The greater the degree of flightness, the higher the probability that the client will report having been on a drinking spree or bout in the past year. Thus, 9% of the nonflight group, 10% of the F1, 22% of the F2 and 26% of the F3 clients reported drinking sprees.

There is supporting evidence for the conclusion that the F3 clients were Skid Row-like people: 33% said that they had lived in a Skid Row area at one time compared with 9% of the nonflight group, 12% of the F1 and 24% of the F2 clients. The conclusion is further supported by differences with respect to difficulties with police and the courts. Strikingly, about half of the F3 clients reported that they had some legal difficulties, and most of them were Skid Row-type offenses, such as vagrancy, panhandling, public drunkenness and the like. Also, the pattern is further evidenced in that, during the last 5 years, the higher the degree of flightness, the greater the likelihood of having been in a jail and the larger the number of jail or prison experiences.

Some of the TAS data suggest that while the F3 clients are most Skid Row-like in important characteristics, some of the other clients were also Skid Row-like. That is, flightness is an important variable, but there may be other variables that are relevant. A limited secondary analysis of the data lends some support to this idea. Clients were asked whether they had ever lived on Skid Row. (The term was not defined for the respondents during the course of the interview and it was assumed that "Skid Row" was a term that was widely understood and more or less standardized in its connotations.) Of the 214 Black men, 18% had some Skid Row experience, compared with 25% of the 341 White men. But the number of Blacks was too small to undertake further analyses, so that conclusions must be limited to the White men. Of these White men, 32% of those who had some Skid Row experience reported that they had been on a drinking spree during the past year, in comparison with 11% of those who had not lived on Skid Row. While spree drinking is not the only drinking pattern to be found in a Skid Row area, and not just alcoholics are to be found in such areas, spree drinking is common and spree drinkers seem to be among those who are most desperate and who turn most often to Skid Row-related social welfare agencies for assistance.

While we would expect the highly mobile people who come to TAS to be limited in their social (friendship) relationships as a consequence of their very mobility, the data suggest that those who had lived on Skid Row were relatively more isolated than those who had never lived on Skid Row. Of the former, 37% said that they had no friends, compared with 21% of the latter.[10] In conclusion, when the data are analyzed in terms of flightness and when they are considered in terms of the clients' having lived on Skid Row at some time in the past, there is reason to believe that men who come to TAS, especially White men, include Skid Row-like transients. The 19th Century–early 20th Century "drifter" pattern has possibly continued into the present as evidenced by some of the clients of private agencies such as TAS, as well as in the lifestyle of the young street people of the last decade.

Finally, are there any predictors suggested by the data? Only 14% of the nonflight clients said that they had ever run away from home, compared with 23, 31 and 39% of the F1, F2 and F3 clients. Further, systematic differences with respect to age of first running away were apparent by the beginning of the 10th year of age to the end of the 18th year. This suggests the need to work with truant children and their families as soon as possible after the first truancy, to "head off" tendencies that may eventually lead to increasingly Skid Row-like behavior.

Demographically and sociologically, there seems to be a continuum of characteristics of those we have called "the wanderers." The street people are the youngest, TAS clients somewhere in the middle, and the Skid Row population the oldest. A similar pattern is found in terms of access to public assistance funds: street people with the least, TAS clients in the middle, and the Skid Row population with the greatest. Finally, the street people come from the lowest social-class backgrounds, at about the level of Skid Row people, with TAS clients a bit more

---

[10] For an extended discussion of friends and friendship among Skid Row men, see Rooney (168).

"advantaged" in terms of social origins. Is there a pattern here of what might be called the "pre-pre-Skid Row population," the "pre-Skid Row population," and the residents of Skid Row? All three groups are part of what Michael Harrington (80) called "the invisible poor." As such, they have been of peripheral concern to welfare and social service agencies, and an extension of comprehensive services to these populations is in order.

It is time to recognize that in classic terminology those whom we call "wanderers" were called "vagrants." Not all vagrants are found in stereotyped Skid Row neighborhoods. Street people and people in flight are special populations which are outside the usual purview of the ordinary citizen, as well as most local authorities and agencies. Sometimes this is because they belong somewhere else and, therefore, are someone else's responsibility, but it is often just because they move frequently and so erratically that they fall through the social welfare network. Rather than high residential mobility within a restricted locality, which is typical of the Skid Row neighborhood, young street people and people in flight are characterized by high mobility on a much larger geographic scale (16, 125). Just as the Skid Row area population is not solely a population with alcohol problems, so with street people and those in flight. It seems likely that out of the most "flighty" will come persons who ultimately "perch" more or less permanently in Skid Row areas or who will be found among the Skid Row-like residents of the poor sections of the big cities when, and if, Skid Row areas themselves "disappear."

Chapter 9

Finding Skid Row-like People[1]

IF WE ARE INTERESTED in the prevention of Skid Row, the problem is how to prevent people from making the transition to Skid Row status from the ranks of the more amorphous destitute residents of the slums. It is especially relevant to interrupt the transformation of the "neighborhood drunk" into the "Skid Row bum." Spradley aptly describes elements of this process, observing the crucial importance of the police and the minor judiciary in the process of transformation (193, *ch. 5, 6, 7*). Our analysis of this process goes well beyond Spradley's.

The transition begins when the "neighborhood drunk" exhausts his "social credit" (his credibility, his ability to get favors done for him) with his relatives and old neighborhood friends (23, *pp. 134, 187, 224*). He may continue to live in his old neighborhood, increasingly relying on kin and friends as resources, but there may come a time when the critical tie is gone (the mother or sister dies, the sustaining employer quits, or the children have "had it"). At that time, given other circumstances such as a jail term or two, he may move out of the old neighborhood into the high density center-city Skid Row locality. The transition, while it has its adjustment and learning problems, is relatively far along before the move takes place. If the home neighborhood is already poor and physically deteriorated, however, he may continue to live there. He may even find some

[1] With the assistance of James Cassidy, Thomas Fedewa, Edwin H. Folk, Zenzo Nhari, and W. Donald Porter. William Hood was a junior author of the urban neighborhood casework section; that work was undertaken under National Institute of Mental Health grant MH 15081, "A Study of the Prevention of Skid Row," and appreciation is expressed to NIMH. We also express our appreciation to Irving Shandler, Howard Sheppard, and Gerald Bouch. The suburban investigation was supported by a contract from the Commissioners of "William Penn" County. We thank the administrators of William Penn County's Mental Health, Mental Retardation, and Alcoholism programs and the directors and staff of the various County agencies who graciously made their files available once matters of confidentiality and their staff limitations were resolved. Responsibility for the data and their interpretation in both projects rests with the authors.

degree of protection and tolerance from the police—a man tends to be treated differently in the neighborhood if he is perceived as an old-timer who "belongs" rather than as a "Skid Row bum." These people, who have characteristics strikingly similar to those of Skid Row neighborhood residents, although they continue to live elsewhere in the slums, are referred to in the present discussion as "Skid Row-like."

One implication of Part III is that in a metropolis that has had an increasingly complex system of both publicly and privately financed social welfare institutions for well over a century, Skid Row-like people have somehow not been reached. They have fallen through the interstices in the social service institutional network. If a program of Skid Row prevention is to be meaningful, it must somehow find them and assist them to develop their own alternatives.

The present chapter discusses several approaches directed to finding Skid Row-like people in their home neighborhoods. If Skid Row were to expand, the new residents would come from among those persons with a Skid Row-like lifestyle. The projects to be discussed assume that the more people remain "anchored" in their home neighborhoods with whatever friendship and family ties there yet remain, the less likely are they to drift into pariah status as participants of the Skid Row community.

The Urban Neighborhood

The caseworker who conducted this project had been involved in a 3-year study of alternative rehabilitation procedures with Skid Row men reported previously (23, *ch. 12*). His work was viewed as a "curbstone social service," or as "aggressive casework"; under the latter term may be subsumed the concepts of intensive casework and neighborhood case-finding. This is an active style of social service, designed to alter the caseworker's job from "waiting behind the desk until the client comes in" to seeking out the client in his own territory and largely on the client's own terms.

The project was conducted in Anglia, a section of Philadelphia described elsewhere in this monograph. The model that was followed was that of the itinerant salesman, the agent "selling" social welfare services. Initially there were no firm leads except the knowledge that Anglia had a high concentration of low-income residents in low-rent rooming houses and furnished one-room apartments, and that long association with Skid Row men as well as reports from other members of the staff of the Diagnostic and Rehabilitation Center indicated the appropriateness of the area. As in any selling, there were "hits" along with the misses, and the favorable interviews were used to develop a chain of additional interviews and relationships. However, social welfare services are not concrete products for many people, and they are likely to become apprehensive: "What's he really here for? Is he really a building inspector or a detective or a police 'stake-out' man, or what?" It was hard to believe that someone representing that he was from a social welfare agency would come into the neighborhood and begin talking with people "on the street" about alcohol and alcohol-related problems directly rather than obliquely.

Rather than simply going from door to door, the caseworker interviewed owners or managers of properties. Efforts were made to elicit problems that the owners or managers or their tenants faced, advice was offered on how to solve these problems more effectively, and an offer was made to talk with the tenants directly. Some of the landlords and landladies themselves had alcohol problems.

One of the most important breakthroughs came after a canvassing interview with an owner; it seems that he was already taking referrals from a State mental hospital which placed patients in the neighborhood and provided ongoing assistance and guidance through a local representative. It was an easy transition for him from the specific casework of the hospital to the alcohol-problem casefinding activities of the project. Once this locally well-known landlord accepted the caseworker, there was no further difficulty with introductions and further referrals to other landlords, managers and tenants. The relationships between the project caseworker and the representatives of the State mental hospital were friendly, possibly another reason why some doors were opened in the neighborhood. Several former clients of the Diagnostic and Rehabilitation Center now lived in the neighborhood and made introductions which further bolstered the acceptability of the project. When no other leads were available, the residents of the locality were approached directly and efforts were made to strike up a conversation which might ultimately lead to an interview.

Over a 3-month period, interviews were conducted with landlords, rooming-house operators, tenants, members of several bottle gangs, and some relatively isolated and homeless men. Whenever there was an interview, or even an introduction, an explanation was given of what the project was about, and a stamped addressed card and the Philadelphia Health and Welfare Council's "Where to Turn" booklet were handed out. The booklet has information on agencies that can be of assistance to people with problems such as blindness, alcoholism and tuberculosis, as well as on public assistance. A directory of the Alcoholics Anonymous groups in Philadelphia was also left if it seemed appropriate.

While the objective was to reach persons with alcohol problems, the approach in the neighborhood was broad. If some other social welfare problem came out during the interview, as it often did, then appropriate advice was given and there was casework follow-through to the degree that seemed justified in light of the limited resources and the major thrust of the project. Had the project continued for a longer period, a substantial caseload would have developed.

The caseworker fully or partly completed interviews with 62 tenants. He gave direct social service to at least 44. The services fell into four categories: information, money management, referral, and counseling.

Tenants were given information on eligibility for public assistance, social security, veterans' benefits, and the availability of part-time jobs. Several older homeowners were told about the Tax Assistance Act which allows rebates on property taxes to elderly low-income homeowners. Information was also provided on such problems as where to go for lower prices on food, clothing and prescription drugs, and for legal advice.

Arrangements were made for three alcoholics to turn their checks over to someone whom they could trust, and that person doled out the money on a daily or weekly basis. Such a system protects a person from drinking up all his money within several days or from having it stolen.

Referrals were made to Medical Assistance (Department of Public Assistance), hospitals and alcohol detoxication centers.

Counseling took place with alcoholics (both before and after detoxication) and with others. A major objective was to encourage tenants to get out of their rooms and into the immediate neighborhood more often and meet other residents of the area. This frequently involved getting other people in the neighborhood to understand how important it was to take a friendly encouraging stance with residents who had a tendency to become withdrawn and isolated.

The caseworker was able to identify an astounding array of needs of Anglia residents. A large number needed to be driven to hospitals, and within the limits of the project's resources this was done. But in addition there is a variety of direct services which should be provided. Many people do not know how to perform a number of elementary tasks which are essential to decent daily living: how to shop for food, clothing and other needs, how to light an oven and cook, how to clean a room and an apartment, to wash clothing, to hang curtains. Neighborhood representatives of the state mental hospital taught many of their former patients how to do these things, and went shopping with them several times. But the lack of these skills is a disability common to many long-term flophouse and mission residents and to many alcoholic men whose mothers have died or whose wives have evicted them. There are many persons who do not know where to go for some needed social services; there are probably more who do know where to go but who do not follow through. It may be because of fear of leaving the neighborhood, of not knowing how to get there, of having had a bad experience with a particular agency, the fear that they may be rebuffed, or the presence of a physical disability, including brain damage, the confusion of alcoholism or other drug abuse, or emotional disorders.

Institutional casework too often ignores or largely overlooks group processes in the neighborhoods where the clients live. Clients from neighborhoods such as those in Anglia are often simply told to change their bad environments, move to a "nice" neighborhood, and to go to Alcoholics Anonymous or some other institutional program. Most such people will not readily uproot themselves. If they do, they are likely to find that they are not at all accepted in the new neighborhood or in the new program.

It takes time to win the confidence of enough people on a particular block or in a neighborhood to see substantial results. During the third month, a cumulative effect began to be evident, particularly where there was a great deal of interaction and communication on the block between members of bottle gangs. In fact, since a good deal of the communication is by word of mouth, if the streetworker made contacts through bottle gangs, his ability to find potential clients for the services he could offer was enhanced.

The following two cases illustrate the work of the casefinder. One client was identified through his landlord, the other through his membership in a bottle gang. Both clients came to use the Center's services after considerable encouragement from the streetworker.

Charles and John

Charles was a former Skid Row resident living in Anglia, with a pattern of part-time use of the residential Skid Row. (This back-and-forth residential pattern is characteristic of what might be called the "Skid Row élite": those spree drinkers who manage to live off the Row until they drink up most of their money and then have to live in very cheap accommodations until their money is completely gone and they stop drinking.) Charles claimed to be a machinist by trade, but his last employment at the time of the interview had been as a muzzler and spot-job man on contract from a local employment agency. During his employment at those jobs he lived on Skid Row and used mission facilities. Charles suffered from conditions characteristic of Skid Row men: an ulcer, a hernia, "bad nerves" and alcohol misuse, and he was receiving welfare checks. Nine days after the first interview, Charles walked into the Center. He reported that he was broke and had spent the last 3 nights at a mission; he also had been drinking heavily. Charles began to use the Center's services and by the time the project ended had found a watchman's job and had not had a drink for 3 months.

John was a member of a bottle gang whose beverage of choice was beer. Occasionally wine was shared but, since the nearest State Liquor Store was some distance away from the gang's usual location, beer drinking was typical for this group (although atypical for Skid Row men). This particular group also included women. These, then, were not Skid Row people but, rather, members of the lower working class.

But John had had some Skid Row experience. He had been a tractor-trailer driver for 24 years and drank heavily during that time. He had never married and for some unknown reason (probably alcohol addiction) became a resident of Skid Row. He had used Center services after a year's Skid Row residence, began to receive public assistance, took a muzzling job to make additional money, and moved off the Row. His drinking pattern was that of a bender every few days.

After a month in which the streetworker spent part of every day with this bottle gang, John asked the worker to get him into Saul Clinic (a 5-day detoxication facility). John entered the Clinic, was discharged, and by the time the project ended had been abstinent for a month and had ended his association with the bottle gang.

Charles was clearly a part-time resident of Skid Row. His drinking pattern, intermittent use of missions, physical ailments and recent employment record were characteristic of Skid Row men. John was a one-time resident of the Row. He had moved into what might be called an incipient Skid Row in Anglia, where he participated in a bottle gang, was a binge drinker, marginally employed, and showed other characteristics associated with Skid Row men. Only aggressive neighborhood case-finding could turn up people like Charles and John, and their cases illustrate that efforts at prevention of Skid Row must take into account the presence of Skid Row-like people throughout the metropolitan area.

We must also understand that what might be called "Skid-rowitis" can be found to a greater or lesser degree in everyone. Skid Row has typically been dealt with as a place, but this is a limitation in our vision. Skid Row or "Skidrowism" is more correctly seen as a human condition. For anyone there can be some event or behavior pattern that will cause a rupture in the web of relationships which holds people together—some behavior which will be unacceptable to family and friends and produce in them a revulsion. In these terms, then, everyone is to a greater or lesser degree susceptible to Skidrowitis, to "ending up on Skid Row." In John's case he had hit the residential Skid Row and had managed to find his way off. Charles was a part-time Row resident. But had these men never been residents of Skid Row, they would still have been Skid Row-like men, though unidentified as such and invisible to scholars and social workers.

This short project suggested, first, that a great many people do not get or benefit from needed social welfare service and they are unlikely to do so without active counseling at the neighborhood level. Second, that an important element in solving social problems is likely to be an active intervention at the local neighborhood level through both individual and group processes. Solutions to problems, including alcoholism, can and must be found at the neighborhood level. And lastly, any successful, massive assault on the problem of alcoholism (and probably other kinds of chemical addiction) will probably require this approach as an essential ingredient. This brief exploration of casefinding directed at Skid Row-like people in a low-income residential section of Philadelphia has given support to the proposition that "on the street" casework is feasible. In addition, it has demonstrated that, while we can conceptualize differences between Skid Row-like people and other poor people in our metropolitan cities, the differences are not only small when we make a comparison of their characteristics, but almost impossible to separate in practice in neighborhood social work. There are interstices in the city in which there are sores, some potential, some incipient, and some festering. These interstices are rarely investigated until the sores break out into a rash and then the police or the morgue are as likely to be involved as the social welfare agencies.

This project started with a plan to find Skid Row-like people with alcohol problems, but it developed into a procedure for finding people who were interstitial to the welfare agencies of the metropolis. Based on this experience we propose a program of aggressive preventive social work to relieve the police and other agencies of some of their social welfare burden. The social workers would have a thorough knowledge of the resources that are available in the metropolis; their task would be to identify potential personal and social problems before they become acute and to assist people in finding ways to rectify their situation. The neighborhood casework agency, being very close to the residents, their problems and their perceptions of the situation, would be a service agency directing people to where they can get help and, at the same time, be engaged in advocacy for them when that seemed indicated. When a husband is drunk and threatens to kill his wife, it may be that the best that can be done at the moment is for her to call the police, but the neighborhood caseworker could step into the situation relatively easily and, being locally known and trusted, offer a less damaging immediate solution as well as a sounder long-run solution.

A Suburban County

The curbstone casework approach proceeded from the view that Skid Row-like people may be found in the poor sections of the central cities. There are large parts of the "inner ring" of the suburbs around these central cities that are similar to sections within them in appearance, population density, socioeconomic condition, and ethnic composition. The differences between the "inner suburbs" and the central cities are really not very great. There are impoverished suburbs as well as wealthy ones, crowded high-density as well as dispersed low-density suburbs, working- and upper-class districts, and predominantly WASP–Italian–Jewish–Irish–Black sections outside the city limits of Philadelphia just as there are within them. In response to suggestions by local police, judiciary, social workers, and personnel of alcoholism treatment agencies that there are "Skid Row people" in a suburb, we looked for the presence of Skid Row-like people in suburban William Penn County (pseudonym).[2]

William Penn County has a land area of about 200 square miles with a 1970 census population of 600,000 persons at a density of a little over 3000 persons per square mile. About 95% of the residents were living in urban areas. In 1970, the county had a civilian labor force of about 250,000 with a median family income of almost $14,000, but there were Census tracts in which the residents had median incomes of less than $2000.

Furthermore, the term "suburban" tends to obscure the fact that in 1974 William Penn County reported about 3700 Part I

---

[2] By advance agreement with County authorities all names of places and organizations are pseudonyms.

offenses[3] per 100,000 population, 9th highest of all the counties in the state. The county also reported about 3400 Part II offenses per 100,000 population, 5th highest in the state.

It is not uncommon for Skid Row-like people to be charged with "disorderly conduct" rather than with drunkenness or vagrancy. Law enforcement agencies in William Penn County reported 663 arrests per 100,000 population for this composite offense category in comparison with 518 per 100,000 in nearby Jefferson County (pseudonym) and about 247 per 100,000 in Philadelphia. However, special tabulations for 1973 and 1974 provided by the State Police strongly suggest that a number of non-Skid Row-like people are probably included and that the data cannot be used as a measure of the size of the county's Skid Row-like population. For example, one well-to-do township had about the same rate of disorderly conduct charges each year as that reported for working-class Logan Borough (pseudonym), a minor civil division that will be given further attention below. In any case, the differences in arrest categories between counties may be a result only of differences in procedures for entering charges.

William Penn County's arrest rate for drunkenness and vagrancy was 53.1 per 100,000 population, in comparison with 480 per 100,000 in Jefferson County and 1802.6 in Philadelphia. This suggests that there are probably some Skid Row-like persons in William Penn County, although not a large number. Insofar as the presence of Skid Row-like persons may be considered a community problem by the citizens of the county, it is quite small in comparison with Philadelphia. Here again the differences reflect, in part, procedural differences between counties.

We examined where Skid Row-like institutions and persons were likely to be found rather than identifying the characteristics of owner-operators, users, or persons receiving counseling.

[3] Part I offenses include criminal homicide, forcible rape, robbery, assaults, burglary, larceny-theft, and motor vehicle theft. Part II offenses include minor assaults, arson, forgery and counterfeiting, fraud, embezzlement, stolen property offenses, vandalism, weapons offenses, prostitution and commercialized vice, sex offenses, narcotic drug law violations, drunkenness, disorderly conduct, vagrancy, curfew law violations, juvenile running away, and violations of local ordinances.

We looked primarily at areas of relatively high population density, with special attention to sections of the county analogous to the central business district (CBD) of Philadelphia. Interest was focused especially on older areas which largely developed by accretion in, around and along the intersections of major transportation routes. Frequently these areas are characterized by commercial strip-zoning. Investigators tried to find the following in association with each other: (1) inexpensive rooming houses, hotels, bar-hotels; (2) cheap bars; (3) missions giving food or lodging either free or at a nominal cost; (4) blood banks; (5) day-labor offices; (6) cheap restaurants (differentiated from fast-food shops); (7) bottle-gang locations; and (8) apparently abandoned structures in slum residential areas or blighted commercial or industrial areas.

A variety of procedures was used in locating Skid Row-like institutions. Local newspapers were examined to pinpoint any concentrations of rooming houses, but the amount of advertising of such housing was negligible. We interviewed a number of knowledgeable informants: police officials of various municipalities, alcoholism treatment agency executives and counselors (who were very helpful), a Black minister–social worker, William Penn County court personnel, and a member of the planning staff in the County Department of Public Assistance. We searched the files of the William Penn County *Daily News* for news of the Pennsport Rescue Mission. Finally, as a check against possible race-blindness by the principal investigator, a Black journalist and alcoholism counselor was hired to conduct an independent examination of the Black residential sections of Logan Borough and Pennsport with an eye to Skid Row institutions and Skid Row-like persons.

The approach yielded suggestive but not conclusive data. There were almost no licensed rooming houses except in the City of Pennsport. Officials in East Girard Township were vaguely aware that there were rooms to rent in the private homes of elderly residents in the area close to the mass transportation terminal in the township, but the number of roomers in any one house was believed to be small and there is no rooming-house district in the township. Information was also gathered while reading clinic case records, and although this turned out to be the best single source of information, the rooming houses are so scattered that it is clear that this criterion alone is not useful for the location of Skid Row-like people in the county. However, it is of no small interest that the Pennsport YMCA is analogous to a Skid Row hotel in that it provides housing for Skid Row-like people and for those for whom a Skid Row-like lifestyle is highly probable in the future.

A number of bar-hotels are located in the predominantly working-class section of the county. Several are readily identifiable as Skid Row-like in their appearance and apparent clientele. These and several others were also on the list of housing used by Skid Row-like and future Skid Row-like persons derived from clinic records. Bar-hotel Skid Row-like housing is located both in the Borough of Logan, a colonial municipality which was long ago "drowned" by the expanding Philadelphia metropolitan complex, and in the City of Pennsport. Most of the bar-hotels, however, seem not to be Skid Row housing. One explanation is that some owners obtained a hotel license so that they could be open on Sundays. In addition, because some of the industries in Pennsport and its industrial satellite suburbs fluctuate widely in their labor force requirements, there is a need for a housing supply that can rapidly expand and contract, and the bar-hotels in the working-class sections of the county supply it.

There has been only one Skid Row mission in the county in recent years. The Pennsport Rescue Mission was first opened in 1927 in the heart of Pennsport, near the CBD. Two years later a local judge facilitated purchase of an abandoned boiler factory building about a block away. From the beginning, the Mission staff prided themselves on being "self-supporting." They engaged in the kind of salvage business which has been typical of Skid Row rescue missions for many years. Before World War II the Pennsport Rescue Mission housed from 90 to 103 men every night with every bed used. Things apparently remained unchanged for a time after the War, for in 1952 they were reported to have 90 beds available. For those who could afford it in that year, the cost of a bed was 50 cents a night, while for those who could not, the beds were free. There seems to have been a 3-day limit for those who came to the Mission but did not enter its work program. The work program in 1952 employed 32 men who were paid a nominal salary: "We do not keep loafers; if a man is able, he must work for his keep."[4] By 1965 capacity was down to 45 men and, with increasing inflation, the number of residents dropped to about 18 persons. Since the store which sold salvaged household goods could not entirely finance the Mission, when the bottom dropped out of the cardboard market in the mid-1970s there simply was not enough money to support the Mission and it closed in the summer of 1975.

The presence of the Mission is consistent with the conclusion reached by direct observation that there has been a longstanding mini-Skid Row in Pennsport. Observation of Skid Row-like men using a nearby bar-hotel leaves no doubt about its location. But visits to the area suggest that this mini-Skid Row is declining and probably has been declining for some time, just as larger East Coast and Midwest Skid Row areas have been declining. Thus, there had been a cheap restaurant as well as a cheap pool hall in the Pennsport mini-Skid Row, but by the time the research was done in 1975 both had closed. Cheap restaurants and pool halls, of course, are not unique to Skid Rows; the "Skidrowness" of urban areas shades off into just plain lower-class poverty and recreational usages.

Since the Salvation Army often provides services to Skid Row-like people, locations of its facilities were examined. The Pennsport facility had recently moved to a new building just outside the city and, while within walking distance of the Pennsport mini-Skid Row, was not convenient to it; the facility clearly served a different clientele. There is a second Salvation Army facility located in the Borough of Logan, however, which is just up the street from the Skid Row-like bar-hotel and within easy walking distance of the cheap bars of Logan. From time to time this facility has Skid Row-like people coming in; they are referred almost immediately to the Philadelphia Salvation Army complex for housing and whatever care may be needed because the Logan unit cannot provide for them.

The balance of the criteria listed above proved relatively useless for the task. A blood bank formerly located on the edge of the Pennsport Central Business District had closed by 1975; no other blood bank was found in the county. There was at least

---

[4] Undated memorandum, ca. 1952, in the files of the William Penn County *Daily News*; other data from newsclippings in the same file.

one day-labor office on the edge of the Pennsport CBD but its help-wanted signs, general appearance and location suggest that it does not recruit Skid Row-like people but a higher class of personnel. With the exception that has already been mentioned, cheap restaurants that clearly served a Skid Row-like population were not readily apparent even in Pennsport; it seems probable that they have been replaced by the ubiquitous fast-food shops or by the bar-hotels. The concentration of Skid Row-like people is not sufficiently large to make a cheap restaurant profitable. With our earlier discussion of Black Skid Rows in mind, we expected to find such facilities in the pervasive slum in which most of the Black residents of Pennsport live and in the racially segregated area of Logan Borough, but here too the cheap eating facilities tended to be fast-food shops and bar-hotels.

Considerable effort was expended in the early stages of the investigation to find bottle gangs. Signs of them were clearly evident along several streets in the slums of Pennsport and there were reports of some bottle-gang activity at the mass transportation terminal located in East Girard Township. But elsewhere in the county there are so many idle pieces of land such as creek bottoms, railroad sidings and underdeveloped weed-grown parcels that this criterion was not useful.

Finally, the slum of Pennsport is pervasive—one could say that large sections of the "inner city" are rotting away. Interviews and observations by our Black journalist–alcoholism counselor confirmed that Skid Row-like Black people were living in the most blighted and abandoned sections. It was not a useful criterion elsewhere in the county.

The search for where Skid Row-like persons live in William Penn County involved the examination of the case records of three alcoholism treatment and counseling centers. Since none of the agencies is very old, and the files are not voluminous, it was possible to examine the entire files of all three centers. The case records of the two major County Medical Health and Mental Retardation Centers were also examined, but these were much larger and sampling procedures were used.

The following categories were used in analyzing the case records:[5]

[5] The categorization of the case records was done by 3 persons, including

A. Persons clearly not Skid Row-like. Although they have a drinking problem, these people seem to have a relatively firm set of social roots, a home and relative job stability. If a Skid Row-like lifestyle lies in the future it is not readily predictable from the present record.

B. Persons for whom a Skid Row-like lifestyle seems likely in the not too distant future, although they are not yet Skid Row-like. (In this discussion they are referred to as "future Skid Row-like.") They have an alcohol problem that is serious, a spree-drinking pattern, considerable personal and social instability, are in relatively low-status occupations if employed at all, and they may have been in jail several times for petty (alcohol-related) offenses or for nonsupport. Nonetheless, they continue to be rooted in family and community. If the present pattern continues, a Skid Row-like lifestyle seems to be a real likelihood in perhaps 5 or 10 years.

C. Persons who are Skid Row-like in their characteristics or lifestyle. These persons are now socially, occupationally and economically marginal and apparently rapidly moving toward a Skid Row-like lifestyle or have already developed such a lifestyle. They are living in an impoverished condition (whether this is due to their "alcoholism" or not) which is usually associated with heavy alcohol consumption. Frequently, they wander around and have been in and out of jail on drunk and disorderly conduct charges. They may be expected to be employed from time to time in temporary low-status jobs, if at all employed, and they are frequently underemployed (under "normal" economic conditions). It is not uncommon for the men to have been picked up and sent to jail on "nonsupport" charges. Many have never married.

Of the 2351 cases examined at the alcoholism treatment centers, 80% were clearly neither Skid Row-like nor was there much evidence to suggest that they would develop a Skid Row-like lifestyle in the near future (Table 8). Fifteen per cent had

---

the senior author, who was project director. A preliminary set of about 15 cases was read and categorized by each of the coders. These were then discussed until differences of interpretation were clarified and general agreement on the case assignment was achieved. The coders then did a series of about 25 or 30 additional cases with the project director nearby to discuss marginal or difficult decisions. A high degree of consensus was secured among the coders as a result of this discussion as well as the relatively easy and friendly communication among the persons involved in the coding process. To categorize the data, the coders read as much of the case file as they considered necessary. The address of the person whose case file was being examined was then recorded under the proper category: not Skid Row, future Skid Row-like, and clearly Skid Row-like. After each address was located in its appropriate census tract and minor civil division, the address list was destroyed to break the link between the data and the case report and to restore the confidentiality of the records.

characteristics which suggested that, if they persisted in the
patterns of behavior that they now evidenced, there was a high
probability of their developing a Skid Row-like lifestyle. (That
the percentage was so high, frankly, came as a surprise to the
coding staff.) It is assumed as a practical matter that the treatment centers will be effective in counseling and treatment with
some of these people, so that the proportion who will actually
come out of the "other end of the pipeline" will probably be
below 15%. Finally, 5% were categorized as having a Skid
Row-like lifestyle at the time that they came to the agencies.[6]

There is some evidence that the numbers of Skid Row-like
people we have identified underestimate the actual or potential
Skid Row-like population. For example, we expect that there
are unidentified probable Skid Row-like Pennsport residents
who did not come into the Pennsport Center for one reason or

TABLE 8.—*Distribution of Patients in William Penn County
Alcoholism Treatment Centers, in Per Cent*

	Not Skid Row-like (N=1890)	Future Skid Row (N=343)	Skid Row-like (N=118)	Totals N	%
Cambridge	4.0	2.9	5.1	92	3.9
Logan–East Girard	15.8	21.0	24.6	399	16.9
Pennsport	80.2	76.1	70.3	1860	79.2
% of Total	*80.4*	*14.6*	*5.0*		

[6] There are several important limitations to the data. First, they were secured from the records of essentially voluntary agencies, that is, while there
were a small number of police and court referrals, almost all of the persons
who came to these agencies did so without pressure from law enforcement
agencies, although they may have been under considerable pressure from family, kinspeople, or friends. There were an indeterminate number of persons
who did not come to the treatment agencies. It seems likely that the largest
number of these "hidden alcoholics" are those who are not Skid Row-like nor
are they future Skid Row-like people for, in general, the more desperate the
person, the more likely that person will seek assistance to handle the sheer
need for physical survival. There is no ready solution to this limitation and the
data must be interpreted as minimal, with probably increasing conjunction between the case record statistics and the prevalence statistics as one moves
from the non-Skid Row-like alcoholic to the future Skid Row-like to the Skid
Row-like alcoholic.

another. We suspect that they outnumber the Pennsport Center cases who were transient or were actually Philadelphia residents at the time they entered the caseloads.

Pennsport is the location of about two-fifths of the Skid Row-like persons and about one-third of the future Skid Row-like persons identified through alcoholism clinic records. That Pennsport should have a number of these kinds of residents was expected, but the proportion of the total is a surprise. Analyzing the data by census tract (not presented here) showed that most of the people came either from the Pennsport mini-Skid Row or from the slums inhabited primarily by Pennsport's Black citizens.

The data support the expectation that East Girard Township is also of some importance as a location of Skid Row-like people. About 6% of the Skid Row-like persons and 11% of the future Skid Row-like persons came from the township. Logan Borough, with 4% of the Skid Row-like persons and 4% of the future Skid Row-like persons, is worthy of mention, but is relatively unimportant in comparison with Pennsport and East Girard Township. Finally, it should be noted that 7% of the Skid Row-like persons had no permanent address. To call them county residents in the traditional sense of a settled abode is a misnomer, but nonetheless they do constitute a part of the Skid Row-like population of the county and demonstrate that stereotyped Skid Row people in the sense of "drifters" do live there.

A considerable literature about the characteristics of Skid Row people suggests that an important fraction of Skid Row residents may drink, and occasionally drink heavily, but they cannot be properly called "alcoholics." Rather they manifest a number of other salient characteristics. With that in mind, we also examined the case records of the two major Mental Health and Mental Retardation (MHMR) agencies in the county.[7] Essen-

---

[7] The files of the Logan–East Girard Mental Health and Mental Retardation Center and the Pennsport Center were divided into adults and juveniles and active–open and closed. The Logan–East Girard adult files were also divided into those who were being provided with aftercare, having been a mental hospital patient and now on some kind of community–home residence plan, and those who were simply in counseling and treatment at the Center itself. The largest single category was the adult closed file: a 20% sample was taken of that file. The entire case record was reviewed in the remaining files. A 25% sample was taken of the entire Pennsport file.

tially, the categories were similar to those used for the alcoholism treatment center case records with one major alteration: the case was first classified as to whether there was good reason to believe that a person's lifestyle was involved with alcohol, i.e., whether there was mention of a pattern of drunkenness or evidence that drunkenness had become a part of the lifestyle. We also looked for evidence of apparent regular use of alcohol that was disruptive of familial relationships and occupational activities, and whether the use of alcohol could be considered one of the presenting symptoms of the mental health problem as it came to the agency. The two major categories thereby established, "alcohol involved" and "nonalcohol involved," were each then further categorized as clearly not Skid Row-like, likely to become Skid Row-like in the future, or Skid Row-like. Thus, there were six final categories instead of three.

About 13% of the Logan–East Girard and about 8% of the Pennsport MHMR patients were classified as alcoholics. With respect to the question of Skid Row-like characteristics, over 80% of the Logan–East Girard patients and over 96% of the Pennsport patients did not have Skid Row-like characteristics; the case records yielded 1% or fewer persons who were Skid Row-like. The most notable finding seems to be that while only about 3% of the Pennsport patients were considered to be future Skid Row-like persons, about 18% of the Logan–East Girard patients were so rated.

Considering the data from both sets of case records, and recognizing that there is some overlap between them, we conclude that there are probably only a small number of Skid Row-like people in William Penn County. Perhaps what is more important from the point of view of the prevention of the Skid Row-like condition is that there are also a number of persons who seem to be headed for a Skid Row-like lifestyle in the next 5 to 10 years.

The findings suggest that Skid Row-like people would be most likely found in three locations in William Penn County and in each case the configuration is quite different. In East Girard Township one might expect to find Skid Row-like people who are merely "Philadelphia's bums" who have moved out to the township. However, the local police report that there is a bottle gang of apparently local residents who gather every day, as well as occasional persons who come into the terminal area from Philadelphia. The local residents apparently live in older homes and rented rooms not very far away. In Logan Borough, there are a Skid Row-like bar-hotel and several cheap bars within a radius of several blocks. In addition, there is a Salvation Army facility which, while it does not house Skid Row-like people, does make referrals to Philadelphia. Thus, there is reason to believe that there are Skid Row-like residents of the borough although the concentration of them is not high. This is in sharp contrast to the stereotype of a Skid Row locality more or less concentrated along a street, although a careful look at Chicago's West Madison Street, or Detroit's Michigan Avenue–West Side, or Philadelphia's Ninth and Vine Street section indicates that Skid Row-like usages are mixed with other kinds of land use and the stereotype of continuous occupancy of the strip is actually a consequence of a relatively high visibility of Skid Row-like men along the sidewalk rather than solid occupancy of Skid Row institutions. That is, the density of Skid Row-like people was relatively high in the big cities before urban redevelopment cleared the land, while in the suburbs it is low: Skid Row in the suburbs is not residential but consists of a number of people with near-Skid Row characteristics.

Finally, in Pennsport, there are several sections close to the downtown area. There is the declining residual mini-Skid Row complex that has been used in the past primarily by Whites. A few blocks away, there is a large slum primarily inhabited by Blacks, with some White and Puerto Rican residents who have Skid Row-like characteristics but whose lives are embedded in the slum and who are, therefore, not easily visible.

It almost seems that we have seen all this before. Despite historical and political differences, the Skid Row-like population and living conditions of Anglia and Pennsport are similar. There are sections of Philadelphia which are similar in many respects to East Girard Township. So, too, there are sections of Philadelphia which are similar in population composition to Logan Borough. The political boundaries of city and county overemphasize the central-city–suburban dichotomy: their essential similarities tend to be obscured. The social conditions that lead to the Skid Row-like lifestyle are present in the old "inner ring" suburbs, as well as in the central cities.

CONCLUSION

This monograph presents a concept of Skid Row as a human condition and not just as a residential location. We have attempted to point out the potential in almost all persons of developing a Skid Row lifestyle, given certain conditions of homelessness, powerlessness, poverty, addiction, alienation.

With this orientation, we have discussed two approaches to identifying Skid Row-like and future Skid Row-like persons who may never have had any identification with the residential Skid Row. One approach sends the urban social caseworker into the streets of a neighborhood to find and identify all who need services, and to offer them, especially to Skid Row-like citizens. It is likely that Skid Row-eligible people may be found throughout the city, but we suspect that they are more likely to be found in areas in which the population is working-class or lower-class, White or Black. The experiences of our caseworker suggest that there is some substantial number of people who may well be missed by social scientists, policy makers and social workers who are concerned with Skid Row.

The second approach involves an investigation of suburban areas from two perspectives: Skid Row institutions and the identification of Skid Row-like and future Skid Row-like persons. Since suburban areas are much less dense than city neighborhoods, the aggressive case-finding method will have much less chance of success in the suburbs than in the cities, and our response was to examine records of alcoholism and mental health agencies to identify Skid Row-like populations. We also used documents to identify Skid Row institutions in the suburbs and interviewed supposedly knowledgeable informants.

As in any new procedure, the results were variable. But we believe that we have demonstrated our point. Scholars and policy makers who focus on the center-city residential Skid Row miss a substantial part of the problem. Clearly, the understanding of Skid Row as a human condition will be more fruitful for future work in this area than a reliance on stereotypes about residential Skid Rows.

Chapter 10

Will There Always Be a Skid Row?

A Summary with Recommendations for Prevention

THIS MONOGRAPH presented two perspectives on Skid Row. First, we have dealt with Skid Row as a residential place in the city found near but not in the central business district, including an agglomeration of "typical" commercial and residential enterprises. Second, we extended the traditional definition of Skid Row to include the idea that people who inhabit the residential Skid Row share certain social characteristics with many others who are only sometimes or never found as Skid Row inhabitants.

The traditional view is that Skid Row occupies a physical space near the central business district where land is being held for its future expansion. This location affords the benefits of easy accessibility for Skid Row-like people to downtown industrial and commercial jobs requiring unskilled labor, to the transportation hub, and to a "main stem" which is used as a locus for panhandling. The commercial and residential enterprises of Skid Row include cubicle hotels (where they are still permitted under zoning regulations), cheap traditional hotels, rooming houses, bars, rescue missions, cheap restaurants, liquor stores, fee-paid blood donor agencies, a park, day-labor agencies and perhaps municipal or private social service agencies. Sometimes a police station, a clinic and other land uses are included in this traditional definition.

The occupants of the traditional Skid Row typically exist at the intersection of the disabling conditions of poverty, homelessness, powerlessness, illness and addiction. They reside in Skid Row because they have fallen through the web of social relationships which connect most people with others. For each there has been some final event, e.g., loss of a job, death of a kinsman or kinswoman, terminal rejection by a spouse, parent, child or sibling, which is related to one or more of the dis-

195

abling conditions and which has cut the web. Bahr (8) has called this phenomenon "disaffiliation."

We believe that every person is more or less susceptible to being "infected" by one or more of the disabling conditions, and that each may thus be seen as potentially a resident of Skid Row. Those persons who have had no Skid Row residence— most of us, to be sure—have not yet been so "infected" and likely never will be. Thus the strength of our web of relationships has not been tested in the same way as that of Skid Row residents, and most of us will never "skid" to the Row.

But some persons who are not Skid Row residents are socially closer to it than others. They still live in their "home" neighborhoods, but they are only one or two events away from Skid Row. Blacks and most women have been kept from the traditional residential Skid Row by external social factors, such as segregation or the protectiveness of American culture toward women; if they had been White and male they would live on Skid Row. In our 15-year examination of all the available data on Skid Row and on what we have called the "disabling conditions," we have been increasingly drawn to formulation of the notion that Skid Row is not just a residential area but rather a human condition to which all of us are in some degree subject.

We contend in this notion that "Skid Rowness" is a continuum, stretching from almost complete immunity in the case of extemely wealthy women to extreme susceptibility in the case of lower-class Black men. If American society were not largely a segregated and male-dominated society, we would find in the central Skid Rows a much higher proportion of Blacks and women than we have. We do find, in fact, Black Skid Rows in Black ghetto areas; we find small satellite White Skid Rows in White slum areas. In both cases the Skid Row-like residents blend in with others who are less Skid Row-like. The residents of the central Skid Row are not like others who live nearby, who are usually upper-middle class. The Black Skid Rows are maintained by the segregation of American society, the satellite White Skid Rows by some remaining ties to "neighborhood."

Thus, we hold, the traditional definition of Skid Row must change if it is to reflect social reality. This monograph has dealt with that social reality and has examined several metropolitan lifestyles which appear to be Skid Row-like in nature.

In Chapter 9 we noted that there exist within White working-class areas collections of men and women who are very similar to the men who reside in Skid Row. Some of the men in these neighborhoods have had some Skid Row experience and others move to Skid Row and back with regularity. Others will be residents of Skid Row as short-timers or permanently. Still others will live out Skid Row-like lifestyles in their "home" neighborhoods. The traditional definitions in sociology and among policy makers of Skid Row as only a residential area do not include these people and so ameliorative efforts overlook the "pre-Skid Row" people.

Another source of Skid Row residents, as Chapter 6 reflects, consists of women and Black men. But for the racial segregation both of Black areas and of Skid Row, the men would have been Skid Row residents. The Black women, like White women, are in a sense "victims" of the overprotective male-dominated culture in which we live. If they were male, they, like their husbands, brothers, lovers, fathers and sons, would have probably been at least part-time Skid Row residents. They have been "saved" from this fate because of their gender. Again, the traditional definitions and stereotypes of Skid Row do not include those who do not live in the residential Skid Row and attention has not been paid to nonresidents. Their residential areas have never been labeled as Skid Row and hence they have avoided opprobrium.

In Chapter 9 we reported recently completed research in a suburban county. We were not surprised to find a small but sociologically and politically important group of pre-Skid Row people there. The traditional definition of Skid Row deals with land uses and occupancy in cities only and usually only in cities of some size. But our discovery of Skid Row-like lifestyles in suburban areas raises serious questions about the adequacy of sociological and political definitions of "the Skid Row problem" which must now be dealt with if we are to be realistic and define it appropriately.

Finally, as discussed in Chapter 8, there appear to be new sources of Skid Row-like populations—male and female and largely White—emerging among young street people. The social origins of this population appear to be quite like those of the residents of the traditional Skid Row. They differ in their educational attainment, but their work histories are similar to those of residents of the traditional Skid Row. This population includes women, and their drug of preference is probably not alcohol, but they use alcohol instead of illegal substances. Clearly we do not know whether, in fact, as street people get older they will continue their vagabondage, become residents of the traditional Skid Row, or become "straight," but we believe that it is important to recognize that they represent a potential Skid Row population.

In sum, we believe that recognition on the part of policy makers and social scientists that Skid Row is not just a residential area in cities but rather a human condition will produce changes in research, practice and policy that have been overdue for decades. We are aware of the origins of the bias toward the residential (and all-male) definition of Skid Row, but all areas are not Seattle or Spokane, and all times are not the late 19th Century—the place and time the term "Skid Row" originated. In a sense, we have been locked into obsolete definitions of Skid Row which have blinded us to a larger social reality.

We come now to the prescriptive part of our work. Residents of Skid Row and also the Blacks, women, suburbanites and street people who do not live on Skid Row for whatever reasons, are all victims of disabling conditions over which they have little control: poverty, homelessness, powerlessness, illness, addiction, and the resultant disaffiliation. In a very real sense, these conditions reduce to two: poverty and addiction. People are able to retain homes, friends, servants, power and probably health in direct relationship to their wealth. Friends, employers, unions, kin and charity organizations are more likely to be able and willing to support retirees, the socially inept and addicts who are not destitute. The very wealthy can be stored in sanitariums (if they are alcoholics) or in nursing homes (if they are feeble or ill) or in private old-age homes or their own houses (when they retire). Most of these facilities are available to middle-class and some working-class people as well. But the poorer one is the more likely that an event which would be taken care of easily by the wealthy or manageably by the middle class will eventuate in Skid Row or Skid Row-like residence.

Our recommendations will thus consist of two sorts of propositions: those aimed at the structural (economic, social and political) factors which produce residential Skid Rows and those which have a shorter aim—the amelioration of more particularly disabling conditions with which we have been concerned earlier in this volume. In the manner of Thomas Malthus (115, *p.* 26), we might call these "preventive" and "positive" checks on Skid Row populations.

Our preventive checks aim at eliminating the two key disabling conditions which produce Skid Row-like subpopulations: poverty and addiction. We envision the end of poverty that a guaranteed income would bring. The guaranteed annual income would provide for all the ability to purchase decent, safe and sanitary housing, food, entertainment, transportation, health care (in the absence of a national health program), and other necessities of life. We believe that most of the population will want to work, and for them the guaranteed annual income program will provide an income floor (74). In the case of those who are ill, old or otherwise unable or unwilling to work (and that unwillingness will be increasingly non-normative and stigmatized but must be accepted by taxpayers as we now "accept" defense cost overruns), the guaranteed income program will replace at the federal level the various state, county and municipal welfare programs which now exist.

There is no question but that the proposal and adoption of a guaranteed annual income will require an ideological shift on the part of the citizenry and its representatives of almost unprecedented proportions. But we believe that such a program must be adopted if poverty is to be eliminated. The social consequences will also be enormous but probably not so fearsome as many might envision. The guaranteed annual income program has the twin virtues of eradicating poverty and increasing consumer demand, both of which will bolster a sagging economy.

Elimination of alcoholism is a task comparable to securing the passage of a guaranteed annual income. Briefly stated, the problem is to eliminate addiction to an agent which the vast majority of people are able to control with relatively little difficulty. Clearly we may prevent alcoholism if we suppress the manufacture and sale of alcoholic beverages. We may discourage alcoholism to some degree if we tax alcohol at a high level. But both of these measures are manifestly unfair to alcohol users who are not addicts and may never become addicted, and, as happened some 50 or so years ago, may merely prevent the un-knowledgeable and those with lower incomes from obtaining the addictive agent. In any case, the constitutional issue is settled.

Drinking is not a disabling condition for a substantial part of Skid Row and for some Skid Row-like populations. About one-third of the men on Skid Row in Philadelphia in 1960 and prior to relocation drank sparingly or not at all. Those men were poor and consequently homeless, powerless, frequently ill and disaf-filiated, but they were not addicted to alcohol. Eliminating al-coholism would leave a residual category of Skid Row and Skid Row-like people who would not be affected and thus would continue to serve as potential sources of Skid Row residents.

In summary, we concede that the aims of eliminating poverty and alcohol from American culture appear to be virtually impos-sible (for poverty) and undesirable (for alcohol). But saving these major tasks, more specific proposals can be made which aim at eliminating or at least making more manageable the human condition which we call "Skid Rowness." These are our "positive checks."

In an earlier book (23), we listed and discussed some 21 proposals which we continue to believe will, if carried out, reduce the harshness of life for those who live a Skid Row-like lifestyle. Our present recommendations include but are not limited to those previously published, and are here presented in the framework of our proposal for a regional comprehensive services facility.

We appreciate the desirability of the ideal of social and eco-nomic independence. We also understand the propensity of the inept to cluster around a source of support. At the same time, we understand that there are many people in city and metropolitan areas who need many different kinds of services which are now being provided in as many bureaucratic settings and, perhaps, in as many locations. We propose to rationalize this system of services by creating a comprehensive social, political, economic and residential services agency for those Skid Row-like people who would use such a place. We believe that as long as the proposals we have here called "preventive" are not carried out, especially the proposal to eliminate poverty, and as long as the disabling conditions of poverty, homelessness, powerlessness, illness and addiction are more or less common, there will be a need for such a facility.

The comprehensive agency will include a branch of the public assistance department, a legal clinic, a relocation bureau, a day-labor employment agency (a branch of the state employment service), a credit union, a carefully supervised liquor store, an emergency room and medical clinic with a detoxication facility, a staff of social workers familiar with Skid Row-like lifestyles, a limited number of single residential rooms which will cost little or nothing, an inexpensive but wholesome restaurant, a day room with the usual furniture, a laundry facility, a barber shop, and an educational facility with a library.[1]

Our intention is not to prevent Skid Row-like people from interacting with the outside city; indeed, the residents of the facility and those who use its services will be encouraged to find a residential neighborhood to move to. But decidedly our intention is to construct a facility which contains Skid Row functions but which is not profiteering from misery. We have tried to include those services commonly associated with Skid Row which provide some positive functions for its inhabitants and for part-time, one-time and pre-Skid Row people. Our chief concern is that the facility be nonprofit, clean and well-supervised, and that it have an atmosphere of nonexploitation.

We expect that there will be criticism of some of our proposals, especially that of the inclusion of a liquor store. But we believe that this facility should provide the same range of services to Skid Row-like people that they had before the facility was built; obviously the liquor store will not serve drunken people, but a fair number of Skid Row people are not "chronic drunks," and we prefer that they not have to involuntarily leave the facility with money in their pockets. Many Skid Row residents who are not alcoholics are old and vulnerable to attack

---

[1] We have included most of the usual Skid Row land uses. We have omitted the fee-paid blood bank. Even though virology has improved in recent years such that viral hepatitis can now be detected in some blood (and the blood thus rejected as contaminated), there is still about a 50% chance that hepatitis will be transmitted through blood transfusion and the chances for this to occur are greater among Skid Row people. Our alternatives are either to pay for blood and then discard it, or to omit the fee-paid blood bank from the facility. We have chosen the latter course.

and we should like to forestall any possible injury to these people.

We intend that the comprehensive facility extend its services city-wide and throughout the region. The detoxication facility should be used instead of the "drunk tank." Courses in the education facility should be aimed at retired people in the style of various "emeritus universities" which are now being founded throughout the country. The barber shop would be open to all. And so on.

We strongly recommend that "typical" Skid Row offenses be decriminalized. We do not believe that proper police functions include jailing street "drunks" or vagrants. In the sense that police functions include actions based on a policy of social control, it is clear that the streets must be policed. But, instead of the police force, a civilian public service corps should be established to deal with petty "violations" as well as with routine and emergency matters and currently take up much police force time and money. As a first step toward this goal, we recommend that the decriminalized "violations" be taken care of by the civilian public service corps' taking vagrants, "street drunks," and obviously ill persons to appropriate treatment and dormitory facilities instead of to jail. Further, we propose that the comprehensive service facility serve as the treatment center and dormitory.

We believe that, with the threatened closing of municipal hospitals and the use of emergency rooms in other hospitals by indigent patients, too great a burden is being placed on the citizenry: no public emergency-room service on the one hand and high hospital rates (to pay for the indigents) on the other. The comprehensive service facility's emergency room might well serve as a replacement for closed municipal hospitals and relieve the burden on other hospitals.

The location of the comprehensive service facility should be carefully planned. We believe that it should be located in or near the central business district, easily accessible from all parts of the region by rail, bus and automobile. We are concerned that it not be located in the outskirts of the city or in the countryside; residents' beliefs about property values being affected by stigmatized agencies will not be mollified and the dubious benefits of a "country" location will be more than offset by inaccessibility to the center of the city.

We reiterate that we do not want to propose a permanent Skid Row. But the numbers of people who might be "permanently homeless" are small, and the expenditure of public funds on them too minuscule to offset the very important benefits which such a comprehensive service facility will offer Skid Row-like citizens and others in need of the facility's offerings. And even if such a facility becomes a permanent home for some, at least that home will not be rat- and roach-infested, dirty, dark and unhealthy.

The opening of the comprehensive service facility should be widely advertised. Citizens should be encouraged to use its services. First priority should be given its funding. In short, the new facility should be as much a matter of course for the metropolitan area as its schools, libraries and organized charities. The advertising campaign should strongly include the notion that the consumers of facility services will not be exploited or "ripped off," but rather given as a matter of right the medical, legal, nutritional, dormitory and other services which the agency offers.

In Chapter 9 we reported on a community-based social work program which identified pre-Skid Row persons living in a working-class neighborhood. We propose that the comprehensive services facility be used as a resource center by community-oriented social workers whose task will be to encourage them to use it. Thus, we are suggesting an outreach program in which neighborhood-based workers will advise, inform and guide people to the use of the comprehensive services facility —in a sense, providing clients. We expect that the supply of such clients will always exceed the facility's "demand," which is a sad commentary on the prevalence of poverty and poverty-related human behavior.

We also hope for a reorientation of attitudes such that those who use the facility's services will not be stigmatized in their home communities as "Skid Row people." Until the role of the facility is clarified for all and accepted as "normal," of course there is a chance that such will be the case. Only a broadly based advertising campaign and a similarly broadly based client population will eliminate such a stigma.

We do not propose that the comprehensive service facility be a Skid Row hotel. Its sleeping facilities should be a temporary expedient only; probably a supervised boarding home or a municipal shelter should be established either in the vicinity or elsewhere downtown, run by a governmental body or by franchise with a guaranteed small profit.

We mean, in sum, to take the profit and the exploitation out of the Skid Row setting, while recognizing that as long as our economic and political systems allow poverty to continue there will always be sources of Skid Row-like people. We believe that if "Skid Row offenses" are decriminalized, a civilian public service corps is established and, most important, a comprehensive services facility is constructed in each metropolitan region, most of the degradation, indignity and pain of Skid Row will be eliminated from our culture.

We propose that the administrator of the comprehensive services facility be a career manager with experience in the social service field. He or she should be given cabinet-level rank in city government but should be exempt from the usual electoral–political context of such rank—for example, he or she must not be removable from office with a change of mayor. The administrator should serve not only as the representative of the comprehensive services facility but also as the political voice of the facility's users, not in an electoral sense but in terms of the region's policies toward those most susceptible to the disabling conditions we have identified as pre-Skid Row in nature. Thus the administrator should be the "ombudsman" for the poor people of the region. The poor are probably the only large collection of people who are not organized and thus not systematically represented. The appointment of the administrator of the comprehensive services facility will end this lack of representation.

We believe that exploitation of those who use the services of the proposed facility will be less likely if the administrator must account to a Board of Directors which is composed of nonpolitical citizens including a large proportion (perhaps a majority) of users of the facility—in effect, a consumer board. In our earlier book (23, *pp. 213–214*) we reported on a proposal for a labor organization in Winnipeg which would be controlled by such a board. We propose that the comprehensive services facility include the same sort of governing structure.

The plan presented in this chapter is admittedly visionary. We have emphasized a multiservice facility as our short-range solution to Skid Row although we understand the tendency that such agencies have of becoming overbureaucratized. We also understand that the same forces which have created a racially and sexually segregated residential Skid Row will operate for our proposed agency as well, at least in the short run. We expect, however, that if there is no other such facility, all will eventually use its services and it will become less segregated than the present residential Skid Row. And we hope that any comprehensive services facility which is constructed will not become so stifled in its bureaucratic organization that the giving of services will become secondary.

This monograph has presented historical and contemporary data on Skid Row in a new light: the idea that Skid Rowness is a human condition. We have identified several sources of possible Skid Row residents, but our emphasis has been on the ways that Skid Row as a social institution interacts with the larger society. Finally, we have recommended some ways to bring Skid Row, its residents, and Skid Row-like people throughout the metropolitan area into the normal political and social mainstream.

Appendix A

List of Supplementary Tables

The following supplementary tables, which are not published in this Monograph, may be obtained by ordering NAPS Document No. 03097 from ASIS/NAPS, c/o Microfiche Publications, 440 Park Ave. S., New York, NY 10016. Remit with order $3 for microfiche copy or $5.50 for full-size photocopy.

Appendix B

Street Name Changes in
Philadelphia and Detroit

Philadelphia

The following list is to assist in the identification of current street names where older names were used as a part of quotations in the text. It will also help those who consult the original sources and find older street names. Where there is more than one older name, an effort has been made to list them in order with the most recent use last. It was common in Philadelphia for a street to be only several blocks long and not to go any further; after an interruption of one or more blocks a street in approximately the same position with respect to Market Street or the north-south streets would begin and run for several blocks. Each of these streets would have a separate name. Over the years a policy was evidently adopted to simplify the street name system not only to clean up the reputation of some of these streets but to facilitate police identification and mail delivery. No effort is made in this list to specify the shorter streets, although they are included in the listing. More complete lists of street names are available in "An ordinance to change the names of certain streets, lanes, courts, alleys, etc., in the City of Philadelphia, 1 September 1858" (148), and the *Public Ledger Almanac* of 1878, pp. 2–15.

Other lists are available at the Historical Society of Pennsylvania. Since none of these sources may prove to be completely satisfactory, it may be necessary to consult maps that were published from time to time: The U.S. Library of Congress, Geography and Map Division, has a large collection.

Present Name	Earlier Name(s)	Present Name	Earlier Name(s)
Addison St.	Little Pine St.	Olive St.	Gilbert St.
	Minister St.	Orianna St.	Dillwyn St.
Arch St.	Mulberry St.	Panama St.	Middle Alley
Bainbridge St.	Shippen St.	Pemberton St.	Baker St.
Bartram St.	Elizabeth St.	Percy St.	Canton St.
Brandywine St.	Depot St.	Perth St.	Prosperous Alley
Cypress St.	Portland Lane	Philip St.	Crown St.
	Bay St.	Produce St.	Margaretta St.
	Budd St.	Quarry St.	Cresson St.
Delancey St.	Barclay St.	Race St.	Sassafrass St.
	Union St.	Reese St.	Gillis Alley
Dock St.	Dock Creek	Rodman St.	Lisbon St.
Ellsworth St.	Prime St.		Pine Alley
Fairmount Ave.	Coates St.		St. Mary St.,
Fitzwater St.	German St.		sometimes abbr.
	Swanson St.		to Mary St.
Florist St.	Graff St.		Trout St.
Hamilton St.	Pleasant St.		Carver St.
	Green St.	St. James St.	Pear St.
	Bacon St.		Stratford Place
Hudson St.	Franklin St.	Souder St.	Wayne St.
Kater St.	Small St.	South St.	Cedar St.
	Trout St.	S. Alder St.	Rye St.
	Bedford St.	S. American St.	Barrow St.
	Alaska St.	S. Camac St.	Dean St.
Kenilworth St.	Metcalf St.	S. Darien St.	Duponceau St.
Latimer St.	Aurora St.		Blackberry Alley
Leithrow St.	Apollo St.	S. Fairhill St.	Smith's Court
Ludlow St.	Shoemaker St.	S. Hancock St.	Annapolis St.
Market St.	High St.	S. Hutchinson St.	Raspberry St.
Marvine St.	Madison St.	S. Jessup St.	Henry St.
Monroe St.	Plumb or Plum St.	S. Marshall St.	Spafford St.
Montrose St.	Marriott St.	S. Randolph St.	Hurst St.
Naudain St.	Cullen St.	S. Schell St.	Acorn Alley
New St.	Key's Alley	S. Warnock St.	Currant Alley
New Market St.	Budd St.	S. Water St.	Penn St.
N. American St.	St. John St.	Spring St.	Sergeant St.
N. Camac St.	Jacoby St.	Twenty-First St.	Schuylkill Second St.
N. Darien St.	Garden St.	Vine St.	Valley Rd.
	Chester St.	Washington Ave.	Love Lane
N. Hutchinson St.	Rugan St.		Prime St.
	Steiner St.	Willow St.	Pegg's Run
N. Randolph St.	Julianna St.	Winter St.	Morgan St.
N. Sheridan St.	Nicholson St.		Graff St.

Detroit

Additional information is available from the Burton Historical Collection of the Detroit Public Library.

Present Name	Earlier Name	Present Name	Earlier Name
Madison	Catherine	Lafayette East	Champlain
Broadway	Miami	Michigan	Chicago Road
Monroe	Croghan	Gratiot	Fort Gratiot Road
Griswold	Rowland	West Jefferson	Woodbridge West
Cadillac Square	Michigan Grant		

Appendix C

The Chinese Quarter[1]

This appendix considers the relationship of the Philadelphia Chinatown, the Skid Row and the Red Light district. While it is a case history, the interpretation it offers is intended to expand on the discussion by Ivan Light (105) of Chinatowns as 19th and early 20th Century vice districts. Light points out that in the "last three decades of the nineteenth century, white men of the laboring class were regular clients of the whorehouses, gambling joints, and opium dens which flourished in major American Chinatowns" (p. 368). These districts prospered under the protection of the corrupt politicians of the time. Basing his discussion mostly on San Francisco and New York, he argues that the criminal activities of Chinatowns received so much publicity that they attracted large numbers of middle-class tourists who "intended only to gaze at the houses of prostitution, opium dens, and gambling halls—rather than to patronize them" (p. 383). However, the tourists were potential customers for the Chinese restaurants and retail stores; and, over a period of years, the Chinese merchants were able to reorganize the Chinese community toward these respectable customers. "As Chinatown became tame enough for middle-class tourists, it became too tame for white ruffians who went elsewhere for excitement. Middleclass tourists were more numerous and more affluent than were ruffians, so tourists shortly proved more profitable than ruffians" (105, p. 392). When this became apparent, the Chinese underworld shifted its capital from vice resorts to restaurants and stores.

Light (105) operates within the framework of the "ethnic neighborhood" or natural area approach which we have com-

---

[1] Appreciation is expressed to Professors Mark Haller and S. M. Chiu and to Ms. Catherine Manning Jackson, all of the History Department of Temple University, for their advice or assistance. Appreciation is also expressed to Ivan Light for his cooperation.

mented on in earlier chapters. He makes mention of New York's "adjacent Bowery district" and says that Chinatown attracted so much vice traffic that Irish, Jewish and Italian gangsters moved their operations into the Chinatown to profit from the high density of potential customers. The argument of the present chapter is that while Chinatown was, indeed, a distinctive area, Light failed to clarify its relationship to Skid Row and the much larger Red Light district. When the relationships between the three are examined, it is suggested that, despite its ethnic singularity, the Chinatown of the late 19th and early 20th Centuries should be considered as a segment of the much larger Red Light district. Put another way, Chinatown, the Red Light district and the homeless-man–Skid Row area shared what amounted to joint tenancy in a territory close to the central business district (CBD), and the same basic factors led to the development of these interrelated areas. If this is so, then the use and the suppression of the Red Light district and the Skid Row as discussed in early chapters and in Appendix D must be considered major factors in the transformation of the Chinatown. The merchants were the parties at interest, but there were more basic factors at work than Light intimates.

Chinese settlement in Philadelphia began at least as early as 1854 (41, *pp. 42–43*; 197, *pp. 42–43*). In 1870, the U.S. Census reported that there were 12 Chinese in Philadelphia and, in 1880, that there were 78. The data for later decennial censuses are less clear because the Census Bureau issued adjusted estimates at subsequent censuses. If we accept the later estimates as the correct ones, there were 1146 Chinese in Philadelphia in 1890, 1165 in 1900, 997 in 1910.[2] The rate of growth was relatively rapid, therefore, even though the exact numbers are in some doubt; however, the proportion of Chinese in Philadelphia during the entire period was at no time very large. That the initial Chinese settlement area in Philadelphia was in the

[2] The following gives the differences in the several Census estimates:

Year	N Chinese	Source	Corrected N	Source
1890	738	1890 Census	1146	1910 Census
1900	1927	1910 Census	1165	1920 Census
1910	1784	1910 Census	997	1920 Census

Seventh Ward is suggested by the fact that all 12 were living there in 1870. Not far away in the Eighth Ward, St. Andrew's Protestant Episcopal Church undertook to give them special attention. (St. Andrew's was located between Walnut and Spruce streets; the building is now occupied by the Greek Orthodox Cathedral of St. George.) St. Andrew's was the church where Yun [Bedell] Ye (Cheng refers to him as Le Yun) was converted and baptized sometime before 1858 (41, *p.* 67). Even after the Chinese began to disperse, St. Andrew's continued to take an active religious interest in the Chinese, as evidenced by the fact that in 1883 "a Chinese School was lately adopted, and is taught Sunday afternoons in the Third story of the Chapel. Its members have shown themselves respectful, docile and industrious" (157, *p.* 8).

During the 1880s there were several other similar efforts to assist the Chinese, as well as to convert them, located in the élite area south of Market Street. The *Public Ledger* of 5 February 1885 reported that the Chinese Union of Philadelphia, Rev. Dr. Paddock, president, had rented a house on Spruce Street near Tenth which they planned to furnish as a "Home for Chinese" with a reading room, a meeting room, and a hospital for poor, sick and disabled Chinese. Several months later, a group calling itself the Chinese–American Union called a meeting and announced its aim "to give a home and needed aid and protection to the Chinamen of Philadelphia." The group had already secured a building and planned a home, school and lecture rooms; about 75 Chinese attended that meeting.[3] In March of the same year, about 40 young Chinese who attended Sunday School of the Tabernacle Baptist Church (which was in Philadelphia's élite area) gave a reception for their teachers.[4] These Sunday School activities apparently did not last out the decade.

As the Chinese population grew, it dispersed. Apparently, residential prejudice did not extend to Chinese laundrymen, who lived above or in back of the store. Laundries and washerwomen were classic local service (neighborhood) institutions and necessary before the era of the small home washing ma-

[3] 1024 Walnut Street; *Public Ledger*, 15, 22 April 1885.
[4] *Public Ledger*, 17 March 1885.

chine. In 1877 at least 32 laundries were listed in Boyd's *Directory* (237, *pp. 339–340*) which had Chinese-like names, and, of these 1 was in West Philadelphia, 14 were south of Market Street and 17 were north of Market Street. This population growth and expansion were facilitated by the activities of "several American ladies and gentlemen who intend collecting the better class of Celestials in San Francisco, and distributing them through eastern cities."[5] In this report, the local committee announced that "A building consisting of a store and three upper floors has been leased on Ridge Avenue by the society, and from thence the work of introducing Chinese servants and laborers will commence. A laundry will be opened whose income . . . will almost defray the expenses of keeping the people while situations are being obtained, and the upper story will be fitted for a workshop. . . . The newcomers are all males, and the establishment will be under the supervision of an American."

Even though the Chinese were dispersed, the Tenderloin, in general, and the 900 block of Race Street became a "rest and recreation" area for them. Other streets in the Tenderloin were also centers of Chinese activity where "specially on Wednesday and Saturday night . . . Chinamen and white men and girls were under the influence of opium."[6] In addition, Lang Sing's place on Callowhill Street was a "resort for Chinamen" on Sundays, where there was also gambling. This location was well away from the Chinatown area but within the developing Red Light district.

Being an almost all male population, the Chinese were also involved with prostitution. Thus, there was a raid on a house where it was believed that five young girls were held in an "opium joint" and, although the girls were not found, a White woman 21 years of age was; similarly, 311 North Randolph (well east of Chinatown) was a house of prostitution in which agents of the Society to Protect Children (SPC) found a case of forcible prostitution; and on Vine Street there was "one of the worst kind of tenement houses and is occupied by drunken and lewd

[5] *North American*, 17 March 1880.

[6] 823 Race St., 205 N. 12th St., 48 N. 10th St., 1022 Ridge Ave., 911 Callowhill St., 803 Buttonwood St. SPC case no. 6411, 5 October 1885, and no. 7356, 29 November 1886. *Public Ledger*, 17 January, 24 June 1885; Philadelphia *Weekly Times*, 12 September 1885.

women. The girl's companions were of the lowest order, some of them being Chinese."[7]

Aside from the usual attitudes toward prostitution and minors, the agents of the SPC seem to have been in part motivated by racial prejudice. Another example of this is a case in 1887 when the SPC reported that "Complt called and said that this girl was with a woman on Filbert Street below 9th over a Chinese laundry and that she did not think it was a proper place for the girl."[8] Apparently the agent agreed, for the girl was removed. Again, in 1888, there is the report that the defendant "lives over a Chinese laundry and from what she (Complt) has heard, she was led to believe that she (Defdt) and the Chinaman were criminally intimate and was an unfit person to have charge of the children." The complainant said that she "saw the defendant in bed with the Chinaman who was the same as a husband to her" and further asserted that she also had different men "calling to see her."[9] In the case record itself, there are no data to support anything beyond a common-law relationship between the Chinese man and the woman, however.

The male sexual pressure did indeed sometimes justify the suspicions of the agents of the SPC, for the *Public Ledger* of 17 July 1890 reports of a laundryman who was charged with keeping his minor daughters for immoral purposes. It is doubtful that these were in fact his daughters, as the following quotation from a 1923 League of Nations (99) report suggests: "The Immigration Authorities find great difficulty in preventing this traffic entirely, though they do not believe it exists in large numbers, because these girls, some as young as eleven years, are entered on the documents as wives, sisters, or daughters of returning Chinese-American citizens, and their papers, secured in China, are, on their face entirely regular. Nevertheless, a dozen of these young girls were rescued from prostitution in 1923" (*p. 177*).

By 1890 the importance of the 900 block of Race Street as a Chinatown was evident and, thereafter, public attention was

---

[7] SPC case no. 6515, 19 November 1885; no. 7420, 4 January 1886; no. 7495, 9 February 1887; no. 6892, 22 May 1886.

[8] SPC case no. 7641, 8 April 1887.

[9] SPC case no. 8774, 6 August 1888.

primarily directed there. Thus, the annual report of the Department of Public Safety for that year lists 911, 913, 915, 916, 917, 918, 920 and 926 Race Street as the locations of Chinese gambling houses that were raided, in which 17 "principals" were arrested as well as 140 "inmates" (142, *p.* 69). It is hard to say what stimulated this harassment, although a press campaign apparently had been launched the previous year against police corruption in which the Chinese gambling provided the impetus. Police in the Sixth District were alleged to protect Chinese gambling for a payment of $5 a week for each gambling table, and the take was thought to be at least $100 a week. "It is believed that this is the beginning of the exposure of a vast system of blackmail and extortion by the police."[10] The initial Chinese response to this harassment apparently was ineffectual, for several men were arrested in July for conspiracy to kill Lee Yuck, a police detective, who himself lived at 926 Race Street.[11]

The initial response of the social welfare community toward Chinese occupancy of the area was positive, for they saw that there had "been a marked improvement in the 10th Ward since the dissolute population in the neighborhood of 9th and Race streets has been supplanted by the Chinese, a people preeminently industrious, and who do not resort to benevolent societies for assistance."[12] The notes do not clarify the reference to "the dissolute population," but our knowledge of the area suggests that these were probably cheap lodging houses or rooming houses in which a good deal of heavy drinking took place. That is, we can infer that they were not very different from the people of the homeless-man area that was developing at the same time along Race and Vine streets.

Thereafter, the pressure continued on the Chinese community, both ideologically and politically, although the two dimensions were not always easy to distinguish in practice. At the ideological level, it assumed the form of Christian missionary

[10] *New York Times*, 17 May 1889. In the year before that, a Chinese gambling house was indicted but the case was "ignored" and never brought to trial. Quarter Sessions Court, Oyer and Terminer, Philadelphia County, bill of indictment no. 430, January 1888.

[11] *Public Ledger*, 3 July 1890.

[12] Philadelphia Society for Organizing Charity, Ward Association Committee Minutes Book (1879–1891), 8 July 1891.

work among the "heathen." At the political level, it assumed the shape of police persecution. In 1894 the Presbytery of Philadelphia was considering a mission among the Chinese "of whom there are about one-thousand-six-hundred in the city. Something has been done among them by Sabbath-school instruction and other evangelistic work. So far as known, there has been no stated or regular preaching of the gospel to them. Those who have labored among them report that there are many who are inquiring to receive the truth."[13]

Apparently, whatever was organized by the Presbytery did not endure, for in 1896 a committee of Episcopal clergymen undertook "a tour of inspection of the Chinese quarters of Philadelphia under the guidance of Frederick Poole, the Chinese missionary. They found a Chinese temple on Race Street where nearly five hundred worshipers of Joss were gathered. They also discovered numerous gambling and opium dens well patronized."[14] Defining Chinatown as a place where the Chinese gather for "religious and shopping purposes," the clergymen then proposed to organize an Episcopal church mission, and, in the Diocesan Convention of that year, they called for a larger appropriation for that purpose (155, *125th, p. 335*). Instead of a major Presbyterian or Episcopalian effort, however, the non-denominational Christian League began to work in Chinatown, after what was locally perceived to be a successful campaign against the vice activities found in the Lombard–Southwark–Moyamensing slum. The League had the support of the police and church leaders, as illustrated by its open-air gospel meeting on Race Street almost opposite the "Joss House"; to counter threats from the Chinese (the "heathen Chinee"), a detail of special officers was provided (156, *38th*).[15] In 1897 a Christian League established a Christian Mission School and YMCA which included a nursery school and kindergarten, a medical dispensary and Christian Endeavor classes (43).

[13] RICE, W. M., *New York Observer*, 17 October 1894. In a clipping collection of articles at the Pennsylvania Historical Society, p. 147.
[14] RICE, W. M., *New York Observer*, 16 April 1896. In a clipping collection of articles at the Pennsylvania Historical Society, p. 170. *New York Times*, 17 May 1899.
[15] *City and State* 4 (No. 3); 42, 21 October 1897.

Official interest in Chinatown was also aggressive. The police conducted a series of raids. The *Evening Bulletin* of 20 January 1905 reports raids on 17 alleged gambling places, in which 93 Chinese were arrested. They and an undisclosed number of White prostitutes and their White "panders" were sent to the House of Correction where detainers were lodged against them so that they would be compelled to serve the full sentence. The annual report of the director of the Department of Public Safety (143, *p.* 8) complains about the fact that the buildings had been modified internally so that there were secret passages, double and triple doors—some inside doors were of oak and were 8 to 10 inches thick—and a system of sentinels. Since the police conducted their activities with the assistance of the American-Chinese affiliated with the Chinese YMCA (i.e., converts under the program of the Christian League), there were threats of reprisals from the operators of the Race Street Chinese Tenderloin, for that is obviously what it was, in addition to being a commercial center.

By 1910 the Christian League seemed to have lost much of its aggressiveness and began to assume a more benevolent stance, combined with a considerable dilution of its ideological pressure on the Chinese (42). Its program now involved the suppression of indecent billboards, postcards and advertisements, eliminating profanity in burlesques and theatrical performances, protection of Chinese laundrymen, rescuing girls who had been lured into Chinatown, abating solicitation on the streets for "disorderly houses," and offering illustrated lectures and providing a roof garden for the children of the Tenderloin. This is in contrast to its vigorous statement of 21 October 1897 when it was announced that the Christian League "Cooperated with the CIVIL AUTHORITIES in enforcing the laws, and with the evangelical CHURCHES in extending the influence of the GOSPEL. It aggressively and successfully strives to improve the conditions of our city, both moral and sanitary, and thus, removes dangerous evils from the pathway of youth, and revolting scenes from the sight of little children. The value of property is increased by the betterment of neighborhoods." The Chinese City Mission was perceived as an extension of that statement of purpose which "seeks to promote the social, moral, and spiritual welfare of these strangers in our midst, and invites the cooperation of Christian men and women in this hitherto neglected work."[16]

One explanation of this change is that during the interim the Christian League had lost most of whatever credibility it had within the Chinese community because of its association with the police, as well as Chinese rejection of the League's cultural pressure. Another explanation is suggested by Light's argument that between about 1890 and 1920 Chinese commercial and business leadership became established and Chinese merchants were able to transform American Chinatowns from vice districts to tourist attractions. From this point of view, the concentrated and hostile attention of the Caucasian "power structure" was no longer justified because the Chinese themselves had found a more permissible way of life and function within the metropolis.

The relationship between the smaller Chinese section and the larger Red Light district also casts a different light on Jackson's discussion[17] of the development of the Chinatown in the 900 block of Race Street in Philadelphia. Jackson notes that Lee Fong opened a laundry on Ninth Street, one door from the intersection of Ninth and Race streets, in about 1876. Within a year, a clansman named Lee Wang had opened another laundry around the corner on Race Street. "By about 1880, Lee Wang, besides operating his laundry, also supplied his compatriots with opium, tea, and incense. He and Lee Fong soon opened a restaurant over the laundry and the place became the acknowledged center of the Chinese in the city." Service facilities (including vice) expanded in the immediate vicinity of the Lee operations on Race Street as a consequence of Lee clan entrepreneurship.

The fact that the Red Light district was already well under way and was much larger than the Chinese section suggests that the vice activities of the Lees were permitted because the area had already been "designated" as a vice district and the Lee activities conveniently fitted a larger scheme of things which

[16] *City and State* 4 (No. 3): 45, 21 October 1897.
[17] JACKSON, C. M. A study of the nature of leadership in the Chinese community of Philadelphia. Honors paper, Department of History, Temple University, December 1972.

had received the sanction of the corrupt Philadelphia power structure. There seems little doubt that the Chinese section and its associated vice activities could have been severely limited by the city government and its supporters.

Not only was the Philadelphia Chinatown a very active part of the larger Red Light district, but it also had characteristics that we associate with the homeless-man area. Almost all of the Chinese in Philadelphia were men and, as the Race Street Chinatown developed other services, it was also necessary to provide housing for the weekly influx from elsewhere in the city, as well as for the resident service personnel. When there was a fire at 922 Race Street in January 1905, for example, the firemen finally chopped their way through the barred doors and found the place occupied by 40 Chinese.[18] They found that the first floor was a grocery, in the front of the second floor were the facilities of the Roslyn Society (Sun Gee Tong), and the third floor front had a meeting hall. In addition, the rear of the second and third floors, and all the fourth floor, were fitted with bunks in little rooms measuring 6 feet by 4 feet. That is, it was a cubicle hotel for members of the Tong, along with everything else; cubicle hotels have been one of the most distinguishing characteristics of homeless-man Skid Row areas.

New York City

The Five Points area of New York City was an undifferentiated slum–Skid Row–vice area before the Civil War and for a few years thereafter (13, *pp. 7–8, 12, 23, 41*; 27, *pp. 94–95, 195–196*; 117, *pp. 47–49, 189–190, 197, 303–305, 312–315, 334, 337, 344–346, 356*; 123, *pp. 34, 49, 94*; 126, *pp. 20–24, 36–42, 48–50, 74–75, 189, 194*). The movement of business and the use of some of the land in the Five Points area for public buildings as well as the insistent pressure from public health workers and various missionaries led to a shift of the "problem" population into the Bowery area. The vice district moved through the Bowery area and further north during the 1870s and 1880s, so that what became known as the Tenderloin was well to the north of the Bowery, but vice continued to be characteristic of the slums

---

[18] *Evening Bulletin*, 9 January 1905.

surrounding the Bowery–Mulberry Bend section. According to Thomas Byrnes (32, *p. 646*) the Skid Row "cheap lodging house" was first developed in New York City about 1877 in Park Row (Chatham Street); by 1892 there were 270 such places with a capacity of 12,317 rooms. Mott, Pell and Doyer streets, the heart of the Manhattan Chinatown, were embedded in this slum–vice district but were not the reasons for the location of the district nor its center (105, *p. 382*). Rather, since the vice activities had moved into and through the area before the coming of the Chinese, it may reasonably be argued that the Chinese "rest and recreation" center located there because it encountered the least resistance from the residents and property owners of the locality and the passive cooperation of the New York City power structure. New York's Chinatown and the homeless-man–Bowery area were distinctive, but adjacent to each other, and distinct from the Tenderloin. The pattern is not exactly the same as Philadelphia's, but clearly it does not fit Light's theory.

San Francisco

Light's description seems to approximate the case of San Francisco, where in the pre-1906 fire era the Barbary Coast saloon section was in the vicinity of the present Portsmouth Square. Inland from the Barbary Coast was a Red Light district along what was then known as Dupont Street, the central street of the Chinatown as well as the vice district. (After the fire, the respectable elements had the name changed to Grant Avenue. This was a common procedure; the "laundering" of street names was done a number of times in Philadelphia.) Meanwhile, and beginning as early as 1870–1880, a district developed south of Market Street characterized by cheap boarding- and lodging houses, inexpensive hotels, immigrant family homes, medium and light industry, and saloons (3). By the 1890s there was also a hobo or homeless-man area along Howard Street centered between Third and Fourth. By 1970 the San Francisco Tenderloin district had moved north to an area bounded by McAllister on the south and Geary on the north and, generally, between Taylor on the east and Polk or Van Ness on the west. The Skid Row continues to be south of

Market Street, but redevelopment has forced it to move a few blocks west to Sixth Street between Mission and Folsom streets. At present, therefore, the Skid Row and the Tenderloin more or less abut each other and are separated from Chinatown.

The Philadelphia Race Street Chinatown, then, was originally a special case of a combined Red Light district and a homeless-man area located on the edge of the larger homeless-man area that began to emerge at about the same time as the Chinatown. Both were on the edge of the much larger Philadelphia Red Light district, both were closely related to but distinguishable from it. And a similar case can be made for New York.

Appendix D

Notes on Some Philadelphia
Social Welfare Agencies

Bremner (28) wrote in a general vein about the "discovery of poverty" in the United States and Rosenberg (171) and Ringenbach (165) discuss it in relation to New York City. Details differ from city to city but there seems little doubt that the development of the "charitable impulse" in Philadelphia was similar to what took place in New York. The predecessor of the New York Tract Society was the Religious Tract Society, founded in 1811. By the depression of 1837–1843, the New York City Tract Society had begun the distribution of religious tracts, with special attention to the needs of the urban poor (171, *pp. 70–96, 188–202, 246–249*). By 1843 it was doing so much charitable work that its name was changed to the New York City Mission and Tract Society. During the 1850s and 1860s, it became the major agency of evangelical Protestantism to the city's slum dwellers. By the 1860s, also, the work was done by full-time professionals in addition to volunteers. The Society established "missions stations" in storefronts, lofts and tenement apartments. In 1868 two mission stations were converted into temporary housing for Skid Row-like persons, while the others continued to give assistance to the rest of New York City's poor.

The "scientific" distribution of charity was the aim of the New York Association for Improving the Condition of the Poor. The city was divided by wards and districts with five volunteer visitors to investigate the requests for charity in each district; the concern was for families, children and the worthy poor. Tramps and vagrants received short shrift.

Ringenbach (165) traced the changes in perception of "tramps" and in the organization of charity in New York City from 1873 to 1916. A superstructure of professional charitable organizations was developed with the assistance of social investigators. This new organizational level was accompanied by a change in point of view toward homeless and vagrant people. In the immediate post-Civil War period, there was a hue and cry about "tramps"; their lack of employment was viewed as evidence of their own deficiency for, it was argued, "any man who really wanted to work could find something to do." By the time of World War I this approach had been largely abandoned by the Charity Organization Society professionals, who recognized that the depressions between the Civil War and World War I were major factors in the large numbers of unemployed and homeless men and that there were many who wanted to work but who just could not find it.

Bremner (28, *ch. 1–5*) undertook a less specific task. We have shown that there were many vagrant and impoverished people in Philadelphia before the Civil War. This was true in all the big cities of the country (28). After the Civil War, Americans became increasingly aware of the poverty that occurred in the midst of their rapidly industrializing society. As Bremner put it, Americans discovered poverty. They learned to conceptualize it, to recognize its concentration in the big cities (rural poverty tended to be ignored), and learned how to gather massive statistical and pictorial evidence of the existence of poverty. This changed perception became an element in the reform movements of the period between 1890 and World War I, which in turn influenced the New Deal of the 1930s.

Prostitution: Magdalen, Rosine, Crittenton, Vice Commission

"Asylums" were an 18th and early 19th Century approach to the rehabilitation of prostitutes; they were similar in some respects to a modern "halfway house" or boarding school but, because of the close confinement and supervision, were also similar to prisons or reformatories. The Boards of Managers of the Magdalen Society and the Rosine Association managed the two pre-Civil War asylums concerned with the reformation of prostitutes.

The Magdalen Society of Philadelphia was organized in 1799. It was modeled after the Magdalen Hospital of London, which was established in 1758 (53). Charles Dingley, the author of the proposal which preceded the actual establishment of the earlier London institution, argued in terms of the prevention of disease, checking libertinism, anarchy and confusion, leading to happiness of those women through marriage, and the lessening of vice among the common people. He claimed that the general belief that there was a system of licensing of prostitutes in certain continental countries was an exaggeration and that the "continental system" did little more than set the formal rules for the behavior of prostitutes and specified legally their pariah status. In the rationalist tradition of the time, Dingley argued the rational inconsistency and immorality of debauching one's neighbor's daughter while insisting that one's own daughter be a virgin at the time of marriage. He stressed a combination of close supervision, strict moral training and job training so that "we rescue their Bodies from torturing pains, and untimely Death; and their Souls from Death eternal."[1]

The Magdalen Society of Philadelphia was formed "To aid in restoring the paths of virtue, to be instrumental in recovering to honest rank in life, those unhappy females, who, in an unguarded hour, have been robbed of their innocence, and sunk into wretchedness and guilt, and being affected with remorse at the misery of their situation, are desirous of returning to a life of rectitude, if they clearly saw an opening thereto."[2] The program adopted by the Philadelphia group remained relatively unchanged over the years—residential seclusion for at least a year, learning the arts of sewing and home maintenance, and religious instruction. Stress was placed on a woman's ability to earn a living without resort to prostitution or leaving her home.

In its first few years, the Magdalen Society placed young women in private homes, but during 1807–1808 it bought three

[1] [Charles Dingley], Plan for Establishing a Charity House or Charity Houses for the Reception of Repenting Prostitutes, to be Called the Magdalen Charity, addressed to the Society for the Encouragement of Arts, Manufactures, and Commerce, 1758. [Van Pelt Library, University of Pennsylvania.]

[2] Constitution of the Magdalen Society, Minutes of the Annual Meetings of the Magdalen Society, Vol. 1, 1800–1824. The discussion that follows is drawn from the minute books of the Society and from the "Record of Daily Occurrences" kept by the Matron in residence. These are in the possession of the White-Williams Foundation, the successor organization to the Magdalen Society. The various annual reports of the Board of Managers are either in the collections of the White–Williams Foundation or the Historical Society of Pennsylvania. For a picture of the Magdalen Asylum building and grounds, see the 4th annual report of the Municipal Court of Philadelphia, 1917 (facing page 18). For another review of the activities of the Magdalen Society, see Teeters (202). For a brief history of the Magdalen Society of New York City, see Rosenberg (171, pp. 99–101).

pieces of property at Twenty-First and Race streets, well away from the center of the city, which it continued to use until just before World War I. Over the years, a policy evolved not to take women over 30 years of age. For many years the Society would not take women who were pregnant, but that policy seemed to have changed about 1878 because "otherwise the Catholics would take them" (114, *100th*; 223).[3] While the age limits were not specified, the records suggest that in practice a woman would probably not be accepted if she were in her late 30s and definitely would not be accepted if she were 40. By 1886 the recruitment focus had shifted to younger and deserving girls who were admitted on request of parents or guardians or on application of the Society to Prevent Cruelty to Children (Society to Protect Children). Over the years a wide variety of techniques of recruitment were used by the organization, including incursions into the houses of prostitution by missionaries with tracts and by detectives and police on legal raids.

The Society bought a lot in 1805 at Twenty-First and Hamilton streets, which was owned by the Bank of North America, and the bank contributed $500 of the $2000 cost. In its early years the Magdalen Society acquired a number of pieces of property through legacies, including a 1000-acre tract of land in New York State valued at a dollar an acre. These properties were rented and later sold. In addition to income from investments, the Society was supported through annual membership subscriptions.

Over the years the Magdalen Society had increasing difficulty in getting support and began to use capital funds. Finally, the asylum property was sold to the City of Philadelphia for a Municipal Court building and in 1918 the Magdalen Society was reincorporated as the White-Williams Foundation; it would try to persuade girls who were leaving school before the legally permitted age of 16 years to return to school. Later the Foundation evolved a program of small grants to young people to assist them to remain in school.

The statement of purpose of the Rosine Association was not greatly dissimilar to the Magdalen's except that it was more feminist. It criticized the Magdalen Society for "in consequence

---

[3] Record of Daily Occurrences, Tuesday, 29 January 1878; 18 April 1885 ff.

of being under the superintendence of Men, its labours have been in a degree inefficient and the reformation of this class [the prostitutes] had been considered almost as a hopeless effort—but we believe, that with Women's sympathy, Women's guiding care, her quick perceptions of the necessities of Women's nature, a regenerating influence may be brought into operation, which may show the world that even the poor degraded prostitute is not irreclaimable" (172, *1851, pp. 7–8*; 173, *1847, p. 5, 1848, p. 11*).

The Rosine Association was more innovative than the Magdalen Society. It was first proposed at a meeting of women who were planning a petition campaign for the abolition of capital punishment in 1847 (172, *1864*; 173, *1857*; 174). Its organization had moderate feminist overtones and, almost from the beginning, a strong antialcohol stand was evident. It established a Home on Eighth Street.[4] It shortly became apparent that a more active effort needed to be made to find jobs for women if they were really to live independent and respectable lives. The Rosine managers called a public meeting and founded a Temporary Home Association for women who were new to the city so that they would not be routed to places that later turned out to be houses of ill fame or houses of assignation. The Rosine and the Temporary Home Association also maintained an "Intelligence Office" (job placement service). By 1857 it was claimed that these joint efforts had provided 11,542 women with homes and employment. By 1864 the Eighth Street location was unsatisfactory (possibly for reasons related to the rise of the Tenderloin) and the Rosine moved some miles away.[5] By the end of the 19th Century the group faded from sight. It had been having financial difficulties since the depression of 1880 and the managers not only dipped into capital but borrowed to have operating funds. Their program also began to shift from appealing to the "self-abandoned" to "saving those who have been unsuspecting victims of unprincipled designing men" (172, *1880, p. 6*).

[4] 320 N. 8th Street (when the houses were renumbered after the consolidation of 1854 this became 204 N. 8th Street). The Temporary Home Association was located at 505 N. 6th Street.
[5] 3216 Germantown Avenue, Philadelphia.

The Florence Crittenton Rescue Mission (230, *pp. 400–406*) had a typical late 19th Century missionary style. The group began with street meetings on Sunday mornings at Sixth and Rodman streets in the spring of 1893. In the fall, after having made "many converts among the depraved women and girls in the surrounding houses of shame," the Florence Crittenton Mission Number 7 was formally organized. It rented 531 Lombard Street which had been a "notorious pool and gambling room," and immediately began services; their meetings were jammed and their collections were sufficient to pay all their bills. This was in the heart of the Lombard–Southwark–Moyamensing slum. In 5 months, 19,960 persons had attended services and 375 had confessed their sins and were converted. The Rescue Band was aggressive; it invaded the saloons and resorts during the late night and early morning hours. The Lombard Street property was not only a preaching station, but a home which took any repentant girl or woman who needed its help, bathed, clothed, fed and lodged her and helped her begin a new life. It made no distinction as to creed, color or nationality, and it laid particular stress from the beginning on convincing the girls approached that the place was not an institution but "a family living in an atmosphere of Christian love."

This was much the same rhetoric that one found in the Magdalen Home and in the Rosine Association homes. The Magdalen program fitted a historically earlier asylum model and its program was oppressive (at least to 20th Century eyes); the Rosine was more liberal than the Magdalen with an emphasis on Christian morals and "women's occupations"; the Crittenton Mission directly challenged sin and was more exciting than the Magdalen or the Rosine.

At least it was at the beginning. The original plan for a combined mission and home lasted only about 7 years, when the mission aspect was abandoned and the Lombard Street location was rehabilitated as a home. In 1904, Lombard Street was no longer satisfactory and the home moved to 139 Queen Street, near the Delaware River. The focus of activities had become assistance to young pregnant women and those with illegitimate babies; an appropriate medical facility was located on the third floor, since it was a considerable distance to the nearest hospital. There were a series of financial crises; and finally, in 1928, the organization moved to the Germantown section of Philadelphia where it developed lying-in and ward–nursery facilities. The Florence Crittenton Mission had progressively redefined its efforts away from the prostitutes and "fallen women" of the Lombard–Southwark–Moyamensing slum and had not followed them to the area north of Market Street; rather, it had become a specialized agency to assist "young women in trouble."

The evolution of these organizations suggests a frustration associated with working with prostitutes, financial problems, and a Victorian–Edwardian orientation toward respectability that progressively led to a displacement from the original concerns of the founders. From prostitutes in general, there was a shift to young prostitutes, to young women who were "ruined" and in danger of becoming prostitutes, to (for the Magdalen) young women who were leaving school at a young age and, therefore, in greater danger of becoming prostitutes. Clearly, these organizations did not prevent the Tenderloin; there were larger societal forces at work.

The Vice Commission of Philadelphia represented an alternative approach to the voluntaristic effort to get prostitutes to change their lifestyle, whether on the basis of entry into an asylum or through conversion and "living a new life based on Christ." The approach through legal suppression was relatively unsuccessful as long as it was based on efforts to define prostitution as simply immoral and a community nuisance. But when it was taken by early 20th Century reformers and related to the politically dominant elements and respectable elements in terms of public health, the woman's movement and the prohibition movement, it acquired a new potency. The Vice Commission, despite its name was a private organization (private commissions investigating public issues were common in Philadelphia); it was probably instigated by the Pennsylvania Society for the Prevention of Social Disease.[6]

The Society was founded in 1906 and in the winter season of 1906–1907 held four public meetings in the Hall of the College of Physicians and another series of four the following year. In 1908 a public meeting which ranged from women's rights to

[6] American Social Health Association Collection, Social Welfare History Archives Center, University of Minnesota Libraries, Minneapolis, Minnesota.

facts about social disease was held under the auspices of the Society by "prominent women of Philadelphia." This suggests either that the Society itself was a "spin-off" from the women's rights movement of the period or that the Society used the highly controversial women's rights approach as a way to focus its meeting and also to attract publicity. A large meeting was held at the College of Physicians in 1910 which inaugurated a state campaign that culminated in a meeting in 1911 under the auspices of the Pennsylvania State Medical Society in the Capitol in Harrisburg. In 1911 a large membership meeting in Witherspoon Hall (a Presbyterian center in Philadelphia) took a legal emphasis, advocating (1) quarantine by the Department of Health of "contagious diseased persons," (2) enforced hospital treatment for contagious or pestilential diseases that could not be treated at home, (3) that pestilential and contagious diseases should be reported by physicians to the Board of Health, (4) that there would be the right of entry and search "where there is just cause to suspect any nuisance to exist," (5) that punishment should be meted out to those keeping a disorderly house, a bawdy house or leasing a house to be so kept, and to those committing adultery and fornication. The Society, therefore, took both a broad public health perspective and a more restricted antivice position without respect to venereal disease.

The outcome of the Vice Commission's report (216) has already been discussed. The Tenderloin was closed down by Rudolph Blankenburg's "quarantine" and, thereafter, it was no longer possible for it to exist in a quasi-legal fashion. Nonetheless, as Mark Mason pointed out, the old Tenderloin continued to operate well into the 1920s. We could, therefore, call the campaign a qualified success, but the Vice Commission did not continue to exist as a watchdog agency to see that its objectives were fulfilled. The fact that Philadelphia's respectables took a strong antiprostitution position may have been a significant factor in the continued suppression of open prostitution, although it is doubtful that the police were successful in the suppression of clandestine prostitution.

Organized Charity: The Union Benevolent Association and its Successors

The Union Benevolent Association of Philadelphia was

founded at the behest of the wife of Judge Joel Jones after the very hard winter of 1830–1831. At that time, the civic leaders and charitable givers developed the theory that "the 'vicious' poor began to discover that it was easier to live by begging than by work." The Association was different from earlier charities in its adoption of a casework approach that had been developed abroad. The city was divided into districts and a board of lady visitors conducted investigations to see whether the case was worthy of charitable assistance. The consequence was undoubtedly that the homeless, especially the homeless men, were excluded. Assistance was usually in kind, rather than in cash, and the Association often sold coal at half price rather than making a gift outright. Not all recipients were "worthy," however, and by 1855 there was a "black book" of "imposters who mulcted the charitable." As with most charitable organizations of the time, the Association was based on annual subscriptions and by 1876 it was declining as its membership grew old and died. The Association consequently narrowed its recipient population to the Kensington area (a predominantly mill district with a population of British origin) and to "gentlewomen reduced in circumstances." Thus the member–subscribers took care of their own, defined either ethnically or in social-class terms (208; 209, 45th).[7]

In the post-Civil War period, the Association lost its charitable coordinative function, suffering a decline in its finances as a part of the process. Its place was taken by the Society for Organizing Charitable Relief and Repressing Mendicancy in 1878.[8] The name was simplified later to the Society for Organizing Charity, but there continued to be a special committee on mendicancy that was assigned the responsibility for recommendations about vagrants and tramps, although the Society's main emphasis was on assistance to families. In fulfilling its purposes, the Society investigated requests for assistance; it rejected temporary relief (e.g., soup, bread, or coal in time of

[7] Minutes of the Board of Directors, Union Benevolent Association, 10 January 1894 to 9 December 1903. [Historical Society of Pennsylvania.].

[8] CITIZENS COMMISSION ON CHARITY ORGANIZATIONS. Report, with proposed constitution, ca. 13 June 1878. And scrapbook items, Family Service of Philadelphia.

emergency) in the belief that this temporary aid merely fostered pauperism (186, *15 February 1880, p. 2*; 188, *2d*).

The Philadelphia Society for Organizing Charity was organized by wards to make both the investigation and fund raising more efficient. The administrative structure was a major effort to coordinate the money, power and influence of the upper and middle classes of Philadelphia insofar as charity was concerned. There was a central Board of Directors, the ward organizations had their own Boards, and ward supervisors met monthly to exchange information and coordinate their activities. The city government responded almost immediately to the argument of the leadership that the Society would save money by weeding out the vagrants, undeserving and cheaters—they discontinued the appropriations for outdoor relief (outside of institutions) that had amounted to $50,000 to $75,000 a year (188, *2d*).

The Society emphasized work rather than direct relief whenever this seemed reasonable from the point of view of the Ward Association's "home visitors." In an 1882 meeting with the Mayor the Committee on Mendicancy reported that, "we have an arrangement with the Pennsylvania Railroad Company to give work to any able bodied man we send them and we are doing this, we have sent scores of men who are now at work. Further than that, as the railroad does not pay at once, if we find a man who is at work and cannot well wait for his pay, we take his power of attorney and collect his wages and then advance the money for his immediate necessities."[9] These referrals were to the West Philadelphia yards and "all able-bodied men applying for employment, or for relief for lack of work" were to be sent there, according to instructions from the General Superintendent to the Ward Association Superintendents. Minimum pay was $1.20 a day and it was reported that some permanent employment was possible for those who worked "faithfully."[10] Just how many actually got a job in this way and how many managed to win a more permanent status is not clear.

[9] SOCIETY FOR ORGANIZING CHARITY, COMMITTEE ON MENDICANCY. Minutes of 17 March 1882.

[10] SOCIETY FOR ORGANIZING CHARITY. Report of the General Secretary, 13 February 1882.

The Society argued that compulsory work was a cure for the tramp-vagrant problem and urged the strict enforcement of the House of Correction Act. The House of Correction Act of 1871 required that every person in the custody of the Board of Managers who was not sick or handicapped was to be employed in quarrying stone, farming or manufacturing items that were needed by the prison, almshouse or other public institutions of the state or city. The Board was also authorized to use jail labor to work for private citizens if they found it to be profitable to the institution and suitable to the health and abilities of the prisoners. The law also specified that those who refused to work were to be kept in their cells and fed bread and water. Commitment for the first offense was for 3 months; for the second, from 9 to 18 months; and for the third, 18 to 24 months.

It was presumed that such stiff sentences would sweep the streets of tramps and vagrants. But they didn't. The Union Benevolent Association complained that "A recent law of Pennsylvania is explicit enough to protect our citizens from the annoyance of tramp begging, and yet the streets of Philadelphia abound with offenders persistently importuning the passersby for alms" (209, *48th, p. 2*). And the Central Board of the Society for Organizing Charity urged that the Mayor and City officials prevent the improper discharge of inmates from the House of Correction (188, *2nd, p. 13*). The Board of Managers used their discretionary power to discharge inmates freely; and the "flagship" social welfare agency of the time, the Society for Organizing Charity, strenuously objected to the leniency of the Board of Managers. This harsh approach was not unusual for the time. In Trenton, New Jersey, in 1883 tramps were compelled to break rocks and split wood; they worked in a fenced location readily accessible to the jeers of the general public, with balls and chains around their legs. The money that was made on the project paid for the raw material, the food and the clothing of the tramps.[11]

In addition to trying to make the House of Correction more effective as an involuntary way of "salvaging" the poor and driving "professional beggars" out of town, the Society planned to establish several semi-involuntary institutions (188, *7th, p.*

[11] Philadelphia *Weekly Times*, 21 March 1885.

15).[12] One institution, known as a "Wayfarer's Lodge," was modeled after those in Boston (190). The Wayfarer's Lodge was a 19th Century approach to the Judeo-Christian ethic: true caring for the poor would lead not only to their own "rescue from pauperism" but would reduce the economic burden on the larger community.

The Society saw this burden as substantial. A minimum estimate of this was given to a conference by members of the Special Committee on Mendicancy with Mayor Stokely in which it was reported that in 1878 there were 2250 beggars on the streets of Philadelphia receiving an average of $2 a day, a total of $4500 a day given to beggars, or about $1.5 million a year (186, *15 April 1880, p. 4; 15 June 1880, p. 3*). To secure the semi-involuntary feature of the Wayfarer's Lodges, the Ward Associations, with the support of the Central Board, solicited and obtained legislation to the effect that, having been notified in advance, any able-bodied person who was fed and sheltered for the night and then refused to do up to 4 hours of work in return was to be sentenced for a term of not less than 30 days nor more than 90 days. Furthermore, the law expressly provided that once the Wayfarer's Lodges were ready to operate, the city was to prohibit overnight lodgers in the station houses, "so far as in their judgement the same may be expedient and practicable" (186, *15 March 1883, pp. 34–35*). This city policy did not last many years and the Society concurred in its abandonment because of the desperate economic conditions in the 1890s (186, *15 April 1895, p. 42*).

Meanwhile it became apparent that the Ward Associations were so locally oriented that they were unable to handle "wayfarers, tramps, and strays." All cases of that sort were centralized in a Department of the Society for Organizing Charity for the Care of Non-Residents. A common technique for getting assistance by many "tramps" was to ask for transportation to somewhere else, presumably to the home community or to where a job was waiting, and the response of the Society was to

[12] The voluntary use of the House of Correction as a resource for survival in the dead of winter was evident soon after the institution was opened; the *North American* reported on 30 December 1875 that "19 men were sent to the House of Correction at their own request" (21, 152).

send the person to the Wayfarer's Lodge while an inquiry was made to a friend or relative in the community to which transportation was sought. The annual report for 1885 says that 965 applications were made (presumably in the previous year) involving 1047 persons. Of these, 100 were sent away on some kind of transportation assisted by the Society or provided by others, 28 were given some assistance by another agency in the city, employment was procured for 5, 12 were assisted with clothes, 57 were given meals and lodging, 28 were refused assistance or turned out of the Wayfarer's Lodges for drunkenness, refusal to work or idleness, and 809 left of their own accord and were not heard from again.

Using techniques such as these, the Society for Organizing Charity was able to show real savings; in 1886 "each lodging and each meal cost the charitable public about two cents in excess of the value received for it" (186, *15 February 1887, p.* 29). Indeed, had the public wholeheartedly cooperated by buying all the wood that was cut, one can infer that the Society might have turned a profit. James W. Walk, M.D., General Secretary for the Society, wrote in 1890 to A. G. Warner that, "we take all men, who apply in a sober condition; but find it difficult in disposing of the product of wood. We could treble the output with our present average of number of laborers."[13]

Mary Richmond, who was to become a leader in the professionalization of social work, came to Philadelphia in 1900. She defined the Society's decentralized system of Ward Associations as the root of its organizational and financial disarray. While she was in Philadelphia from 1900 to 1909 she reorganized the Society into a strongly centralized casework-oriented agency. On the basis of this structural reorganization, there developed a reevaluation of the purpose of the Society itself that took some years to be worked out.

As early as 1911 there was careful discussion of the pros and cons of the establishment of a municipal lodging house in Philadelphia.[14] The Society had been opposed to this as a solu-

[13] Letter from James W. Walk, M.D., General Secretary, to A. G. Warner, Esq., 15 April 1890.
[14] FAMILY SERVICE OF PHILADELPHIA. Preliminary statement as to the advisability of urging the establishment of a municipal lodging house in Philadelphia, 1911.

tion to the housing problems of the city's Skid Row population. By November 1914 the Society's position on municipal lodging houses had jelled, according to a letter from R. M. Little, General Secretary of the Society, to Bernard J. Newman, Executive Secretary of the Philadelphia Housing Commission (now known as the Housing Association of the Delaware Valley): "In reply to your letter of the 4th, I wish to say that the Society for Organizing Charity does not contemplate making an extensive study of the lodging houses in Philadelphia. We have made several surveys—once since I came here—and have a general knowledge of the situation, quite sufficient to base our judgement upon, that Philadelphia should have a municipal lodging house and exercise a close supervision over all private lodging houses and missions."[15]

By 1915 the Philadelphia Society for Organizing Charity had reached the position that the care of the homeless was peculiarly a municipal responsibility and tried to get the city to take up this responsibility (131). The development of such municipal facilities was common in many cities in the country after 1908 (48, 133). Mayor Blankenburg agreed, but the City Councils rejected the idea. The Society, nonetheless, began to implement its position by closing the 16th Street Lodge in 1915 and the Lombard Street facility in 1918. In 1921, the Society joined other charities to form a new centralized fund-raising agency, the Welfare Federation, which could only require a further recognition that it was necessary to reformulate the purposes and client population or quit the field entirely. The consequence of this was a change in name to the Family Society of Philadelphia in 1925 and a further change in 1950 to Family Service.

Again, we see that over time the private charitable organizations were progressively defined away from the socially unrespectable; in this case, the direction was away from "organizing charity" and "suppressing mendicancy" to a derivative but somewhat different set of objectives in which the homeless, whether workingmen or vagrant men, were excluded. Tramps,

[15] Correspondence in files of the Philadelphia Housing Commission (renamed Philadelphia Housing Association and then Housing Association of Delaware Valley). These materials should now be in the Urban Archives, Paley Library, Temple University.

vagrants and "bummers" continued to be a part of the life of Philadelphia long after the Society "withdrew" its concern from them.

Slums and Urban Renewal: Neighborhood Houses and Octavia Hill

The long campaign against the Lombard–Southwark–Moyamensing slum was conducted by a series of religious agencies, culminating in the work of several settlement houses and the Octavia Hill Association. The Bedford Street Mission was founded in 1853 at 619 Kater Street in the heart of the slum. In its earliest days, it was known as "The Young Men's Central Home Mission of the Episcopal Church," and, high on the building, this may still be found carved into a white marble block. Its early religious orientation is illustrated by the fact that in 1854 its Board of Directors rented a small church building at 23d and Lombard streets where preaching services and a Sunday School were designed to replace open-air preaching under the trees on Gray's Ferry Road. But this location, known as the Pitman Chapel, was overshadowed by the work on Bedford Street. At the core of the religious activities at the Mission were about 90 young Methodist men and women, with additional volunteers from the Presbyterians, Lutherans, Episcopalians and Friends (Quakers). In 1866 the organization became nonsectarian and known as the Bedford Street Mission.

The Bedford Street Center continued to operate a neighborhood house program until about 1946 when it merged with the Friends Neighborhood Guild, located in the Old Spring Garden District just north of the Skid Row area. The Guild developed as Friends Mission Number 1, a project of the Friends First Day School Union. After some organizational politics, it assumed ownership of a Meeting House that had fallen into disuse. Its program was also a settlement house program aimed at the residents of the densely populated family area in which the Tenderloin was located.[16] By the time the Bedford Street Center

[16] HEACOCK, E. Friends Neighborhood Guild . . . Sixtieth Anniversary, 1879–1939; letter of Horace Lippincott to Friends Neighborhood Guild, dated 4 May 1950; MATLACK, T. Brief historical sketches concerning Friends Meet-

and the Friends Neighborhood Guild merged, both were perceived as Quaker settlement-house projects and, given financial
limitations, the merger seemed logical.

The activities on Rodman Street were similar, although the
development was somewhat more complex. Settlement work on
St. Mary Street began with a Sunday School established in 1857
by William David Stuart, a student at the University of Pennsylvania. William Stuart died and his work was continued by his
father, George H. Stuart, who operated a Mission Chapel there
for many years. Other efforts to provide a "good influence" in
the neighborhood were the establishment of a day nursery in
1880 and a kindergarten school in 1881; each was an autono-
mous agency developed and operated by concerned persons.

Starting in 1880, plans developed for the physical rehabilitation of the area. Theodore Starr began to acquire properties on
St. Mary, Naudain and Lombard streets, among them the lots
surrounding the church and graveyard property, which he
turned into a garden. When Starr died, he gave the garden to
Anna Hollowell, a member of the Board of Education and a
founder of the City Parks Association. She, in turn, gave the
property to the City Parks Association for the use of the College
Settlement.

Down the street, Hannah Fox acquired 615–617 St. Mary
Street and evicted Mom Hewitt in 1886. In 1893 her property
became the location of the College Settlement. To help obliter-
ate the stereotype of St. Mary Street as a place of vice, crime,
poverty and vagrancy, the name was changed to Carver Street
(though later it was again changed to Rodman Street). To further
assist in driving out the previous residents, the entire block
between Sixth and Seventh and from Lombard to Carver was
cleared with City Council support, and the Starr Garden Centre
replaced the College Settlement with an educational and recreational program.

By 1893 several approaches had developed in response to the
social and moral conditions of the slum. There were two
settlement-house programs operating in the heart of the slum
within two blocks of each other. There was also housing renova-

ings of the past and present with special reference to Philadelphia Yearly
Meeting, 1938, pp. 480 ff. [Friends Historical Collection.]

tion (urban renewal) which had been expressed on a small scale
by the Beneficent Building Association and, on a larger scale,
by Theodore Starr, Hannah Fox and Anna Hollowell. During
the latter part of 1895 and in 1896 the housing approach was
organized more systematically and placed on a stable business
basis with the encouragement of the Civic Club of Philadelphia.
The Octavia Hill Association was incorporated late in 1896 as a
limited dividend corporation, selling shares at $25 each. It was
the belief of the members that it could both raise the moral
character of the area and raise its rent-paying capacity at the
same time.

The Octavia Hill Association expanded rapidly. In July 1896
it acquired 518 South Seventh Street and 4 houses in the 700
block of Rodman Street. The following year, still feeling their
way, the Managers of the Association reported that "the eight
houses in Smith's Court and the adjoining house, 529 Lombard
Street—both in May 1897—have been difficult to rent owing to
the previous reputation of the Court. Its name has now been
changed to Fairhill Street and the locality gives excellent opportunity to test the efficacy of the Association's methods as
landlord in raising the moral character of a neighborhood and its
rent-paying capacity." Apparently, these properties continued
to "severely test the methods of the organization" up through
1898, but then the Octavia Hill Association seemed to "take
off." Near the end of 1899, it had 553 outstanding shares
capitalized at $33,835 and owned 31 houses and was rental
agent for 28 other properties (129, *1895, 1897, 1 January 1899,
November 1899*). Its ownership was now focused in 2 zones, the
first being the heart of the slum and the second relatively close
to the Delaware River and a little down in the old Southwark
district.[17] Some of the properties were acquired as a part of
earlier private antislum campaigns; the Association managed
the properties of the Starr Estate and other houses in the heart
of the slum.[18]

[17] Zone 1, 4 houses in the 700 block of Rodman Street; 518 and 529 Lombard Street; 8 houses on Fairhill Street. Zone 2, 956 and 958 Otsego Street; 14
houses on League Street; 955 Front Street.
[18] 529 Reese Street; 9 houses on Naudain Street; 502, 506 Kater Street; 11
houses in the 2600 block of Webster Street.

The tenants of the Octavia Hill Association varied both racially and ethnically. Fairhill Street was Black, Webster was Irish and American, Rodman Street and the Starr properties were Jewish (129, *1899*). In 1901 the Association owned 26 properties and managed 42; among the rental properties were 4 in the 700 block of Clymer Street occupied by Italians (129, *1901*). The Association continued to expand into other parts of the city as it continued its dual commitment for improving housing quality for the poor, as well as assured (although limited) profits for its investors. Thus there were further acquisitions in the Italian section of the 400 block of Montrose Street, the Black slum area on Rittenhouse Street in Germantown, the Slavic residential area on both South and North Front streets (129, *1903, 1907, 1910, January 1912*). By 1913 the Association owned 124 houses with 171 residents and was agent for 178 houses with 404 families (129, *1913*). But it had reached the threshold of its easy expansion, for in 1914 it was having difficulty in getting properties at a price which it could afford and, for the first time, it reported a deficit (129, *1914*).

During all this time the Association continued its social commitment. In 1902 the Association bought 4 houses on Prosperous Alley [Perth Street] which were formerly a "notorious resort" (129, *10 November 1902*). In 1904 it sponsored a study of housing conditions in Philadelphia by Emily W. Dinwiddie (51) which described housing conditions in an Italian, an ethnically mixed Russian–Jewish, Polish, Irish, German and American section, and a Black residential section, and did a special substudy of slum dwelling located in the densely populated and deteriorating alleys and courts of the inner-city areas.

The Association is still active in the field of housing improvement in the poorer sections of the city but is having difficulty finding adequate financing. In the short run, the Octavia Hill Association was successful as a part of a larger effort to expel the slum residents of the Rodman Street area. As a demonstration of privately sponsored urban renewal, it was unable to expand its activities to the point where it could be a significant influence in turning back the more extensive slums of the city and should therefore be viewed as very limited in its significance.

Salvaging Alcoholics: Franklin Home and Rescue Missions

The Franklin Reformatory Home for Inebriates was oriented to the larger population which might have had considerable contact with the slum residents nearby but did not. Founded in 1872, the Home occupied three adjacent row houses at 911–15 Locust Street by 1890. Recovered alcoholics assisted the incoming resident; the fact that the recovered alcoholics had gone through the experience themselves made them sensitive to new residents' sufferings. Regarded as a physically sick person, the inebriate was also perceived as a victim of his society rather than as a "slave of his appetites" or as a "victim of heredity." That is, Franklin Home regarded the inebriate as someone who, by conforming to social customs, had acquired a taste for intoxicants, then developed an appetite, and then became habituated to their use.

The Home provided a "shelter from temptation" and a "place to recover from excesses." But it was more than that, for the home adopted a religious point of view. A man's condition was not only physical and mental, but spiritual, and the task of the program was to "arouse his conscience to a realization of his moral and religious duties and responsibilities." Provided with a warm (Protestant) Christian family atmosphere, the men went to the meetings held by the Godwin Association (the group of graduates from the Home) where present and former residents discussed their own alcohol problems on the basis of the following principles (68, *32d, pp. 30–31*):

"(1) Rigorous and unshrinking examination of the cause of his downfall; (2) acknowledgement that his course has been a continued offence against God and His Laws; (3) admission of the necessity of God's mercy and pardon; (4) recognition of his inability to do the right, except by God's grace and assistance; (5) acceptance of mercy and forgiveness in the faith that strength is never withheld from him who earnestly seeks it; (6) recognition that ultimate and permanent reformation is in his own hands; (7) realization that the Home not only seeks to remove drunkenness but teaches how to change association, habits, thoughts, and feelings which lead to drunkenness."

This formulation is remarkably similar to the principles set forth by Alcoholics Anonymous many years later.

The Home's program was free to those who could not afford

to pay; between April 1872 and March 1890, it had 4634 residents, of whom 38% were cared for free. During the same period, the Home claimed that 40% "have been rescued from lives of drunken depravity and have become useful sober citizens," a surprising proportion to those experienced in alcoholism treatment.

Notwithstanding this statement of success, it seems probable that few of the residents were "hardcore" vagrant alcoholics. The Home expressed a concern for reaching these vagrants. "They are not all, as they appear in the mass, indolent nonentities, who are happy in and prefer their present life, no; many of them have moments of bitter remorse, the remembrance of a once happy home . . . hunted like wild beasts as 'tramps' by police officers and shunned as something loathesome by the passerby, how in God's name, are these men to raise themselves? It is next to impossible" (68, *12th, pp. 109–110*). The 1884 annual report showed some effort to implement this concern. Eight men were persuaded to move into the Home who did not have enough money to provide themselves clothes nor to "maintain them until they are restored to Christian manhood that will enable them to live by the labor of their own hands." Nothing more was said about the matter, however, and we assume that the experiment died.

While the Franklin Reformatory Home went in one direction, the Sunday Breakfast Association went in another. The Sunday Breakfast was adapted to incorporate the vagrant as a major reason for continued support and survival, while the Franklin Home concentrated on alcoholism treatment. It is worthy of note that the work ethic and the easy equivalence between work and rehabilitation have continued down into our own time; it is a view of "rehabilitation" that is not easily put to rest. It is of some interest also that organizationally the Sunday Breakfast Association ultimately absorbed the Franklin Reformatory Home.

In addition to the Sunday Breakfast Association, other agencies developed which used the rescue mission approach; the Florence Crittenton Mission is an example. Rescue missions were largely expressions of concern by churches and church-related groups elsewhere in the city; and, consistent with the advent of the late 19th and early 20th Century, they were mostly oriented to the proposition that the person should accept Christ and be "saved," and that food and lodging are merely the means to bring the prospective convert into a position where he or she would hear the message. If the person was truly saved, then Christ would have entered his life, he would have been "born again," and he would, as a consequence, abandon a drunken and vagrant lifestyle, or a life of prostitution, and so forth. He would, in a word, be "rehabilitated."

In this section we consider several gospel missions to the alcoholics and the vagrant men of Philadelphia, selecting those that have been important to Skid Row men in recent years, being located either on Vine Street or within relatively easy walking distance from the Skid Row area. They were a significant part of the institutional survival network during the 1950s and 1960s, i.e., a man could go from one to the other and piece out food and shelter for most of the month.

The historical origins of the missions varied considerably. The Brotherhood Mission, which is actually located on East Girard Avenue in Fishtown–Lower Kensington rather than in the old Skid Row–Tenderloin area, was a consequence of Russell Conwell's leadership of the Men's Brotherhood of the Grace Baptist Church (more commonly known as the Baptist Temple), located along Broad Street in a then affluent upper-middle-class neighborhood. In 1906 the Brotherhood made the final payment on the $100,000 debt that they had incurred to construct the Baptist Temple and Conwell suggested that they support a project that was outside of their regular routine of Church work. Conwell "asked for twelve men who would pray every day at the noon hour for the leadership of the Spirit, for two weeks, at which time we held our regular meeting, in order to tell what we felt led to do. Deacon Gillen thought we should do something for the drunkard, drug addict, homeless men of the street, discharged prisoners" (29, 75).[19] Oriented to the poor of Fishtown, the Brotherhood Mission still serves a modest number of vagrant men from the Philadelphia Skid Row area.

Fitting somewhat more closely to Skid Row in its historical origins was the Methodist Episcopal Mission. As early as 1892 the Philadelphia Conference of the Methodist Episcopal

[19] Cf. "The Temple Review," 1 June 1906. [Grace Baptist Church.]

Church, held at Simpson's Grove (Trevose Heights), was attracted to "rescue" work among "criminals, gamblers, drunkards, and women of shame" (122, *105th, p. 130; 122d, pp. 118, 120*). Until a few years ago the Mission maintained a "ministry of love and saving grace to the fallen men and women who throng that locality and many are rescued from lives of vice and shame" (122, *125th, p. 157*). That the area was still a family area is evidenced by the fact that in 1910 the Mission reported an attendance of 26,151 with 728 conversions (less than 3%) and a Sunday School with 125 children. The close tie which its supporters saw with the Prohibition campaign is evidenced in the following defensive statement in 1919 by Charles E. Carroll of the Board of Home Missions and Church Extension of the Methodist Episcopal Church: "The present location for a mission of this type is claimed to be ideal by the leaders of the present work. Many influential friends of the mission also, it is claimed, believe it would be unwise to 'touch' the mission as far as changing location is concerned. There are located in the heart of this district, many saloons and low grade picture houses, besides the city's 'reddest' vice section. Not until the changes which are anticipated through national prohibition come, is there much prospect for this particular mission losing its present reputation for marked success."[20] The decline of the Skid Row area and its redevelopment in the late 1950s and 1960s led to the closing of this mission.

The Galilee Mission was probably almost as important to the Philadelphia Skid Row as the Sunday Breakfast Association, although it was founded at a much later date. Arthur Lewis mentions it as "the last stop in Skid Row" and a "source of many a non-paying Patterson client and recipient of whatever money Chippy had left in his pockets by that time of the night" (103, *p. 122*). The name of the Mission is said to have come from that part of the old English Cathedral porch or chapel which was provided for penitents and catechumens; the Philadelphia Galilee Mission was adapted from the Galilee Mission of the

---

[20] CARROLL, C. E. Report on the religious and social survey of the downtown district, Philadelphia, Pennsylvania. Methodist Episcopal Church, Board of Home Missions and Church Extension, 19 February 1919. [Methodist Historical Center.]

Calvary (Protestant Episcopal) Church and the Galilee Coffee House that opened on Christmas Eve 1890 at 338 East 23d Street, New York City (186, *May 1891, pp. 50–51*).[21] It was conceived as an effort to promote temperance among workingmen through the sale of inexpensive food, coffee, tea, cocoa, the availability of billiards, a game and reading room, and inexpensive baths. Bishop Potter was among those who gave an address.

In 1897 the Northeast Convocation of the Protestant Episcopal Diocese of Pennsylvania began a rescue mission, "the object of which is to rescue men and women who have been wrecked by sin, and who are willing, by God's help, to undertake to live a better life." In that first year, the Convocation spent $500 on the mission, which was located at Ninth and Carleton streets, "in the midst of one of the worst sections of American-born people in our city" (155, *113th, p. 67*; 156, *40th, p. 25*). Initially the Galilee was oriented to children as well as adults and women as well as men. A small Sunday School was established for "young people," and the emphasis was placed on the need for a Deaconness to "visit the careless and immoral who live in the vicinity of the Mission" (156, *39th, pp. 26–27; 40th, p. 25*). As usual, there are the claims to success (albeit without statistics): "many have been reclaimed from their past lives of vice and misery, and some are known to be doing well, and leading good, honest, and useful lives" (156, *40th, p. 25*). By 1904 the location at the northeast corner of Vine and Darien streets was purchased; this was "in the heart of the Tenderloin opposite the most used patrol box," according to the *Evening Bulletin*, 28 January 1905. What was reported as the "most modern mission in the country" was dedicated the previous day; Bishop Whittaker spoke at the ceremony and warned against "over-zealous converts." The new building was oriented to the homeless men of the area and, in clear competition with the cheap lodging houses of the vicinity, the Galilee made a small charge: in 1915 meals were 5 and 10 cents, beds were 10 cents a night (and no double deckers!), laundry and bath were 5 and 10 cents.[22] The general principle of small payment continued,

[21] HARTSHORNE, F. Historical sketches of the parishes of Pennsylvania, 1915–1916. In a collection of clippings at the Protestant Episcopal Diocese of Pennsylvania Church House.
[22] Ibid.

although rates were somewhat higher, and the details vary from the pre-World War I period until it was closed in late 1973.

While there was some early attention toward families in the locality, both the Sunday Breakfast Association and the Galilee Mission came to focus their attention on homeless people (the Sunday Breakfast has always maintained a small program for homeless women who are referred to it). This policy was reinforced on the part of the Galilee by a continuity of leadership.[23] George Wilkins, the last executive director, came to the Galilee in 1908 from a wealthy Utica, New York, family; apparently he came to Philadelphia just out of college and began as a volunteer helper. Over the years, he moved up to be business manager, superintendent and, finally, executive director. An able and vigorous man, he was also active in business, civic and fraternal affairs. Thus, by the time he was 48 years of age in 1937, he had founded and operated a textile company, was president of a hardware firm and associated with two building and loan societies; he was vice-president of the Pennsylvania Prison Society, vice chairman of the Central Division of the Welfare Federation of Philadelphia, chairman of the Red Cross Community Flour Distribution Committee of Philadelphia, member of the Board of Directors of the Red Cross, member of the Board of Administration of Episcopal Hospital and a vestryman of Old Christ Church (which had roots deep in Colonial Philadelphia); he was the past chancellor of the Knights of Pythias, and a member of the Grand Lodge of Pennsylvania Masons. At the same time, he managed also to be executive director of the Galilee Mission during the Depression, when the demands on its services were extremely heavy.

Indeed the Depression had led to his assuming the directorship of what amounted to a municipal shelter as well. In November 1930 the Mayor and the Director of Public Safety expressed concern for the health of the hungry and homeless men who were then sleeping on the floors of the cellars of the

[23] Most of the data on George Wilkins are from the files of the American Foundation, Philadelphia, Pennsylvania, which makes the annual Bok Award. The award consists of $10,000 and a gold medal. This file contains nominations with supporting statements, clippings from newspapers, and other materials.

police stations.[24] On 28 November a private fund drive by the "Committee for Unemployment Relief" made it possible to open a shelter for the homeless in an abandoned 8-story building of the Baldwin Locomotive Works at Eighteenth and Hamilton streets. The shelter was opened to 891 men and by 1 December 1930, 1350 men had received shelter, supper and breakfast.[25] By the time it closed, 4 years later, 3629 men had been cared for.

Wilkins instituted a system of registration, identification, and work expectations that were evidently directly adapted from his experience in working with Skid Row men; after a preliminary interview, there was a fumigation and a medical examination, then the man was given a bath card, an identification card, vaccination, bed and meal tickets; he was expected to work 30 hours a week, the meal tickets were renewed daily, and he had to be in the building by 11 PM. There was some protest by labor unions at the work requirement on the familiar grounds that attention was being given to homeless men rather than to families and children,[26] but, apparently, Wilkins and his supporters had their way. In 4 years the men in the Shelter contributed 10,260,199 hours of labor. When the Eighteenth and Hamilton facilities were closed, Wilkins obtained a factory building in Kensington without cost to the city in which 248 men lived and worked. When the Mayor insisted that the city could not afford even this, the counterargument (to no avail) was that at $3 a day the men had put in 8000 man hours of labor (or $24,000 of earned value) which had cost the city only about 31 cents a day per man to maintain. Wilkins sent homeless boys across the street to a house he bought in 1933 for this purpose; in 3 years, 300 boys were cared for.

It was for this work, as well as his supervision of the distribution of over 21 million pounds of flour through the Red Cross Flour Distribution Committee, that George Wilkins received the Bok Award in 1937. It was a recognition by those in positions of power and influence that George Wilkins had been

[24] Philadelphia *Inquirer*, 18 November 1930.
[25] Wilkins file, American Foundation; *Public Ledger*, 1 December 1930.
[26] *Union Labor Record*, 5 December 1930. In the clipping collection of the Family Service of Philadelphia.

an important force in terms of humanitarian values, as well as in the reduction of the political threat posed by the Depression.

The problems of prostitution, slums, drunkenness, and vagrancy were too large for the social welfare institutions to handle. They had undertaken a job which was too big for them in the first place and they knew it. The additional factor which they believed was present in the situation was the possibility of divine intervention; some expected this to be made manifest in conversion, or at least a sincere desire to change, and accompanied by subsequent changes in lifestyle, while others sought to use the state as a way to remove the sources of evil. But, in general, the scale of the problem they sought to remedy was too large and the hard-won sought-after results were pitifully small. Some agencies sought to be more "efficient" through the separation of the "worthy" from the "unworthy" poor and, in the process, transformed the problem on which they were actually working and then abandoned it altogether. The rescue missions, which developed to provide assistance and service to Skid Row people (albeit at a price), attracted needy homeless and unemployed men from elsewhere in the metropolitan region while the missions were, at the same time, engaged in efforts to get them off Skid Row. Their methods repelled many who needed help.

The social welfare agencies neither created poverty and homelessness nor provided much more of a remedy for them than did the House of Correction and the rescue mission. Just as prostitution, slums, drunkenness and homelessness are products of larger societal conditions, so the disappearance of the (White) Skid Row is a consequence of larger conditions in our society. It is worth noting that while social reformers were discovering poverty and unemployment and organizing professional social work from earlier church-related private charitable institutions, the Skid Rows and the Tenderloins became differentiated from the more general poverty–slum–vice–vagrancy area and became acceptable as specialized complexes of social institutions. Indeed, the Social Reform's most successful effort in Philadelphia, which led to the actual ejection of the population and the physical and social "reconstruction" of parts of the Lombard–South-

wark–Moyamensing slum, was a factor in the further segregation of the institutions of the "unworthy poor." It would not be
too far from the truth to suggest that the Social Reform was a
major factor in the development of Philadelphia's Vine Street
Skid Row neighborhood.

Bibliography

1. ANDERSON, N. The hobo; the sociology of the homeless man. Chicago; University of Chicago Press; 1923.
2. ANDERSON, N. The homeless in New York City. New York; Welfare Council of New York City; 1934.
3. AVERBACH, A. San Francisco's south of market district, 1850–1950; the emergence of a Skid Row. Calif. hist. Quart. **52:** 197–223, 1973.
4. BAHN, A. K. and CHANDLER, C. A. Alcoholism in psychiatric clinic patients. Quart. J. Stud. Alc. **22:** 411–417, 1961.
5. BAHR, H. M., ed. Dissaffiliated man; essays and bibliography on Skid Row, vagrancy, and outsiders. Toronto; University of Toronto Press; 1970.
6. BAHR, H. M. The gradual disappearance of Skid Row. Social Probl. **15:** 41–45, 1967.
7. BAHR, H. M. Homelessness and disaffiliation. New York; Columbia University Bureau of Applied Social Research; 1968.
8. BAHR, H. M. Skid Row; an introduction to disaffiliation. New York; Oxford University Press; 1973.
9. BAHR, H. M. and CAPLOW, T. Old men drunk and sober. New York; New York University Press; 1974.
10. BAHR, H. M. and GARRETT, G. R. Disaffiliation among urban women. New York; Columbia University Bureau of Applied Research; 1971. [Mimeographed.]
11. BALTZELL, E.D. Philadelphia gentlemen; the making of a national upper class. New York; Free Press; 1958.
12. BARKER, C. Philadelphia in the forties. Philadelphia; City Historical Society; 1931.
13. BARNARD, W. F. Forty years at the Five Points. New York; The Five Points House of Industry; 1893.
14. BARSKY, S. F. Representations of community. Ph.D. dissertation, University of Chicago; 1974.
15. BAUMOHL, J. I don't have a home and I live there all the time. Pp. 9–30. In: ROSENBERG FOUNDATION. Annual report. San Francisco; 1973.
16. BAUMOHL, J. and MILLER, H. Down and out in Berkeley. Berkeley; City of Berkeley and University of California Community Affairs Committee; 1974.
17. BERNSTEIN, S. American labor in the long depression, 1873–1878. Sci. Soc. **20:** 59–83, 1956.
18. BITTNER, E. The police on Skid Row; a study of peace keeping. Amer. sociol. Rev. **32:** 699–715, 1967.
19. BLUMBERG, L. U. Segregated housing, marginal location and the crisis of confidence. Phylon **25:** 321–330, 1964.

20. BLUMBERG, L. U., HOFFMAN, F. H., LoCICERO, V., NIEBUHR, H., JR., ROONEY, F. and SHIPLEY, T. E., JR. The men on Skid Row; a study of Philadelphia's homeless man population. Philadelphia; Temple University Department of Psychiatry; 1960.

21. BLUMBERG, L. U., SHIPLEY, T. E., JR. and MOOR, J. O., JR. The Skid Row man and the Skid Row status community; with perspectives on their future. Quart. J. Stud. Alc. 32: 909–941, 1971.

22. BLUMBERG, L. U., SHIPLEY, T. E., JR. and SHANDLER, I. W. Relocation services to Skid Row men; final report to the Greater Philadelphia Movement and the Redevelopment Authority of the City of Philadelphia. Philadelphia; 1968. [Mimeographed.]

23. BLUMBERG, L. U., SHIPLEY, T. E., JR. and SHANDLER, I. W. Skid Row and its alternatives; research and recommendations from Philadelphia. Philadelphia; Temple University Press; 1973.

24. BLUMBERG, L. U., SHIPLEY, T. E., JR., SHANDLER, I. W. and NIEBUHR, H. The development, major goals and strategies of a Skid Row program; Philadelphia. Quart. J. Stud. Alc. 27: 242–258, 1966.

25. BOGUE, D. J. Skid Row in American cities. Chicago; University of Chicago Community and Family Study Center; 1963.

26. [BOYER, H.] North of Market Street; being the adventures of a New York woman in Philadelphia. Philadelphia; Avil; 1896.

27. BRACE, C. L. The dangerous classes of New York and twenty years of work among them. Montclair, N.J.; Patterson Smith; 1967. [Reprint of the 3d ed., 1880.]

28. BREMNER, R. H. From the depths; the discovery of poverty in the United States. New York; New York University Press; 1972.

29. BROTHERHOOD MISSION, PHILADELPHIA. 50th anniversary; 1906–1956. Philadelphia; 1956. [Jubilee Dinner pamphlet.]

30. BURGESS, E. W. The growth of the city. Pp. 47–62. In: PARK, R. E., BURGESS, E. W. and McKENZIE, R. D., eds. The city. Chicago; University of Chicago Press; 1925.

31. BURTON, C. M., STOCKING, W. and MILLER, G. K., eds. The city of Detroit, Michigan, 1701–1922. 2 vol. Detroit; Clarke; 1922.

32. BYRNES, T. (CAMPBELL, H., ed.) Darkness and daylight or lights and shadows of New York life. Hartford; Worthington; 1892.

33. CAPLOW, T., LOVALD, K. A. and WALLACE, S. E. A general report on the problem of relocating the population of the lower loop redevelopment area. Minneapolis; Minneapolis Housing and Redevelopment Authority; 1958.

34. CAREY, M. Essays on the public charities of Philadelphia intending to vindicate the benevolent societies. . . . Philadelphia; Clarke; 1829. [Historical Society of Pennsylvania.]

35. CAREY, M. A plea for the poor. Philadelphia; Bailey; 1837. [Historical Society of Pennsylvania.]

36. CARSON, A. The history of the celebrated Mrs. Ann Carson, widow of the late unfortunate Lieutenant Richard Smith. . . . Philadelphia; 1822. [The Library Company of Philadelphia.]

37. CATLIN, G., ed. Historic Michigan. *Vol. I.* Dayton, OH; National Historical Association; 1940.
38. CAVAN, S. Liquor license; an ethnography of bar behavior. Chicago; Aldine; 1966.
39. CENTRAL NORTH BROAD STREET PRESBYTERIAN CHURCH, PHILADELPHIA. Manual and historic sketch. Philadelphia; 12 October 1914. [Presbyterian Historical Society.]
40. CHAFFEE, Z., JR., POLLAK, W. H. and STERN, C. S. Report on lawlessness in law enforcement. Washington, DC; U.S. National Commission on Law Observance and Enforcement; 1931.
41. CHENG, E. T. Acculturation of the Chinese in the United States. Ph.D. dissertation, University of Pennsylvania; 1948.
42. CHRISTIAN LEAGUE OF PHILADELPHIA. Annual report. Philadelphia; 1910.
43. CHRISTIAN LEAGUE OF PHILADELPHIA. Christian League echoes. Philadelphia; First quarter, 1899. [Historical Society of Pennsylvania.]
44. CLARK, D. The adjustment of Irish immigrants to urban life. Ph.D. dissertation, Temple University; 1970.
45. CLARK, V. S. History of manufactures in the United States. *Vol. II.* 1860–1893. New York; McGraw-Hill; 1929.
46. CLARKE, M., ed. The memoirs of the celebrated and beautiful Mrs. Ann Carson, daughter of an officer of the U.S. Navy and wife of another, whose life terminated in the Philadelphia prison. 2d ed. Philadelphia; 1838. [The Library Company of Philadelphia.]
47. CLOSSEN, C. C., JR. The unemployed in American cities. Quart. J. Econ. 8: 168–217, 453–477, 1894.
48. CUNNINGHAM, J. Municipal lodging houses. St. Louis publ. Libr. mon. Bull., New Ser. 10: 326–348, 1912.
49. DALY, J. and WEINBERG, A. Genealogy of Philadelphia County subdivisions. 2d ed. Philadelphia; Philadelphia Department of Records; 1966.
50. DICKENS, C. American notes. Boston; Ticknor & Fields; 1867.
51. DINWIDDIE, E. W. Housing conditions in Philadelphia. Philadelphia; Octavia Hill Association; 1904.
52. DITTER, D. E. C. The cultural climate of the centennial city; Philadelphia, 1875–1876. Ph.D. dissertation, University of Pennsylvania; 1947.
53. DODD, W. An account of the rise, progress, and present state of the Magdalen Hospital. . . . 4th ed. London; 1769.
54. DRAKE, S. and CLAYTON, H. Black metropolis. Rev. ed. New York; Harper & Row; 1962.
55. DU BOIS, W. E. B. The Philadelphia Negro; a social study. (University of Pennsylvania Series in Political Economy and Public Law, Study No. 14.) New York; Schocken Books; 1967. [Reprint of 1899 edition.]
56. DUNBAR, W. All aboard; a history of railroads in Michigan. Grand Rapids, MI; Eerdmans; 1969.

57. DUNHAM, H. W. Skid Rows—past, present and future. Pp. 50–61. In: Proceedings of the 4th Annual Institute on the Homeless and Institutional Alcoholic. New York; National Council on Alcoholism; 1959.

58. EDWARDS, G., HAWKER, A., WILLIAMSON, V. and HENSMAN, C. London's Skid Row. Lancet 1: 249–252, 1966.

59. EMERSON, H., PINCUS, S. and PHILLIPS, A., eds. Social hygiene. In: PHILADELPHIA SURVEY COMMITTEE. Hospital and health survey. Philadelphia; 1930.

60. EPISCOPAL MISSION, DETROIT. Fourth annual report. Detroit; 1930.

61. ERICKSEN, M. Helping through the group. San Francisco; Travelers Aid Society of San Francisco; ca. 1968.

62. FARMER, S. History of Detroit and Michigan. 2d ed. Detroit; Farmer; 1899.

63. FELS, R. American business cycles. Chapel Hill; University of North Carolina Press; 1959.

64. FEMALE DOMESTIC MISSIONARY SOCIETY OF PHILADELPHIA FOR THE SUPPORT OF THE GOSPEL IN THE ALMS HOUSE. Annual reports. Philadelphia; 1817— [Historical Society of Pennsyvania.]

65. FLYNT, W. J., pseud. [WILLARD, F. E.] Tramping with tramps. New York; Century; 1901.

66. FOSTER, C. The urban missionary movement. Penn. Mag. Hist. Biog. 75: 47–65, 1951.

67. FOSTER, G. C. (TAYLOR, G. R., ed.) Philadelphia in slices. Penn. Mag. Hist. Biog. 93: 23–72, 1969. [Orig. New York Tribune, Oct. 1848–Feb. 1849.]

68. FRANKLIN HOME FOR THE REFORMATION OF INEBRIATES. Annual reports. Philadelphia; 1883— [Historical Society of Pennsylvania.]

69. FRANKLIN HOME FOR THE REFORMATION OF INEBRIATES. The Franklin Home and its work. Philadelphia; ca. 1904.

70. FRETZ, F. K. The furnished room problem in Philadelphia. Ph.D. dissertation, University of Pennsylvania; 1910.

71. GARRETT, G. R. and BAHR, H. M. Women on Skid Row. Quart. J. Stud. Alc. 34: 1228–1243, 1973.

72. GIFFEN, P. J. The revolving door; a functional interpretation. Canad. Rev. Sociol. Anthrop. 3: 154–166, 1966.

73. GOLDBERG, M. The runaway Americans. Ment. Hyg. 56: 13–21, 1972.

74. GOODWIN, L. Do the poor want to work; a social-psychological study of work orientations. Washington, D.C.; Brookings Institution; 1972.

75. GRACE BAPTIST CHURCH OF PHILDELPHIA, THE BAPTIST TEMPLE. Years of grace, 1872–1967; a sketch of the history of the Grace Baptist Church. . . . Philadelphia; n.d.

76. GROGAN, E. Ringolevio; a life played for keeps. Boston; Little, Brown; 1972.

254 LIQUOR AND POVERTY; SKID ROW AS A HUMAN CONDITION

77. HALE, W. B. An empire of illusion and its fall. Leslie's Mon. **60:** 451–459, 1905.
78. HANDLIN, O. Boston's immigrants; a study in acculturation. New York; Atheneum; 1959.
79. HANDLIN, O. The newcomers; Negroes and Puerto Ricans in a changing metropolis. Cambridge, MA; Harvard University Press; 1959.
80. HARRINGTON, M. The other America; poverty in the United States. New York; Macmillan; 1962.
81. HARRIS, C. and ULLMAN, E. L. The nature of cities. Ann. Amer. Acad. polit. soc. Sci. **242:** 7–17, 1945.
82. HARTSHORNE, F. Historical sketches of the parishes of the Dioceses of Pennsylvania, 1915–1916. Philadelphia; n.d.
83. HAWLEY, A. H. Human ecology; a theory of community structure. New York; Ronald; 1950.
84. HAWLEY, A. H. Urban society; an ecological approach. New York; Ronald; 1971.
85. HOFFMAN, C. The depression of the nineties. J. econ. Hist. **16:** 137–164, 1956.
86. HOOD, W., BLUMBERG, L. [U.] and SHIPLEY, T. E., JR. The intensive counselor; a more detailed analysis. In: BLUMBERG, L. [U.], SHIPLEY, T. E., JR. and SHANDLER, I. W. Skid Row and its alternatives; research and recommendations from Philadelphia. Philadelphia; Temple University Press; 1973.
87. HUNEKER, J. G. Steeplejack. *Vol. I.* New York; Scribner's; 1920.
88. HUTTER, M. Summertime servants; the Schlockhaus waiter. Pp. 204–225. In: JACOBS, G., ed. The participant observer. New York; Braziller; 1970.
89. IRWIN, W. The city that was; a requiem of Old San Francisco. New York; Huebsch; 1906.
90. JELLINEK, E. M. "Death from alcoholism" in the United States in 1940; a statistical analysis. Quart. J. Stud. Alc. **3:** 465–494, 1942.
91. JELLINEK, E. M. Phases of alcohol addiction. Quart. J. Stud. Alc. **13:** 673–684, 1952.
92. JELLINEK, E. M. and KELLER, M. Rates of alcoholism in the United States of America, 1940–1948. Quart. J. Stud. Alc. **13:** 49–59, 1952.
93. JULIANI, R. Historical and demographic aspects of Italian immigration to Philadelphia. In: JULIANI, R. The social organization of immigration; the Italians in Philadelphia. Ph.D. dissertation, University of Pennsylvania; 1971.
94. KANE, J. J. The Irish immigrant in Philadelphia, 1840–1880; a study in conflict and accommodation. Ph.D. dissertation, University of Pennsylvania; 1950.
95. KATZMAN, D. M. Before the ghetto; Black Detroit in the nineteenth century. Urbana; University of Illinois; 1973.
96. KNACK, J. H. Skid Row and its relocation; a Detroit case study. M.A. thesis, Wayne State University; 1966.

97. KYNETT, H. K. For better or for worse? Rambles with progress and otherwise. Philadelphia; 1949.
98. LAW AND ORDER SOCIETY, PHILADELPHIA. Annual reports. Philadelphia; 1881—
99. LEAGUE OF NATIONS. SPECIAL BODY OF EXPERTS ON TRAFFIC IN WOMEN AND CHILDREN. Report, part 2. Geneva; 1927. [American Social Health Association Collection, Social Welfare History Archives, University of Minnesota Library.]
100. LEAVITT, S. The tramps and the law. Forum 2: 190–200, 1886.
101. LEBERGOTT, S. Manpower in economic growth. New York; McGraw-Hill; 1964.
102. LEVINSON, B. M. A comparative study of northern and southern homeless men. J. Negro Educ. 35: 144–150, 1966.
103. LEWIS, A. H. The worlds of Chippy Patterson. New York; Harcourt, Brace; 1960.
104. LIEBOW, E. Tally's corner. Boston; Little, Brown; 1967.
105. LIGHT, I. From vice district to tourist attraction; the moral career of American Chinatowns, 1880–1940. Pacific hist. Rev. 43: 367–394, 1974.
106. LOFLAND, J. The youth ghetto. J. high. Educ. 39: 131–143, 1968.
107. LOVALD, K. A. From hobohemia to Skid Row; the changing community of the homeless man. Ph.D. dissertation, University of Minnesota; 1960.
108. LOVALD, K. [A.] and STUB, H. R. The revolving door; reactions of chronic drunkenness offenders to court sanctions. J. crim. Law Criminol. 59: 525–530, 1968.
109. MACCABE, J. P. B., ed. Directory of the city of Detroit, 1837. Detroit; Harsha; 1837.
110. MCGREGOR HELPING HAND MISSION. Witnesses. Detroit; April 1894.
111. MCGREGOR, T. [W.] The gospel for the masses; the body as well as the soul. Detroit; ca. 1890. [Offprint pamphlet, Burton Historical Collection, Detroit Public Library.]
112. MCGREGOR, T. W. An introduction to twenty thousand men. Detroit; McGregor Institute; 1916.
113. MCKENZIE, R. D. The ecological approach to the study of the human community. Pp. 63–79. In: PARK, R. E., BURGESS, E. W. and MCKENZIE, R. D., eds. The city. Chicago; University of Chicago Press; 1925.
114. MAGDALEN SOCIETY, PHILADELPHIA. BOARD OF MANAGERS. Annual reports. Philadelphia; 1867— [Historical Society of Pennsylvania, The White–Williams Foundation.]
115. MALTHUS, T. R. An essay on the principle of population. New York; Modern Library; 1960. [Reprint of 1798 edition.]
116. MALZBERG, B. New data on mental disease among Negroes in New York State, 1960–61. Albany; Research Foundation for Mental Hygiene; 1965.
117. MARTIN, E. W., pseud. [MCCABE.] The secrets of the great city; a

work descriptive of the virtues and the vices, the mysteries and crimes of New York City. Philadelphia; Jones, Brother; 1868.

118. MARTINDALE, D. American social structure. New York; Appleton-Century-Crofts; 1960.

119. MASON, P. F. Some characteristics of a youth ghetto in Boulder, Colorado. J. Geogr., N.Y. **71**: 526–532, 1972.

120. MASON, P. F. Some spatial and locational relationships relevant to youth ghetto disorder. Proc. Ass. Amer. Geogr. **5**: 165–169, 1973.

121. MELTZER, B., CAMINS, B. and COHEN, M. R. A technical report on incipient Skid Rows; prepared for the Philadelphia Redevelopment Authority. Philadelphia; Greenfield; 1966.

122. METHODIST EPISCOPAL CHURCH. Minutes [official journal, year book] of the Philadelphia annual conferences. Philadelphia; 1892—

123. METHODIST EPISCOPAL CHURCH. NEW YORK LADIES' HOME MISSIONARY SOCIETY. The old brewery and the new mission house at the Five Points. New York; Stringer & Townsend; 1854.

124. MINEHAN, R. Boy and girl tramps of America. New York; Farrar & Rinehart; 1934.

125. MONTELIUS, M. Final report of the Travelers Aid Society demonstration project on transient young adults in San Francisco. San Francisco; November 1968.

126. NASCHER, I. L. The wretches of Povertyville. Chicago; Lanzit; 1909.

127. NASH, G. The habitats of homeless men in Manhattan. New York; Columbia University Department of Applied Social Research; 1964. [Mimeographed.]

128. OBERHOLZER, E. P. Philadelphia; a history of the city and its people. Philadelphia; Clarke; 1911.

129. OCTAVIA HILL ASSOCIATION, PHILADELPHIA. Annual reports. Philadelphia; 1897— [Octavia Hill Association.].

130. OCTAVIA HILL ASSOCIATION, PHILADELPHIA. Certain aspects ot the housing problem in Philadelphia. Ann. Amer. Acad. polit. soc. Sci. **20**: 111–120, 1902.

131. ORMSBY, R. A brief history of Family Service of Philadelphia, 1879–1956. Philadelphia; ca. 1956. [Mimeographed.] [Family Service of Philadelphia.]

132. ORWELL, G. Down and out in Paris and London. New York; Harcourt, Brace, Jovanovich; 1961. [Orig. 1933.]

133. OVERSEERS OF THE POOR, BOSTON. Fiftieth annual report. Boston; 1913–1914.

134. PALMER, F. Early days in Detroit. Detroit; Hund & June; 1906.

135. PARRISH, I. Report on the sanitary condition of Philadelphia. Trans. Amer. med. Ass. **2**: 466, 1849.

136. PENNSYLVANIA SOCIETY FOR THE PROMOTION OF PUBLIC

ECONOMY. Report of the library committee . . . of February 1, 1817. Philadelphia; 1817. [American Philosophical Society Library.]

137. PENNSYLVANIA STATE POLICE. BUREAU OF RESEARCH AND DEVELOPMENT. Uniform crime report, Commonwealth of Pennsylvania; annual report. Philadelphia; 1974.

138. PHILADELPHIA. BUREAU OF POLICE. Annual report. Philadelphia; 1896.

139. PHILADELPHIA. CHIEF OF POLICE. Annual reports. Philadelphia; 1877—

140. PHILADELPHIA. CHIEF OF POLICE. Annual report . . . for 1881. In: SELECT COUNCIL. Appendix of the Journal. . . . Philadelphia; 1882.

141. PHILADELPHIA. MAYOR. Annual message of Mayor Stuart for 1894, Vol. II. Philadelphia; 1895.

142. PHILADELPHIA. MAYOR. Annual message of Mayor Edwin H. Fitler, 1891. In: PHILADELPHIA. DEPARTMENT OF PUBLIC SAFETY. Report for 1890, Vol. 2. Philadelphia; 1891.

143. PHILADELPHIA. MAYOR. Annual report of Mayor John Weaver for year ending December 31, 1904. Book 2. [Free Library of Philadelphia, Logan Circle.]

144. PHILADELPHIA. MAYOR. Mayor's message. In: SELECT COUNCIL. Appendix 140 of the Journal . . . January 1 to July 1, 1870.

145. PHILADELPHIA. MAYOR. Third annual report of Samuel G. King, Mayor, for 1883. In: SELECT COUNCIL. Appendix 172 of the Journal. . . . Philadelphia; 1884.

146. PHILADELPHIA. MUNICIPAL COURT. Fourth annual report. Philadelphia; 1917.

147. PHILADELPHIA. OFFICE OF THE DIRECTOR OF FINANCE. Report on real property assessments and real estate tax revenue. Philadelphia; January 1971.

148. PHILADELPHIA CITY COUNCILS. An ordinance to change the names of certain streets, lanes, courts, alleys, etc., in the City of Philadelphia, September 1, 1858. Philadelphia; Bicking & Gilbert; 1859. [The Library Company of Philadelphia.]

149. PHILADELPHIA STARR CENTRE. History of a street. Philadelphia; 1901.

150. PITTEL, S. M. The current status of the Haight Ashbury Hippie Community. San Francisco; Haight Ashbury Research Project; 1968.

151. PITTMAN, D. J. Alcoholism treatment and referral demonstration project, final report. St. Louis; Washington University Social Science Institute; 1967. [Mimeographed.]

152. PITTMAN, D. J. and GORDON, C. W. Criminal careers of the chronic police inebriate. Quart. J. Stud. Alc. 19: 255–265, 1958.

153. PITTMAN, D. J. and GORDON, C. W. Revolving door: a study of the chronic police case inebriate. (Rutgers Center of Alcohol Studies, Monogr. No. 2.) New Brunswick, NJ; 1958.

154. PIVAR, D. J. Purity crusade; sexual morality and social control, 1868–1900. Westport, CT; Greenwood; 1973.
155. PROTESTANT EPISCOPAL CHURCH OF THE DIOCESE OF PENNSYLVANIA. Journals of the annual conventions. Philadelphia; 1896— [Protestant Episcopal Diocese of Pennsylvania.]
156. PROTESTANT EPISCOPAL CHURCH OF THE DIOCESE OF PENNSYLVANIA. BOARD OF MISSIONS. Annual reports. 1898— [Protestant Episcopal Diocese of Pennsylvania.]
157. PROTESTANT EPISCOPAL CHURCH OF ST. ANDREW'S. Twenty-first annual report of the parochial work, 1883–1884. Philadelphia; 1884.
158. RADICE, R. Sacred Heart Center counseling program; Sacred Heart Center for the Treatment of Alcoholism. Philadelphia; ca. 1971. [Mimeographed.]
159. RECKLESS, W. C. The natural history of vice areas in Chicago. Ph.D. dissertation, University of Chicago; 1925.
160. REITMAN, B. L., ed. Sister of the road. New York; Macauley; 1937.
161. REPS, J. W. Town planning in frontier America. Princeton; Princeton University Press; 1969.
162. REZNECK, S. Distress, relief, and discontent in the United States during the depression of 1873–78. J. polit. Econ. **58:** 494–512, 1950.
163. RICHMOND, J. F. New York and its institutions, 1609–1871. New York; E. B. Treat; 1871.
164. RIIS, J. How the other half lives. New York; Hill & Wang; 1957.
165. RINGENBACH, P. T. Tramps and reformers, 1873–1916; the discovery of unemployment in New York. (Contributions from American History, No. 27.) Westport, CT; Greenwood; 1973.
166. ROBERTS, R. E. Sketches of Detroit. Detroit; R. J. Johnstone; 1855.
167. ROBERTS, R. R. Sketches of the city of the straits. Detroit; Free Press Book and Job Printing House; 1884.
168. ROONEY, J. [F.] Friendship and reference group orientation among Skid Row men. Ph.D. dissertation, University of Pennsylvania; 1973.
169. ROONEY, J. F. Group processes among Skid Row winos; a reevaluation of the undersocialization hypothesis. Quart. J. Stud. Alc. **22:** 440–460, 1961.
170. ROONEY, J. F. Societal forces and the unattached male; an historical review. Pp. 13–38. In: BAHR, H. M., ed. Disaffiliated man; essays and bibliography on Skid Row, vagrancy, and outsiders. Toronto; University of Toronto Press; 1970.
171. ROSENBERG, C. S. Religion and the rise of the American city; the New York City mission movement, 1812–1870. Ithaca; Cornell University Press; 1971.
172. ROSINE ASSOCIATION OF PHILADELPHIA. Annual and semi-annual reports of the managers. Philadelphia; 1851— [Historical Society of Pennsylvania.]

173. ROSINE ASSOCIATION OF PHILADELPHIA. Constitution and address. Philadelphia; 1847—
174. ROSINE ASSOCIATION OF PHILADELPHIA. Reports and realities from the sketchbook of a manager of the Rosine Association. Philadelphia; John Duross; 1855. [Historical Society of Pennsylvania.]
175. RUBINGTON, E. The bottle gang. Quart. J. Stud. Alc. **29:** 943–955, 1968.
176. SACRED HEART CENTER FOR THE TREATMENT OF ALCOHOLISM. Sacred Heart Center for the treatment of alcoholism. Detroit; June 1969. [Mimeographed.]
177. ST. MARY STREET COLLEGE SETTLEMENT OF PHILADELPHIA. Third annual report. Philadelphia; 1894. [Historical Society of Pennsylvania.]
178. SAN FRANCISCO. DEPARTMENT OF CITY PLANNING. The Haight Ashbury; a brief description of the past. San Francisco; 1971.
179. SAN FRANCISCO. DEPARTMENT OF HEALTH. City agencies report on new start for south of Market residents. San Francisco; 1 September 1970.
180. SAN FRANCISCO REDEVELOPMENT AGENCY. New Start Center; results. San Francisco; 28 September 1970.
181. SAN FRANCISCO REDEVELOPMENT AGENCY. Program reports, domiciliary project . . . protective care [and] . . . detoxification [of] patients. San Francisco; February 1971.
182. SEWELL, B. T. Sorrow's circuit, or five years experience in the Bedford Street Mission. Philadelphia; 1859.
183. SHAPIRO, J. Single room occupancy; the community of the alone. Soc. Wk, N.Y. **11:** 24–33, 1966.
184. SKOLNICK, J. H. A study of the relation of ethnic background to arrests for inebriety. Quart. J. Stud. Alc. **15:** 622–630, 1954.
185. SOCIETY FOR ORGANIZING CHARITY, PHILADELPHIA. Cities within the city; six short stories. In: Twenty-sixth annual report. Philadelphia; 1904. [Family Service of Philadelphia.]
186. SOCIETY FOR ORGANIZING CHARITY, PHILADELPHIA. Monthly register. Philadelphia; 1880—
187. SOCIETY FOR ORGANIZING CHARITY, PHILADELPHIA. Report of the citizens commission on charity organizations, with proposed constitution. Philadelphia; ca. 13 June 1878.
188. SOCIETY FOR ORGANIZING CHARITY, PHILADELPHIA. CENTRAL BOARD OF DIRECTORS. Annual reports. Philadelphia; October 1880— [Family Service of Philadelphia.]
189. SOCIETY FOR ORGANIZING CHARITY, PHILADELPHIA. FIFTH WARD ASSOCIATION. Report of the Board of Directors . . . for 1879–1882. Philadelphia; n.d.
190. SOCIETY FOR ORGANIZING CHARITY, PHILADELPHIA. SPECIAL COMMITTEE FOR SUPPRESSING MENDICANCY. Report. In: CENTRAL BOARD OF DIRECTORS. Second annual report. Philadelphia; 1 October 1880.

191. SOCIETY FOR ORGANIZING CHARITY, PHILADELPHIA. TENTH WARD ASSOCIATION. Annual reports. Philadelphia; 1892— [Family Service of Philadelphia.]
192. SOLENBERGER, A. W. One thousand homeless men. New York; Survey Associates; 1914.
193. SPRADLEY, J. P. You owe yourself a drunk; an ethnography of urban nomads. Boston; Little, Brown; 1970.
194. SPROGLE, H. O. The Philadelphia police force past and present. Philadelphia; 1887.
195. STEFFENS, L. The shame of the cities. New York; McClure, Phillips; 1905.
196. STERNE, M. Drinking patterns and alcoholism among American Negroes. (Social Science Institute, Occasional Paper No. 7.) St. Louis; Washington University; 1966.
197. STEVENS, W. B. The past and present of St. Andrew's; two discourses preached in St. Andrew's Church, Philadelphia. Philadelphia; Sherman & Son; 1858.
198. STRAUS, R. and MCCARTHY, R. G. Nonaddictive pathological drinking patterns of homeless men. Quart. J. Stud. Alc. 12: 601–611, 1951.
199. STRAYER, R. A study of the Negro alcoholic. Quart. J. Stud. Alc. 22: 111–123, 1961.
200. SUNDAY BREAKFAST ASSOCIATION OF PHILADELPHIA. Thirteenth annual report. Philadelphia; 1891. [Historical Society of Pennsylvania.]
201. SUTTLES, G. D. The social construction of communities. Chicago; University of Chicago Press; 1972.
202. TEETERS, N. K. The early days of the Magdalen Society of Philadelphia. Social serv. Rev. 30: 158–167, 1956.
203. THEODORSON, G., ed. Studies in human ecology. Evanston; Row, Peterson; 1961.
204. THOMPSON, R. E., ed. The life of George H. Stuart. Philadelphia; J. M. Stoddart; 1890.
205. THORP, W. L. Business annals. . . . New York; National Bureau of Economic Research; 1926.
206. TRICE, H. M. Alcoholism in America. New York; McGraw-Hill; 1966.
207. TRICE, H. M. and WAHL, J. R. A rank order analysis of the symptoms of alcoholism. Pp. 369–381. In: PITTMAN, D. J. and SNYDER, C. R., eds. Society, culture, and drinking patterns. New York; Wiley; 1962. [Orig., Quart. J. Stud. Alc. 19: 636–648, 1958.]
208. UNION BENEVOLENT ASSOCIATION OF PHILADELPHIA. The Union Benevolent Association of Philadelphia, 1831–1931; a history commemorating the centennial anniversary of the founding of a society for ameliorating the conditions of the poor. Philadelphia; 1931.

209. UNION BENEVOLENT ASSOCIATION OF PHILADELPHIA. LADIES' BOARD OF MANAGERS. Annual reports. 1876—

210. U.S. BUREAU OF THE CENSUS. Statistical abstract of the United States; 1973. 94th ed. Washington, DC; U.S. Govt Print. Off.; 1973.

211. U.S. DEPARTMENT OF LABOR. Sub-employment in the slums of Philadelphia, by the U.S. Department of Labor in cooperation with the Pennsylvania Bureau of Employment Security. Washington, DC; ca. 1966.

212. VANDER KOOI, R. C. The mainstem; Skid Row revisited. Society 10: 64–71, 1973.

213. VANDER KOOI, R. C. Relocating West Madison Skid Row residents; a study of the problem, with recommendations. Chicago; Chicago Department of Urban Renewal; 1967.

214. VANDER KOOI, R. C. Skid Rowers; their alienation and involvement in community and society. Ph.D. dissertation, Michigan State University; 1967.

215. VICE COMMISSION, CHICAGO. The social evil in Chicago. Chicago; 1914.

216. VICE COMMISSION, PHILADELPHIA. A report on existing conditions. . . . Philadelphia; 1913.

217. WALLACE, S. E. Skid Row as a way of life. Totowa, NJ; Bedminister Press; 1965.

218. WATSON, J. F. (HAZARD, W. P., ed.) Annals of Philadelphia and Pennsylvania in olden time. . . . 3 vol. Philadelphia; Edwin S. Stuart; 1897. [Reprint of 1857 edition.]

219. WEBER, J. M. Final evaluation report; the St. Louis detoxification and diagnostic evaluation center. St. Louis; Social Science Institute, Washington University; ca. 1967. [Mimeographed.]

220. WEIMER, A. M. and HOYT, H. Principles of urban real estate. New York; Ronald Press; 1939.

221. WEIMER, A. [M.] and HOYT, H. The structure and growth of residential neighborhoods in American cities. Washington, DC; U.S. Federal Housing Administration; 1939.

222. WESTERN SEAMEN'S FRIEND SOCIETY, DETROIT. Fourth annual report. Detroit; 1851. [Burton Historical Collection, Detroit Public Library.]

223. WHITE–WILLIAMS FOUNDATION FOR GIRLS. One hundred and nineteenth annual report. Philadelphia; 1918.

224. WHITEMAN, M. Philadelphia's Jewish neighborhoods. In: DAVIS, A. F. and HALLER, M. H., eds. The peoples of Philadelphia; a history of ethnic groups and lower class life, 1790–1940. Philadelphia; Temple University Press; 1973.

225. WILKINSON, R. L. The prevention of drinking problems; alcohol control and cultural influences. New York; Oxford University Press; 1970.

226. WILLIAMS, M. H. The new era of church work in Philadelphia.

The Open Church, pp. 53–75, April–June 1897. [Presbyterian Historical Society.]

227. WILLINGS, J. Directory of the city of Detroit for 1845. Detroit; Harshal & Wilcox; 1845.

228. WILLOUGHBY, C. W. Prostitution and its repression in New York City; 1900–1931. New York; AMS Press; 1968.

229. WILLOUGHBY, W. F. The measurement of unemployment; a statistical study. Yale Rev. 10: 188–202, 268–297, 1901.

230. WILSON, O. Fifty years' work with girls, 1883–1933. Washington, DC; National Florence Crittenton Rescue Homes; 1933.

231. WISEMAN, J. P. Stations of the lost; the treatment of Skid Row alcoholics. New York; Prentice-Hall; 1970.

232. WOMAN'S CHRISTIAN TEMPERANCE UNION, PHILADELPHIA. Twelfth annual report. Philadelphia; 1886. [Historical Society of Pennsylvania.]

233. WOODFORD, F. B. and WOODFORD, A. M. All our yesterdays; a history of Detroit. Detroit; Wayne State University; 1969.

234. WRIGHT, C. Industrial depressions. In: U.S. COMMISSIONER OF LABOR. First annual report, March 1886. Washington, DC; U.S. Govt Print. Off.; 1886.

235. YOUNG, C. A. The downtown church; a study of a social institution in transition. Ph.D. dissertation, University of Pennsylvania; 1912.

236. ZAX, M., GARDNER, E. A. and HART, W. T. A survey of the prevalence of alcoholism in Monroe County, New York, 1961. Quart. J. Stud. Alc. 28: 316–327, 1967.

237. Boyd's Philadelphia city business directory. Philadelphia; Central News Co.; 1877.

238. Daily advertiser directory for the city of Detroit for 1850. Detroit; Duncklee, Wales; 1850.

239. Detroit McAuley Mission; its origin and history. 2d ed. Detroit; Eby; 1885. [Burton Historical Collection, Detroit Public Library.]

240. Guide to the stranger or pocket companion for the fancy, containing a list of the gay houses and ladies of pleasure in the City of Brotherly Love and Sisterly Affection. Philadelphia; ca. 1849. [Library Company of Philadelphia.]

241. Standard & Poor's trade and securities; statistics, price indexes, commodities, wholesale, cost of living. New York; August 1968.

242. Thrilling narrative from the lips of sufferers of the late Detroit riot, March 6, 1863. Hattiesburg, MS; The Book Farm; 1945.

243. Will Allen's Rescue Mission and Workingmen's Home. Detroit; 1900. [Burton Historical Collection, Detroit Public Library.]

Index of Names

Index of Subjects

Abbott Street, Detroit, 66
Adams Street, Detroit, 59
Addiction, *see* Alcoholism; Drugs
Advertising, 203
African Baptist Church, Detroit, 67
African Church (Fort Street), Detroit, 67
Age groups, 141, 199
  charity and, 128, 129, 198
  crime rates and, 93, 148, 201–202
  drinking and, 107–108, 124, 134, 135, 136, 137
  homeless women and, 131, 132, 165
  inner city ratios, 49
  Philadelphia TAS clients, 168, 169
  prostitutes and, 226, 229
  runaways, 173
  site clearance and, 103–104
  young street people, 143, 156, 158, 160–66, 168, 171
Alaska Street, *see* Kater Street, Philadelphia
Alcoholics Anonymous, 31, 137, 178, 179
  principles of, 241
Alcoholism, 86, 104, 121, 141, 151, 241–49
  Blacks and, 124, 125, 126, 132
  job exploitation of, 146–48
  prevention efforts, 109, 114, 118, 175, 177, 178–83, 199–200, 241–42
  public assistance and, 149, 201

Alcoholism (*cont.*)
  stereotypes of, *xix*, 6–7, 31–32, 152–53
  suburban, *xxi–xxii*, 188–90
  women and, 124, 130, 131, 132–38, 181
  See also Drinking
Alcoholism treatment facilities, 93, 101, 104, 178, 181
  detoxication and, 31, 201, 202
  in Detroit, 111, 114
  in St. Louis, 145–46
  suburban, *xxi*, 183, 185, 188–91, 192
  women in, 132, 133, 137
Aliases, 139, 145, 149
Alienation, 121, 138, 194, 195, 198
  "flightness" and, 171, 173
  helplessness and, 139–40, 145, 148–49, 200
Allen's (Will) Rescue Mission and Workingmen's Home, 64
Almshouses, 30, 46
  drunkards in, 61
American Hotel, Detroit, 55n1
American Indians, 162, 165
American Revolution, 7, 9–10, 105
American Street, Philadelphia, 15
Amphetamines, 156, 161, 163
"Anglia" area of Philadelphia, 100, 101, 104–10, 118, 141, 154
  casefinding in, 176–83
  suburban quality of, 193
Ann Arbor, Michigan, 164

267